Making
a Difference

*Trudy W. Banta
and Associates*

Foreword by C. Robert Pace

Making a Difference

*Outcomes of
a Decade of Assessment
in Higher Education*

Jossey-Bass Publishers • San Francisco

Substantial discounts on bulk quantities of Jossey-Bass books
are available to corporations, professional associations, and other
organizations. For details and discount information, contact the
special sales department at Jossey-Bass Inc., Publishers.
(415) 433-1740; Fax (415) 433-0499.

For sales outside the United States, contact Maxwell Macmillan
International Publishing Group, 866 Third Avenue, New York,
New York 10022.

Manufactured in the United States of America

 The paper used in this book is acid-free and meets the
State of California requirements for recycled paper
(50 percent recycled waste, including 10 percent
10% POST
CONSUMER postconsumer waste), which are the strictest guidelines
W A S T E for recycled paper currently in use in the United States.

Library of Congress Cataloging-in-Publication Data

Making a difference : outcomes of a decade of assessment in higher
   education / Trudy W. Banta and associates. — 1st ed.
      p.   cm. — (The Jossey-Bass higher and adult education series)
   Includes bibliographical references and index.
   ISBN 1-55542-578-X
    1. Education, Higher—United States—Evaluation—Case studies.
   2. Educational tests and measurements—United States—Case studies.
   3. Higher education and state—United States—Case studies.
   I. Banta, Trudy W.   II. Series.
   LA227.4.M35 1993
   378.1'664—dc20   93-19501
                                            CIP

FIRST EDITION
HB Printing   10 9 8 7 6 5 4 3 2 1   *Code 9377*

To
Logan and Holly,
who keep me smiling
and inspire me
to keep trying to make a difference

Contents

Foreword

Despite the fact that I have been engaged for nearly sixty years in many of the activities that are now called assessment, I have gained some important new insights about higher education and about the scope of the assessment movement from reading the chapters in this book.

In the early years of educational research, tests and measurements, and evaluation, the field was characterized by innovation and diversity. Here, for example, are some of the devices and practices I recall from the 1930s, 1940s, and 1950s: rating scales; profiles; tests of attitudes, interests, and appreciation; measures of critical thinking; alumni surveys; inventories of life goals and values; analyses of time logs; diaries; performance tests; personal essays about educational plans and progress; cumulative records; self-evaluation; the familiar tests of general and special abilities; and achievement tests measuring knowledge of facts and principles, methods, and applications. Many practitioners in those days were devising new types of objective tests. Indeed, in the mid 1950s, a book was published titled *Specimen Objective Test Items,* which included many examples of items for measuring understanding, applications, activities, appreciation, attitudes, interests, and adjustments. Moreover, specific colleges and universities became well known for their creativity and expertise in measuring students' progress toward important educational objectives: the College at the University of Chicago, the General College at Minnesota, and the Basic College at Michigan State, for example. Also in the early years, much attention was given to the role of tests in the evaluation and improvement of teaching. Evaluation and learning were closely connected. One of the purposes of the former was to improve teaching and student learning.

Following World War II — with greatly expanded college enrollments, the push toward universal higher education, and the experience of mass testing in the armed forces — educational testing became increasingly focused on a mass market: machine-scorable, objective multiple-choice tests constructed by the dominant testing agencies: the Educational Testing Service (ETS), American College Testing (ACT), and the College Entrance Examination Board (CEEB). Unfortunately, with the dominance of mass testing and production, the educational and personal values of evaluation became somewhat obscured by economic and administrative concerns.

With the advent of the assessment movement in the 1980s and 1990s, the virtues of variety and creativity are now being reclaimed, redefined, and extended. The student and the teacher are again the central figures in many of the current activities described in *Making a Difference*. The educational merit of student self-evaluation is widely recognized. The ways in which assessment contributes to teaching and learning are emphasized. At some colleges, curriculum, teaching, learning, and assessment are all part of a coherent enterprise. Teachers are together exploring meaningful ways to assess student development and also to judge program effectiveness.

What accounts for this current movement? Several conditions have probably been influential. Given the diversity of student characteristics, the fairness of any single objective achievement test has been questioned. Given the political concern about competition in a global economy, interest in the quality of student

training has grown. Given public perception that colleges are
not as effective as they should be, demands for greater accountability have increased. Given the perception that many teachers
do not teach enough, or well enough, the need for a fuller analysis of teaching and learning is recognized. And given changes
in curricula and courses — women's studies, ethnic studies, ecology, and new perspectives about general education and Western
civilization and history — corresponding changes in examinations
and expected outcomes are necessary. Indeed, changes in curriculum require modifications in the content of assessment. All
these conditions are reflected in the present book.

    Because the stimulus for assessment is different at differ-
ent colleges, their responses are also quite different. At some
colleges, assessment is centrally orchestrated, in response to external demands, and results are disseminated locally as well as
externally; however, faculty and students have relatively little
involvement in the activity. The results may show improvements
in student satisfaction, performance, retention, or other variables; they may by themselves be a valuable contribution to institutional research, but they may have little impact on faculty
or students. At other places, assessment has become a faculty-
and student-centered experience, influencing classroom teaching and student learning. At still other institutions (perhaps the
majority), a combination of administrative leadership and faculty
enthusiasm, sometimes aided by supplemental funds, has helped
to make assessment a viable and important part of the institutional culture.

    One of the recurrent themes in *Making a Difference* is col-
laboration — working together to raise the quality of teaching
and learning and to find evidence that programs are effective.
Participation in assessment has generated enthusiasm about being a college teacher and seeing that one's efforts are effective.
Almost all the chapters illustrate how this participation has occurred. The accounts provide guidance for colleges to get the
most out of campus assessment activities. Moreover, we know
from educational research that good outcomes and good processes go together; and when assessment is seen as a worthwhile
process, we can be sure that its influence on outcomes will be

positive, especially when they are measured by gains in faculty motivation and morale, as well as by student learning and development.

The other lesson to be learned from this book is simply this: leadership in higher education comes from many places. Leadership in assessment has come from unfamiliar places. Of the colleges and universities whose activities are described here, none are Ivy League institutions (except that there are a few localized projects at Harvard), none are Big Ten state universities, none are high-prestige private universities such as Chicago or Stanford, and none are the very selective liberal arts colleges such as Amherst, Swarthmore, Oberlin, Carleton, and Pomona. Instead, exciting approaches to assessment have come from places many people know little about: Alverno, Northeast Missouri, Fredonia, Sonoma, Kean, James Madison, Austin Peay, and many others, including community colleges. We are thus reminded again that the capacity for creativity and ingenuity exists everywhere.

August 1993   C. Robert Pace
                                  Emeritus professor of higher education
                                  University of California, Los Angeles

Preface

Are we making a difference? According to Darrell Krueger, formerly chief academic officer at Northeast Missouri State University, that question — posed persistently to him by Charles McClain, then president of Northeast — motivated him to undertake a comprehensive program of assessment of student learning that virtually transformed Northeast by the early 1980s. Since that pioneering work during the 1970s by Krueger and his colleagues and by the faculty at Alverno College, calls for demonstration of accountability on the part of states and evidence of effectiveness on the part of accrediting bodies have spurred virtually every institution in the country to undertake some kind of investigation into the impact of higher education on students. According to the latest American Council on Education *Campus Trends* survey (El-Khawas, 1993), 97 percent of U.S. colleges and universities conduct or are planning to conduct assessment activities.

Genesis of the Book

By 1990 — the beginning of the second decade of intense interest in measuring the outcomes of higher education — the practice of assessment had been described in several books, scores of journal articles, and hundreds of informal publications from institutions and higher education associations, as well as in a bimonthly periodical, *Assessment Update*. But to date, no one has attempted a systematic study of the results of all this assessment activity in colleges and universities. Have campus programs actually improved? Is the student experience fuller and richer? Are faculty members teaching more effectively? Are students learning more? In short, is assessment itself making a difference?

In early 1992, I embarked on a project designed to answer these questions. I sent a letter to approximately 115 individuals who were doing noteworthy work in outcomes assessment on their own campuses. I asked if they would be willing to contribute a chapter to an edited work that would summarize improvements in students' experiences in the years since *assessment* became a part of the campus lexicon. More than half these individuals replied favorably to my letter.

Obviously, I could not include sixty separate chapters. With some trepidation, I took the rash step of grouping most of the proposals I had received and suggesting that people who had proposed to write about similar aspects of assessment combine their efforts and collaborate on a single chapter. Yet I wondered how it could possibly work, since scholarship is most often viewed as an individual undertaking and the idea of collaboration seems to many faculty members to be a needless complication to the task of writing.

To my surprise and delight, virtually everyone accepted my proposal. The authors agreed to form working groups and to describe their combined experiences. Some even went so far as to offer to conduct their own surveys of other institutions in order to be able to contribute the most comprehensive chapters possible. Readers hold in their hands the results of these unselfish collaborators' efforts.

I have long considered my colleagues in outcomes assessment around the country to be among the most pleasant, generous, conscientious, optimistic, energetic, hard-working, and highly motivated people that I have encountered in all my professional life. The experience of assembling this book has strongly confirmed that perception. First, as I have pointed out, most of those who offered to contribute to the volume agreed to work with collaborators, some of whom they had never met. They observed deadlines and then responded with grace and even good humor to my many suggestions for adjusting the focus of their chapters. I have special admiration and appreciation for the authors of four chapters who agreed in effect to start over in order to achieve the focus that I wanted for this book — on the actual outcomes of assessment as opposed to particular methods or institutional contexts. *Making a Difference* presents the only comprehensive collection of first-person accounts by people who have developed and implemented campus assessment practices with the help of their campus colleagues.

Audience

My coauthors and I hope that our descriptions of methods that have proven effective (or ineffective) in producing change on campuses will help faculties and academic and student affairs administrators decide which measures hold the most promise for their own settings.

Our current students and those who have now graduated — the most important participants in assessment and recipients of its benefits (or of its impotence) — are also potential consumers of the information assembled here. Finally, we hope our answers to the question, Are we making a difference? will help inform governors, legislators, and higher education policy makers in state, regional, and national associations and agencies who fashion the assessment mandates for institutions.

Overview of the Contents

The book is divided into five parts, each with its own introduction. Although the chapters are grouped to illustrate the contributions of various assessment approaches to campus improvement efforts, they need not be read consecutively. Each tells its own complete story. Thus if one is interested, for instance, in learning about methods that could be used to assess the impact of general or liberal education programs, Chapters One, Five, Seven, Nine, Twelve, Sixteen, and Seventeen will be helpful. Chapters Ten, Eleven, and Twelve are concerned particularly with assessment in major fields. Readers interested in assessment in community colleges will find resources in Chapters Six, Thirteen, Fourteen, Nineteen, Twenty-One, and Twenty-Two. All the chapters in Part Five consider the impact of externally imposed templates to assess institutional accountability for the use of public funds.

Part One presents the stories of five institutions in which assessment has effected a marked change in the way faculty and staff do their work. In Chapter One, Georgine Loacker and Marcia Mentkowski characterize assessment at Alverno College as the judgment by the faculty of whether students demonstrate eight abilities. Since 1973, the entire curriculum at Alverno has been directed toward assisting students to develop those abilities. Perhaps no institution in the world has been more profoundly transformed by attention to evaluation than Alverno. But at Northeast Missouri State University and Kean College, strong, visionary, courageous presidents used assessment to focus attention on the improvement of student learning as a distinctive institutional competence. In Chapter Two, Candace Cartwright Young and Michael E. Knight describe the impact of the assessment initiatives championed by those two presidents, Charles McClain at Northeast Missouri and Nathan Weiss at Kean.

In Chapter Three, A. Michael Williford and Gary O. Moden demonstrate the commitment to institutionwide outcomes assessment that has been linked closely to the strategic plan at Ohio University since 1980. Albert M. Katz, author of Chapter Four, likens the impact of the assessment process at the University of Wisconsin, Superior (UWS), to the effects of angioplasty on an arteriosclerotic patient. Effective administrators and faculty leaders at UWS employed outcomes assessment as a major component in an effort that transformed their institution from one with dangerously low enrollment and a questionable public image in 1985 to one with rising enrollments and much-improved public regard in its region today.

Part Two describes some of the broad approaches to assessing institutional effectiveness that have been used on a variety of campuses with a diverse array of learners. In Chapter Five, MindaRae Amiran, Karen Maitland Schilling, and Karl L. Schilling illustrate several approaches undertaken by the faculty at two liberal arts colleges. The approaches raised more questions than they answered but stimulated some positive initiatives. For Chapter Six, R. Dan Walleri and Jeffrey A. Seybert conducted a national survey to find out how community colleges are using assessment results to improve students' experiences. Chapter Seven, by James H. Watt, Nancy Hungerford Drennen, Raymond J. Rodrigues, Nancy Menelly, and Erica K. Wiegel, details the difficulties of capturing the attention of a research-oriented faculty for assessment activities. They demonstrate that significant work in outcomes assessment can nonetheless take place even at research universities, particularly if assessment is made the topic of scholarly inquiry. For their work on Chapter Eight, Carol E. Kasworm and Catherine Marienau cast a wide net to find institutions that were doing exceptional work in meeting the needs of adults and were using the results of assessment to make their programs even more effective.

Whereas the chapters in Parts One and Two focus primarily on the outcomes of institutionwide approaches at the institutions that have employed them, the chapters in Part Three describe specific *methods* that can be used in a variety of college settings. For instance, Lendley C. Black's topic in Chapter Nine — the use of portfolios — is arguably the most widely discussed assessment method in higher education today, regardless of setting. And Chapter Ten by Reid Johnson, Robert D. McCormick, Joseph S. Prus, and Julia S. Rogers presents results from a panoply of methods for assessing student achievement in the major.

John A. Muffo and Mary Anne Bunda discuss in Chapter Eleven the use of surveys, interviews, and other strategies for gathering data on the perceptions of the stakeholders in higher education. While drawing on the programs at their own institutions to illustrate their points in Chapter Twelve, R. Stephen

RiCharde, Cynthia A. Olney, and T. Dary Erwin describe cognitive and affective measures of student development that are appropriate for any campus. C. Robert Pace's work on establishing the important link between student involvement and student achievement provides the theoretical base for the Community College Student Experiences Questionnaire (CCSEQ) described by Jack Friedlander, Patricia H. Murrell, and Peter R. Mac-Dougall in Chapter Thirteen. These writers summarize evidence from several community colleges on the usefulness of the CCSEQ in promoting improvements in student learning. Classroom assessment, based on the work of Patricia Cross and Thomas Angelo, has proven to be extraordinarily helpful to faculty interested in improving their own teaching. In Chapter Fourteen, Susan Sellman Obler, Julie Slark, and Linda Umbdenstock describe the impact that classroom assessment techniques have had on student learning in community colleges.

Parts One, Two, and Three thus include descriptions of institutional approaches and specific methods that are in widespread use across the country. Part Four presents information on some strategies that have not yet been applied broadly but show promise for increased application in the future. In Chapter Fifteen, Robert E. Millward discusses the use of assessment centers in diagnosing the beginning teaching skills of undergraduate majors in teacher education. Carl J. Waluconis, in his presentation (Chapter Sixteen) of the application of student self-evaluation techniques, illustrates the power of student voices to stimulate change. In Chapter Seventeen, James L. Ratcliff and Elizabeth A. Jones describe a method for using cluster analysis to link assessments of undergraduates' general learning with the coursework in which they enroll. In Chapter Eighteen, Darrell W. Krueger provides a vision of higher education in which outcomes assessment, viewed as part of total quality management (TQM), serves the purpose of continually improving institutions.

Part Five demonstrates the power of external pressures to influence campus assessment practices. In Chapter Nineteen, Janice Van Dyke, Linda B. Rudolph, and Karen A. Bowyer attest to the ways performance funding in Tennessee (and later the institutional effectiveness criterion of the Southern Association of Colleges and Schools) stimulated campus interest in outcomes assessment at public colleges and universities in that state. The effects of the less prescriptive approaches on campuses in Virginia and New Jersey are the subjects treated respectively in Chapter Twenty by Barbara S. Fuhrmann and Karen M. Gentemann and in Chapter Twenty-One by Nina Dorset Jemmott and Edward A. Morante. In Chapter Twenty-Two, Dorothy Bray and Martha J. Kanter discuss an array of state initiatives that have led California colleges to pay more attention to the outcomes of their work. Peter T. Ewell draws on his vast experience as a consultant in a majority of the states to comment in Chapter Twenty-Three on how policies formulated by state governments and regional accrediting agencies have shaped campus assessment practice.

In Chapter Twenty-Four, the last chapter in the book, I consider several significant difficulties encountered in answering the question, Are we making a difference? First, substantive change takes time to effect, and even more time must elapse before the results become apparent. Second, the measures that might be employed to show that improvement in student learning has occurred are technically inadequate for the task. Despite these problems, however, there is an excellent case to be made that assessment *does* create positive change. In Chapter Twenty-Four, I show that the changes that have been made — most often by faculty who had not previously studied the literature about the impact of college on students — are generally actions that research has shown to be most likely to enhance student learning and development now and in the future.

Acknowledgments

I would like to acknowledge the detailed, thoughtful, constructive comments of three prepublication reviewers. I tried to address all their substantive criticisms in the final draft of my own contribution to the volume, and I believe the impact of the work has been strengthened in consequence.

Much of the energy and inspiration for assembling the final manuscript came from my closest associates at Indiana

University–Purdue University, Indianapolis. Karen Black, assistant to the vice chancellor, and Caitlin Anderson, graduate assistant, assumed major responsibilities for editing chapter drafts and communicating with authors. Frances Oblander, a colleague on the higher education faculty, also helped in the editing process. Invaluable work was accomplished by Linda Durr, Betty Dorsey, Victoria Cook, and Patricia Laskowski in preparing and revising the typed manuscript. In a very real sense, the completion of this volume is due to the enthusiasm and diligent efforts of this wonderful team of colleagues.

Indianapolis, Indiana   Trudy W. Banta
August 1993

Reference

El-Khawas, E. *1993 Campus Trends Survey.* Washington, D.C.: American Council on Education, 1993.

The Authors

Trudy W. Banta is professor of higher education and vice chancellor for planning and institutional improvement at Indiana University–Purdue University, Indianapolis. Before assuming that position in 1992, she was professor of education at the University of Tennessee, Knoxville (UTK). In 1982, she was named campus assessment coordinator at UTK. In 1986, with the assistance of a grant from the Fund for the Improvement of Postsecondary Education, Banta established the national Assessment Resource Center at UTK, which became the Center for Assessment Research and Development in 1989. Banta has written or edited five books, contributed a dozen chapters to other works, and had more than 120 journal articles, monographs, and research reports published. She has addressed meetings on the topic of outcomes assessment in twenty states and made more than seventy visits to campuses across the country to assist in establishing assessment programs. In 1988, Banta was honored by the American Association for Higher Education for her contributions to the field of assessment in higher education. She became the founding editor of *Assessment Update,* a bimonthly Jossey-Bass publication, in 1989. Banta's baccalaureate degree in education (with majors in biology and history) and master's degree in counseling were earned at the University of Kentucky. Her Ed.D. degree in educational psychology was awarded by the University of Tennessee.

MindaRae Amiran is professor of English at the State University of New York, Fredonia, where she also served as dean for liberal and continuing education. She received her B.A. degree (1953) in psychology from Swarthmore College, her M.A. degree (1954) in English from Radcliffe College, and her Ph.D. degree (1968) in English from Hebrew University in Jerusalem.

Lendley C. Black is associate dean for the College of Liberal Arts and Sciences and director of undergraduate studies at Emporia State University, where he is also associate professor of theater arts. He was a member of the study group that co-authored *Time Will Tell* (1990); he has written about portfolio assessment for the *NCA Quarterly* and *Assessment Update;* and he serves as an assessment consultant. He received his B.A. degree (1974) in English from the University of Tennessee, Martin; his M.A. degree (1977) in dramatic arts from the University of Connecticut, and his Ph.D. degree (1984) in theater from the University of Kansas.

Karen A. Bowyer is president of Dyersburg State Community College. She received her B.A. degree (1963) in mathematics from Knox College; her M.A. degree (1967) in mathematics from Rutgers, the State University; and her Ph.D. degree (1971) in mathematics education from the University of Alabama.

Dorothy Bray is vice president of educational services at College of the Desert in California. A longtime practitioner and proponent of assessment, she was the founding president of the Learning Assessment Retention Consortium (LARC) and coeditor of *Issues in Student Assessment* (1987, with M. J. Belcher). She received her doctorate in educational psychology with a specialty in learning theory from the University of Southern California.

Mary Anne Bunda is director of university assessment and professor of educational leadership at Western Michigan University. She has been consulting editor for several scholarly journals and chair of the Topical Interest Group on Higher Education Assessment for the American Evaluation Association. She received her B.A. degree (1965) in mathematics, her M.Ed. degree in measurement and research from Loyola University of Chicago, and her Ph.D. degree (1971) in research, measurement, and evaluation from the University of Illinois, Urbana–Champaign.

Nancy Hungerford Drennen is professor of consumer sciences and interim director of the University Accountability Program at Colorado State University. She received her Ph.D. degree (1978) in family ecology from Michigan State University.

T. Dary Erwin is currently director of the Office of Student Assessment and professor of psychology at James Madison University. He is a past recipient of the Annuit Coeptis Award of the American College Personnel Association (1983) and of the Ralph F. Berdie Memorial Research Award of the American Association for Counseling and Development (1985). He also served as chair of the Measurement Services Association (1985–86). He is author of *Assessing Student Learning and Development: A Guide to the Principles, Goals, and Methods of Determining College Outcomes* (1991). He received his B.S. degree (1972) in business administration and psychology and his M.S. degree (1975) in educational psychology, both from the University of Tennessee, and his Ph.D. degree (1978) in student development and measurement from the University of Iowa.

Peter T. Ewell is senior associate at the National Center for Higher Education Management Systems (NCHEMS) in Boulder, Colorado. Since joining the NCHEMS staff in 1981, he has consulted on assessment policy and technique with more than two hundred colleges and universities and twenty-three state agencies or higher education systems. He is the author of six books on assessment and evaluation in higher education and of numerous articles and papers commissioned by such agencies as the National Governors' Association, the Education Commission of the States, the National Conference of State Legislators, and the National Institute for Education. He edits a column on state policy for *Assessment Update* and is a frequent speaker on the topic at national and international meetings. A graduate of Haverford College, he received his Ph.D. degree (1976) in political science from Yale University.

Jack Friedlander is dean of academic affairs at Santa Barbara City College. He earned his B.A. degree (1973) in psychology from Florida International University and both his M.A. degree (1976) in learning and instruction and his Ph.D. degree (1980) in higher education from the University of California, Los Angeles. Friedlander has written more than fifty published articles and chapters on a variety of topics related to community colleges. He coedited *Models for Conducting Institutional Research* (1990, with P. MacDougall) and, with C. Robert Pace and Penny Lehman, published *The Community College Student Experiences Questionnaire* (1990).

Barbara S. Fuhrmann is professor of education and director of assessment at Virginia Commonwealth University. She has acted as consultant on assessment issues for the State Council for Higher Education in Virginia; she has also written in a variety of books and journals about the integration of liberal and professional education. She received her B.A. degree (1962) in English from Beloit College; her M.S. degree (1969) in counseling from Wisconsin State University, Oshkosh; and her Ed.D. degree (1973) in teacher education from the University of Massachusetts.

Karen M. Gentemann is director of institutional assessment at George Mason University. Her publications have been in the areas of assessment, minority education, energy policy, and domestic violence. She has presented papers and served on panels discussing assessment and institutional research. She is active in national, regional, and state organizations focusing on those interests. She is currently on the board of the Southern Association for Institutional Research and is president of the Virginia Assessment Group. She earned a B.A. degree (1967) in social sciences from Webster University and M.Ed. (1974) and Ph.D. (1978) degrees in higher education administration from the University of Pittsburgh.

Nina Dorset Jemmott has been involved in assessment at the state and local levels in New Jersey for more than ten years. She has served on the state Basic Skills Council, the College Outcomes Evaluation Program Council, and the Assessment and Accountability Task Force. Currently, she is involved in research on and statewide implementation of faculty development programs through the New Jersey Institute for Collegiate Teaching and Learning, whose mission is the improvement of teaching and learning at the college level. She earned her doctorate (1992) in higher education administration from Seton Hall University.

Reid Johnson is professor of psychology at Winthrop University and coordinator of the South Carolina Higher Education Assessment Network, a forty-five–member consortium housed in the Office of Assessment at Winthrop. Some eighteen of his articles, newsletters, book chapters, and monographs on higher education assessment topics have been published. He has also delivered more than forty presentations, workshops, and consultations, particularly emphasizing methods for evaluating student progress as a primary indicator of institutional effectiveness. He received his B.A. degree (1966) in mathematics and psychology from the University of North Carolina, Asheville, and both his M.A. degree (1969) in psychology and his Ph.D. degree (1971) in school psychology from the University of South Carolina.

Elizabeth A. Jones is research associate at the National Center for Postsecondary Teaching, Learning, and Assessment at Pennsylvania State University, where she is also a special assistant to the vice provost and dean for undergraduate education, and assistant editor of the *Journal of General Education*. She received her B.S. degree (1981) in music education from West Chester University and both her M.Ed. degree (1983) in counselor education and her Ph.D. degree (1991) in higher education from Pennsylvania State University.

Martha J. Kanter is president of DeAnza College in Cupertino, California. A community college educator for more than fifteen years, she was awarded her bachelor's degree (1970) by Brandeis University, her master's degree (1974) in education (with a concentration in clinical psychology and public practice) by Harvard University, and her doctorate (1989) in educational administration by the University of San Francisco. She is a nationally recognized expert on the effects of college placement testing on access to higher education for underrepresented students and related issues of educational equity and access.

Carol E. Kasworm is professor of adult education and associate dean for research in the College of Education at the University of Tennessee, Knoxville. She has written extensively on adult undergraduates and is currently conducting research funded by the U.S. Department of Education on the topic. She received her B.A. degree (1967) in psychology and sociology from Valparaiso University, her M.A. degree (1970) in higher education administration from Michigan State University, and her Ed.D. degree (1977) from the University of Georgia.

Albert M. Katz is professor of communicating arts at the University of Wisconsin, Superior, where he is also coordinator of assessment. His primary area of academic and professional interest is conflict management. He received his B.A. degree (1958) in English from Union College and his M.A. (1960) and Ph.D. (1966) degrees in speech and theater from the University of Michigan.

Michael E. Knight is professor of early childhood and family studies at Kean College of New Jersey, where he is also coordinator of assessment of student learning and development. He has made numerous presentations at the American Association of Higher Education Assessment Forum, has acted as consultant at more than forty colleges and universities, has had six articles on assessment published, and has contributed to and edited two anthologies on the subject. He received his B.A. degree (1966) in elementary education and his M.A. (1968) degree in reading from

Newark State College and his Ph.D. degree (1973) in curriculum and reading from Fordham University.

Darrell W. Krueger, president of Winona State University, is a nationally recognized leader in the area of outcomes assessment. In 1991 and 1992, he convened conferences of national leaders in higher education on the subject of total quality management and improving undergraduate education. Krueger holds a B.A. degree (1967) in political science and history from Southern Utah State College. He earned his master's degree (1969) and his Ph.D. degree (1971) from the University of Arizona. His areas of study have focused on government.

Georgine Loacker is professor of English at Alverno College, where she directs the Council on Student Assessment. She received her B.S.E. degree (1947) in education and English from Alverno, her M.A. degree (1956) in English from Marquette University, and her Ph.D. degree (1971) in English language and literature from the University of Chicago. She continues to be a major contributor to the development of Alverno's ability-based education and student assessment process begun in 1973. In 1989, she was a visiting fellow at the Higher Education Research and Development Society of Australia. Her recent publications include "Designing a National Assessment System: Alverno's Institutional Perspective," commissioned by the U.S. Department of Education in 1991.

Robert D. McCormick is professor of Spanish and psychology and director of the Office of Institutional Assessment at Montclair State College. He is coordinator of the Montclair State national assessment conference and has presented papers on outcomes assessment at conferences throughout the United States. He received his Ph.D. degree (1976) in eighteenth-century Spanish literature from the City University of New York and a second doctorate (1986), in psychology, from Rutgers University.

Peter R. MacDougall is president of Santa Barbara City College. He received his B.A. degree (1961) in education from the University of Rhode Island, his M.A. degree (1965) in education from Rhode Island College, and his Ed.D. degree (1969) in counselor education from Pennsylvania State University. He has published articles and chapters on topics related to community colleges. MacDougall has also coauthored a New Directions for Community Colleges sourcebook, *Models for Conducting Institutional Research* (1990, with J. Friedlander).

Catherine Marienau is associate professor in the School for New Learning at DePaul University in Chicago. She is the founding and current director of the School of New Learning Master of Arts for Practicing Professionals program. She has worked in alternative adult higher education for twenty years as a program developer and administrator, teacher, and adviser. She received her B.A. (1971), M.A. (1976), and Ph.D. (1982) degrees, in anthropology, the social and philosophic foundation of education, and curriculum and instruction, respectively— all from the University of Minnesota.

Nancy Menelly is a lecturer in communication sciences at the University of Connecticut, Hartford, and a Ph.D. candidate in the Department of Communication Sciences at the University of Connecticut. She was formerly a project assistant in the University Assessment Office. She received her B.A. degree (1984) from Simmons College and her M.A. degree (1987) in communication from Fairfield University.

Marcia Mentkowski, director of research and evaluation and professor of psychology at Alverno College, earned her B.A. degree (1961) in psychology and education from Milwaukee-Downer College (now Lawrence University) and her M.A. (1965) and Ph.D. (1971) degrees in educational psychology from the University of Wisconsin, Madison. In 1975, she was visiting scholar at the Harvard Graduate School of Education. She initiated Alverno's approach to institutional assessment, including the Alverno Longitudinal Study, in 1976. Her recent papers include "Designing a National Assessment System: Assessing Abilities That Connect Education and Work," commissioned by the U.S. Department of Education in 1991.

Robert E. Millward is professor of education in the College of Education at Indiana University of Pennsylvania, where he is also director of the Teacher Assessment Center. He received his B.S. degree (1965) from California University of Pennsylvania, his M.Ed. degree (1968) from Duquesne University, and his D.Ed. degree (1973) from Pennsylvania State University.

Gary O. Moden is associate provost at Ohio University and assistant professor in the School of Applied Behavioral Science and Educational Leadership. From 1977 until 1990, he served as director of the Office of Institutional Research at Ohio University. He received both his B.A. degree (1966) in international relations and his M.A. degree (1970) in political science from Mankato State University, and his Ph.D. degree (1978) in higher education from the University of Missouri.

Edward A. Morante is dean of educational resources, research, and technologies at the College of the Desert in California. He was formerly director of both the College Outcomes Evaluation Program and the Basic Skills Assessment Program for the New Jersey Department of Higher Education. He also teaches testing and evaluation at the Kellogg Institute of the National Center for Development Education. He received his B.S. degree (1965) in psychology from Manhattan College and both his M.Ed. (1967) and Ed.D. (1974) degrees in counseling psychology from Teachers College, Columbia University.

John A. Muffo is director of program review and outcomes assessment at the Virginia Polytechnic Institute and State University, where he also teaches higher education administration. He has been a consulting editor for several scholarly journals and is currently president of the Association for Institutional Research. He earned a B.A. degree (1969) in philosophy from Saint Francis College of Pennsylvania, an M.Ed. degree (1971) in student personnel administration from Ohio University, and both an M.B.A. degree (1976) and a Ph.D. degree in higher education administration from the University of Denver.

Patricia H. Murrell, director of the Center for the Study of Higher Education at Memphis State University, received her B.A.

degree in religion from Millsaps College in Mississippi and both her M.Ed. and Ed.D. degrees in counseling and student personnel services from the University of Mississippi. She serves on the advisory board of the ERIC Clearinghouse on Higher Education and was a recipient of the Melvene Hardee Award of the Southern Association for College Student Affairs (1990). She has written extensively on outcomes assessment, learning styles, and student development.

Susan Sellman Obler directs the Teaching-Learning Center at Rio Hondo College and a Title III Consortium of four colleges doing classroom assessment with diverse students. She taught writing for many years and has worked with colleges in the United States, the United Kingdom, and Canada on writing across the curriculum, writing assessment, and teaching and learning programs. Her involvement with various colleges and consortia has helped them develop models for initiating and assessing alternative classroom teaching and learning strategies. She is president of LARC, the California statewide network of some eighty colleges. She earned her B.A. (1968) and M.A. (1969) degrees in English from California State University, Fullerton, and her Ph.D. degree (1985) in higher education from the University of Texas, Austin.

Cynthia A. Olney is assistant assessment specialist in the Office of Student Assessment and assistant professor of psychology at James Madison University. She earned her B.A. degree (1981) in English from Pennyslvania State University, her M.A. degree (1985) in speech communication from the University of Arizona, and her Ph.D. degree (1991) in educational psychology at the University of Arizona. Her research emphases include assessment of developmental outcomes of college students and cognitive development.

Joseph S. Prus is professor of psychology at Winthrop University, where he also directs the Office of Assessment and the school psychology program. He is coauthor of *Assessing Assessment,* a report on a national assessment survey published by the American Council on Education (1991, with R. Johnson, C. J. Anderson, and E. El-Khawas), and has presented numerous papers and workshops on assessment in higher education. He received his B.A. degree in psychology, his M.A. degree in educational and counseling psychology, and his Ph.D. degree in school psychology from the University of Kentucky.

James L. Ratcliff is professor of education at Pennsylvania State University, where he is also director of the Center for the Study of Higher Education; director of the National Center for Postsecondary Teaching, Learning, and Assessment; and editor of the *Journal of General Education.* He received his B.A. degree (1968) in history and political science from Utah State University, his M.A. degree (1972) in history from Washington State University, and his Ph.D. degree (1976) in higher education and community college education from Washington State University.

R. Stephen RiCharde, associate dean of the faculty and director of institutional analysis at the Virginia Military Institute, earned his B.A. degree (1970) in history from the University of Central Florida and his M.A.T. (1972) and Ph.D. (1979) degrees in behavioral sciences from the University of Florida.

Raymond J. Rodrigues is vice president for academic affairs at North Adams State College. He developed the assessment program at Colorado State University. Rodrigues received his Ph.D. degree (1974) in secondary education (English education) from the University of New Mexico.

Julia S. Rogers is director of institutional evaluation and associate professor of psychology at University of Montevallo in Alabama. She has been extensively involved in assessment since 1985, has presented numerous papers at regional and national conventions, and has spearheaded implementation of outcomes assessment on her own campus, in addition to serving as consultant to other institutions. She is a member of the Association for Institutional Research, the American Evaluation Association, the American Educational Research Association, and related regional and state professional bodies. She received her B.S. degree in business from the University of Louisville, her M.S. degree in psychology from the University of Georgia, and her Ph.D. degree in educational research from the University of Alabama.

Linda B. Rudolph is assistant vice president for planning and institutional effectiveness at Austin Peay State University in Tennessee, where she is also professor of psychology and director of the president's Emerging Leaders Program. She has had numerous articles published in the area of assessment and has presented programs and workshops at state, regional, national, and international conferences. She has also served for years on the state committee that oversees Tennessee performance funding. She received her bachelor's and master's degrees in psychology from Austin Peay State University and her Ed.D. degree in counselor education from the University of Tennessee, Knoxville.

Karen Maitland Schilling is university director of liberal education and associate professor of psychology at Miami University. She completed her B.S. degree (1971) in psychology at Tufts University and her M.A. (1972) and Ph.D. (1975) degrees in clinical psychology at the University of Florida.

Karl L. Schilling is associate dean of the Western College Program at Miami University and assistant professor of interdisciplinary studies. He is currently on leave, serving as director of the American Association of Higher Education Assessment Forum. He received his B.A. degree (1971) in English and psychology from Adrian College and his M.A. (1972) and Ph.D. (1975) degrees in clinical psychology from the University of Florida.

Jeffrey A. Seybert is director of research, evaluation, and instructional development at Johnson County Community College, Kansas. He serves as consulting editor and columnist for *Assessment Update* and consults nationally on assessment in two-year colleges. He is former president of the National Council for Research and Planning, an affiliate council of the American Association of Community Colleges. He received his B.A. degree (1970) in psychology from California State University, Long

Beach, his M.A. degree (1971) in psychology from the University of Oklahoma, and his M.A. degree (1983) in public administration from the University of Missouri, Kansas City. He holds a Ph.D. degree (1974) in psychology from the University of Oklahoma.

Julie Slark has been the director of research, planning, and resource development at Rancho Santiago College in California for fifteen years. She has conducted evaluation and learning outcomes studies, many of which have appeared as monographs, for numerous multiple-college projects in California. She has held office in the Southern California Community College Institutional Research Association, among others. She received her B.A. degree (1971) in sociology from the University of California, Riverside, and her M.A. degree (1980) in public administration from California State University, Fullerton.

Linda Umbdenstock, director of institutional research and planning at Rio Hondo College, was the project director of a Title III grant that launched various programs in assessment. Her expertise, gained both nationally and regionally, lies in systems management, cultural change, program planning and evaluation, policy and trend analysis, and learning outcomes. She is former president of the sixty-college Southern California Community College Institutional Research Association. She serves with the Research Advisory Group for the Community College League of California as cochair of the league's Futures Commission and the Chancellor's Task Force on Innovation: Planning for Growth and Diversity. She earned her B.A. degree (1968) in social science from Alverno College and her Ph.D. degree (1981) in systems science from Portland State University.

Janice Van Dyke is assistant dean for academic support at State Technical Institute at Memphis. She received her B.S. degree in mathematics from Concord College in West Virginia, her M.S. degree, in mathematics also, from the University of Tennessee, Knoxville, and her Ed.D. degree in educational research methodology and statistics from Memphis State University.

R. Dan Walleri is director of research, planning, and computer services at Mount Hood Community College in Oregon. He is former president of the National Council for Research and Planning, an affiliate council of the American Association of Community and Junior Colleges. He was awarded his B.A. degree (1971) in political science by the University of Portland and M.A. (1973) and Ph.D. (1976) degrees, also in political science, by the University of Hawaii. He has authored or co-authored several articles and book chapters on assessment and student outcomes.

Carl J. Waluconis is professor of English and humanities at Seattle Central Community College. He earned his B.A. degree in English from Towson State University and his M.A. degree, also in English, from Western Washington University.

James H. Watt is professor of communication sciences at the University of Connecticut. He directs the University Assessment Office and is chair of the faculty-administration-student University Assessment Committee. He received a B.S. degree (1966) in electrical engineering and an M.S. degree (1969) in journalism from Ohio University, and a Ph.D. degree (1973) in mass communication research from the University of Wisconsin.

Erica K. Wiegel, project assistant in the University Assessment Office at the University of Connecticut, is a graduate student in the Department of Communication Sciences. She received her B.S. degree (1988) in business administration from the University of Florida and her M.A. degree (1992) in communication from the University of Connecticut.

A. Michael Williford is director of institutional research at Ohio University and assistant professor in the School of Applied Behavioral Science and Educational Leadership. He received his B.S. degree (1979) in psychology from Manchester College, his M.S. degree (1983) in social science from Syracuse University, and his Ph.D. degree (1989) in higher education from Ohio University.

Candace Cartwright Young is associate professor of political science at Northeast Missouri State University, where she is also chair of the university assessment committee. Young teaches courses in American politics, public policy, and public administration and was honored as Northeast's 1992 educator of the year. She completed her B.A. degree (1973) in history and government at Columbia College and her M.S. (1975) and Ph.D. (1987) degrees in political science at the University of Missouri.

Making
a Difference

Part One

Transforming
Campus Cultures
Through Assessment

Twenty years ago, the faculty at Alverno College began to create a unique educational environment based on the concept of
"assessment as learning"—assessment as an integral part of a
curriculum designed to develop in each student eight generic
abilities. The faculty, administrators, and students at Alverno
work together on a continuous research and development process
aimed at improving teaching, curricular organization, academic
administrative structures, and academic support services and
resources. Over the years, Alverno faculty have influenced thousands of educators in the United States and around the world
by sharing ideas about assessment instruments and processes
and their validation and about the importance of helping students develop the capacity to assess their own work. Part One
begins with Alverno's story, as told by two of the people most
responsible for it, Georgine Loacker and Marcia Mentkowski.

   At almost the same time that faculty were beginning to
make assessment the touchstone for curricular and pedagogical
metamorphosis at Alverno, a similar unfolding of a "new" institution began in Kirksville at Northeast Missouri State Univer-

sity. In 1970, the new president of Northeast Missouri, Charles McClain, made academic quality and the assessment thereof the principal theme for transforming a teachers college with a declining enrollment into a comprehensive regional university. By using assessment to demonstrate that Northeast Missouri graduates were nationally competitive in their chosen fields and that their university experience had added value to their knowledge and skills, the institution acquired a national reputation for academic quality. This achievement caused significant increases both in the number and in the academic potential of students applying for admission to Northeast Missouri. Faculty member Candace Young describes the Northeast Missouri experience in Chapter Two.

In 1985, another president—Nathan Weiss at Kean College—launched a crusade to use outcomes assessment to stimulate a campuswide self-consciousness about the quality of student learning. Michael Knight, coordinator of Kean's assessment program, writes in Chapter Two that a principal outcome of this program is increased satisfaction and feeling of empowerment on the part of Kean faculty as they have worked with each other, with students, and with alumni and employers of their graduates to define goals and objectives for individual programs, to develop assessment strategies, and to make warranted improvements. The student experience at Kean is much richer as a result of the assessment initiative, and student satisfaction with that experience has increased.

Strong presidential leadership aimed at using evidence of program quality to improve overall institutional quality was also the impetus for the Institutional Impact Project at Ohio University, begun in 1980. A. Michael Williford and Gary Moden, who have shepherded this project since its inception, describe in Chapter Three the testing, surveying, and student-tracking components that have provided direction for numerous improvements in programs and services. Ohio University can now document increases in students' scores on national exams, more involvement by freshmen in the campus experience, more faculty-student contact, higher levels of satisfaction among seniors, and improved freshman retention.

In Chapter Four, Albert Katz credits strong administrative and faculty leadership and a 1986 grant from the Fund for the Improvement of Postsecondary Education for the establishment of a program that is improving teaching, increasing affective support for students, and raising levels of expectation and performance on the part of students at the University of Wisconsin, Superior (UWS). Enrollment at UWS has increased since 1986; faculty are more satisfied; freshmen report a more positive initial impression of the institution than was the case in 1986; and enrolled students say they find their classes more challenging.

All five of these "transformed" institutions were headed — and most still are — by strong leaders who believed outcomes assessment could make a difference and stated their conviction often and strongly. All five also had strong campus coordinators drawn most often from faculty ranks. These individuals knew how to create a strategy for the assessment implementation process because they were well-established, respected faculty leaders before they were appointed to take charge of assessment.

In all five institutions, assessment initially was given time to develop in an orderly way, with a clear purpose, and with widespread participation by all concerned with the education of students: faculty, students, administrators, graduates, employers, and others. Assessment findings are disseminated broadly, in an atmosphere of trust — trust that negative findings will not be used to punish students or faculty.

Data collection and the reporting of findings are built into established procedures such as institutional planning, curriculum development, and programs designed to enhance the teaching effectiveness of faculty. This factor, coupled with careful, persistent follow-up, has helped assessment to be viewed as part of the fabric of the institution rather than an addition with a special, perhaps temporary, purpose.

Creating a Culture Where Assessment Improves Learning

Georgine Loacker
Marcia Mentkowski

Over the past twenty years at Alverno College, the educational process has become a dynamic system that involves ongoing examination, evaluation, and refinement. Alverno is a four-year liberal arts college for women, located in Milwaukee, Wisconsin. It presently serves over 2,500 degree students who attend classes either on weekdays or on weekends. Since 1973, Alverno students graduate only if they have demonstrated eight specified abilities to an explicit level of effectiveness in the context of disciplinary or professional content. The educational beliefs and values of the institution expressed in the current curriculum were already present in the late 1960s, when we began raising issues that led to a new curricular design. The faculty had always seen themselves as accountable for what happened to students as a result of their college education and began to ask questions about how to find out whether each student was developing her full potential.

In 1973, we set out to improve the way our students learn and the way we teach by articulating and making public the abilities that they must demonstrate. At that time, the word *assessment* was in limited use in higher education. We chose it to describe a concept that was a logical part of a curriculum designed to assist students to develop eight identified abilities: communication, analysis, problem solving, valuing in decision making, interacting, global perspectives, effective citizenship, and aesthetic responsiveness. It seemed clear then as now that assessment needed to be based on performance using specific abilities essential for student learning.

Assessment at Alverno College is an integrating developmental experience, assisting the student in developing her own strengths. Assessment processes are integral to a curriculum that assures students of appropriate direction, resources, and the coherence of instruction to enhance the developmental experience.

Leadership for the Assessment Initiative

In the late 1960s, our president, Sister Joel Read, started us on a process of critical inquiry that led to curricular action. She challenged each department to set forth the questions being raised in the discipline, our position on them, the ways we were dealing with them in our major and in general education, and the concepts we were teaching that students could not afford to miss. In exploring these, we came to a key question that drove our curricular reform and assessment process: what kind of person were we as educators seeking to develop?

The inquiry triggered extensive discussion and generated additional questions. What outcomes or characteristics or abilities would students need as part of their lives? What would be the expected and required outcomes? How would we assist the student to develop them? The results of these conversations led us to a transformation of many aspects of the campus that embody and create its culture: curricular organization, academic administrative structures, and academic support services and resources.

The process of asking questions and probing for implications gradually developed into a dynamic, interactive system, supporting individual student development. Through that system, both the faculty and administrators took responsibility for their roles in that development. Because we require our students to develop and demonstrate abilities incorporating their knowledge, we need to reexamine continually their learning processes and our teaching. We now see our work as constantly creating and recreating a system that provides for ongoing review. This work involves assessment design and curricular development, as well as constant improvement of our teaching through research and redesign of learning experiences.

Organizing Framework: Underlying Assumptions and Principles

Underlying our original work is a set of assumptions that gradually became informing principles. We believe that education means being able to do what one knows. Inherent in this principle is the concept that learning outcomes are abilities that students develop in order to use the knowledge they have constructed. Because these outcomes characterize someone liberally educated, we see the abilities as multidimensional, cumulative, and integrated; as having affective as well as cognitive components; as open to further development; and as transferable to new experiences. Our key specific assumptions about individual learning and assessment came out of an examination of what it would mean for students to develop abilities and out of our best understanding (based on our teaching experience) of ways students learn best, including insights from any study of theory we had done to assist us to improve our teaching. (For a more extensive articulation of these assumptions, see Alverno College Faculty, 1993.)

A result of such a view of abilities and assessment is that the demonstration of abilities is more contextual. One of the outcomes now required for a chemistry major, for example, is that she use the "methodology and models of chemistry to define and solve problems independently and collaboratively" (problem-solving ability). History majors must be able to "identify and critique the theories, concepts, and assumptions that historically have been used to create coherent interpretations of the past" (ability to analyze). Business and management majors must be able to "use organizational and management theory to interact effectively in organizational contexts that require leadership of groups or other types of interpersonal interactions" (effective citizenship). Students are not expected to perform in a vacuum. They are expected to demonstrate competence within a range of situations in which they might find themselves.

A culture already supportive of student growth gradually took new shape through the flexibility we had to exercise to create and implement a curriculum that focuses systematically on the development of the student. In order to create and maintain an effective system for learning that includes assessment, we found that it was important regularly to revisit and review our educational values, assumptions, and principles in relation to the mission statement of our institution and to assure ourselves that assessment theory and practice were consistent with these and with the dynamic expectations of the work and civic world that our graduates experience.

Student Assessment as Learning: How It Works

Students who come to Alverno immediately begin a process of consciously developing their abilities. They engage in performance assessments of their communication abilities including quantitative and computer literacy, reading, and speaking. After some preliminary input and practice in self-assessment, they evaluate each of their own performances and receive feedback on their specific strengths and areas needing improvement.

All the students' general education courses provide them with the opportunity to expand and demonstrate each of the eight abilities. Through their study in major and minor areas, students continue to develop skills identified as essential learning outcomes by faculty in each discipline and professional area. These outcomes, distinctive to each major and minor, relate to and extend general education abilities. For example, to meet general education requirements, the student will show analytical skills at the four basic levels: observing, making inferences, making relationships, and integrating concepts and frameworks. All these are integrated with the content of her general education courses. When the student enters a major, she will advance the abilities two more levels, to comparing disciplinary frameworks and using professional frameworks within the context of the field.

During the educational process, each student completes performance assessments to find out how well she is doing and to qualify her to move ahead. These assessments may include reports, letters, journals, oral presentations, individual and group projects, recitals, and exhibits. Many are simulations, which come as close as possible to actual situations in which a student might use the given abilities. The simulations require her to take a clear perspective, one that is her own or an assumed one (consumer, guest editorialist, or member of a citizens' advisory group, for example). She must also address a specific audience — a group of her peers, for instance, or the readers of a professional journal. We try to make sure that each assessment is designed to elicit a range of responses that clearly demonstrates developmental progress.

Most assessments are within courses, but some are more comprehensive, interdisciplinary ones that are administered by the Assessment Center on institutionwide assessment days. Select performances are accumulated in portfolios. All the assessments meet specified guidelines: demonstration of an ability according to public criteria, feedback to the 'student, and self-assessment.

As students progress academically, they play an increasing role in selecting their own learning experiences and assessing their own performance. Advanced students regularly engage in independent projects or field experiences shaped by needs and opportunity in the community, for which learning and assessment plans are adapted or improvised. Although faculty members primarily do the assessing, approximately four hundred seasoned professionals from the business and professional urban community assist as external assessors of student performance. They participate in a training program designed and administered by the faculty. On an ongoing basis, they seek to improve their ability to interpret criteria, exercise judgment, and provide meaningful feedback.

The basic responsibility for articulating our assessment principles and practice and constantly refining the process by which they inform each other lies with the group of representative faculty members who make up the Assessment Council. They direct the development of collegewide instruments and criteria that assess abilities across disciplines. This work is carried on simultaneously in the academic and professional departments and the interdisciplinary departments that focus on the eight abilities. Council members also monitor student assessment techniques for comparability.

Institutional and Program Assessment: How It Works

In 1976, three years after the start of our program, we established the Office of Research and Evaluation to undertake the validation of the program and its process, including performance assessment techniques designed by the faculty. The office investigates how curricular elements caused learning, how college-learned abilities influenced the performance of our alumnae, and how these abilities compared to competencies that outstanding professionals use in practice. The resulting information contributes to continuous improvement, demonstrates quality and effectiveness, enables us to critique our own educational assumptions, and compares student and alumna performance to educator, employer, and public expectations.

An important principle that informs this evaluative work is that approaches and strategies must be consistent with the educational values, assumptions, and principles that inform the curriculum, including the psychometric implications inherent in ability-based performance assessment theory (Mentkowski, in press; Mentkowski, 1991a; Mentkowski and Loacker, 1985). Thus, office members collaborate with the faculty to create processes and structures—including a Research and Evaluation Committee of senior faculty and administrators—for generating questions, researching essential ones, providing feedback from multiple data sources that focuses on broad patterns, thus encouraging positive change.

The researchers draw standards from many internal and external sources, including descriptions of cognitive-developmental trajectories, ability models of professional performance, student and alumna constructions about their learning, and expectations of what graduates will need (Mentkowski, 1991b). A range of measurement techniques, drawn from diverse theoretical frameworks, also reinforce the adequacy of the standards and their dynamic nature.

From the start we felt it was important to create multiple strategies that can ensure diverse perspectives and data sources and that can yield both short- and long-term results. For example, instruments were drawn from outside the college to represent a number of theoretical frameworks in abilities, learning, and development and to give a picture of what is possible for humans to achieve. The researchers also developed many instruments and methods on their own, with an emphasis on in-depth, perspectives interviews of students and alumnae and performance interviews of graduates, to make possible a comparison with outstanding professionals who are not Alverno alumnae (DeBack and Mentkowski, 1986; Mentkowski and Rogers, 1993; Mentkowski and others, 1991).

Some of Alverno's current strategies are

1. Longitudinal analysis of student and alumna learning, development, and performance as a result of curriculum; analysis of who changes and why as a result of curriculum
2. Analysis of graduates' and other professionals' performance in work, personal, and citizenship roles
3. Evaluation of general education and the major field
4. Practitioner-based inquiry studies
5. Evaluation and validation of ability-based performance assessment (for example, defining contextual validity, developing strategies for validating faculty-designed performance assessment measures, defining criteria for "good" assessment)

Faculty Design and
Refinement of Assessment Strategies

Alverno faculty members design all the student assessments within the curriculum, on the basis of the abilities they have articulated as expected outcomes and the developmental criteria they have researched and assigned as standards each student must meet. The design process itself involves the constant discovery of data for improvement based on a model that the faculty have developed out of their practice. This model assures the inclusion of crucial elements and feedback in an evaluation of each aspect of design and implementation so that changes can be made as soon as data suggest them. The process can be seen as a cyclical progression that begins with identification of the particular ability to be assessed and identification of its components. Stimulus and performance criteria are then developed. The implementation includes eliciting student performances, exercising expert judgment, providing student feedback, and finally evaluating the entire process. Faculty members, when designing, and administering assessments, include all these elements (Alverno College Faculty, 1985, 1993; Loacker, 1988, 1991; Loacker, Cromwell, and O'Brien, 1986). After administering an assessment, we find it second nature to ask several questions. Did the stimulus evoke the abilities we wanted it to? Were the criteria clear and sufficient? Was there some aspect that no one learned? One faculty member's findings in designing and revising of a course instrument illustrates what goes on throughout the campus.

An In-Basket Assessment
Instrument in an Accounting Class

An accounting instructor uses as his midsemester assessment an in-basket, a collection primarily of memos, letters, and phone messages typical of a given day, incorporating multiple problems to be handled. At first, he had aimed to assess how students used the accounting concepts and skills they had learned thus far to solve a variety of problems in an organizational context. At the same time, he thought he would assess their judgment in setting priorities, in determining which problems required immediate attention and which could wait.

By studying the students' performances, the instructor discovered that he needed to emphasize different skills in the learning experiences of the course and in the assessment criteria. In the process, the students' ability to assign priority to tasks became irrelevant because the students generally did all of them, directly using the concepts they had learned. However, the teacher learned that they demonstrated little sensitivity to varied communication needs, to whether a situation required explanation, analysis, evaluation, decision, or recommendation. Nor did they select appropriate styles for different audiences (top management, peer managers, or staff employees). The instructor found that in his teaching he needed to concentrate more on the thinking processes that the student needed to use in responding to varied situations. He also had to provide the students more practice in adapting their responses to the specific contexts.

Through the same kind of process, faculty produce helpful findings that result in revision each time they administer more comprehensive assessments designed by departments or interdisciplinary teams. A general education assessment in the arts and humanities using across-the-curriculum portfolios provides another example.

Writing Portfolios

An example of how abilities may be demonstrated in diverse contexts can be seen in the development of portfolios. Since the start of the program, Alverno faculty members had kept copies of key performances, especially writing samples, as a cumulative record of each student's development. They found that they had bulging portfolios of products that had already been individually assessed. They soon saw that they could gain only limited understanding of patterns of development by reviewing final products. They could report changes but not how they had occurred.

At the same time, faculty members realized that they had incorporated into their teaching practice contemporary writing process theory, and they were committed to have their assessment reflect their instructional principles. As a result, they began to keep fewer writing samples, but each one represented as much of the process (pre writing and brainstorming notes, successive drafts, self-assessments, peer feedback, instructor feedback, final drafts) as possible (O'Brien, 1990).

In the meantime, the communication department, one of the interdisciplinary groups that provides direction and as-

sures quality in learning and assessment opportunities for a given
ability, was continuing its process of refining writing criteria
for individual products. This entailed work analyzing student
performance against existing criteria, synthesizing conclusions,
restating the criteria, and bringing them to the entire department and then to the entire faculty for feedback.

In addition to the gradual improvement of criteria for individual writing samples, the work led to consideration of standards for the entire process of development represented by a
student's portfolio. Communication department members are
now designing criteria by which both a student and her adviser
can study overall writing development in relation to expectations apt to be met at differing times. For instance, they look
at when a student begins to make more than surface revisions
and when she begins to revise on the basis of her own assessment, not only in response to feedback from others.

Design and Refinement of
Institutional Assessment Strategies

The Office of Research and Evaluation designed several studies
to respond to the question "Does the curriculum work?" They
were carried out to test educational assumptions, to find out
if students really were developing the abilities required of them.
Most of all, the faculty wanted to know what components contributed most, in the students' minds, to student learning, and
in what ways, so that they could better use those components
across the curriculum.

Thus, improvement and accountability were intertwined
in our goals almost as two sides of the same question. If faculty
members wanted to improve, they knew that they had to find
out what aspects were working best. If they wanted to continue
to improve, they knew that they had to keep probing precisely
how and why those aspects were working. The issue then becomes a matter of who changes over time, how, and why.

Students Learn Abilities Across Contexts

One key set of findings contributing to our ongoing commitment to improvement was that students learn general abilities

(Mentkowski and Doherty, 1983, 1984). Data revealed that these abilities, in performance, were visible to the faculty, students, and professionals from outside the college. Despite the various forms that the abilities took on in different disciplines and professional environments, they were recognizable. Performance also demonstrated that abilities were developed sequentially to increasingly complex levels.

Such findings confirmed the value of requiring students to develop abilities and of striving continually to develop their meaning. The findings also identified needs that faculty members have continued to address. One was the importance of continually refining how they articulate the sequential levels of each ability and to study them in relation to classroom experience, individual patterns of learning, and the expectations of other higher education faculty members and members of the professions.

Improved Definition of Abilities

Departments representing each ability constantly improve their statements of ability levels. Major, meaningful revisions have been published by the Communication, Analysis, Problem-Solving, and Social Interaction Departments (Alverno College Faculty, 1993; Loacker, Cromwell, Fey, and Rutherford, 1984; Loacker and Jensen, 1988; O'Brien, Matlock, Loacker, and Wutzdorff, 1991; Halonen, 1992). Within the past two years, reconceptualizations of ability levels have come from the Valuing, Aesthetic Responsiveness, Effective Citizenship, and Global Perspectives departments, each of which is gathering data to determine the significance of the incorporation of these levels into learning experiences across the curriculum.

Work in the Majors

The finding that abilities are recognizable in varied forms in different disciplines and professional environments has also influenced the effort of every department with a major or minor. Each has worked to produce an improved statement of expected outcomes unique to its discipline or profession but building on the basic abilities students develop in their general education

(Alverno College Faculty, 1990). The articulation of these departmental outcomes has resulted in more focused and developmentally coherent course designs, evident both in course proposals to the Curriculum Committee and syllabi for students. It has had the same effect on departmental plans for assessment incorporated into the student learning process. When education students present their pre-student-teaching portfolios, they know what stage of abilities is expected of them and how what they are doing relates to what is expected at graduation. When art students do a public presentation and explanation of their current "best piece" each semester, they understand where they are in relation to where they should be then and for graduation.

Learning to Learn

Our studies show that students become self-sustained learners and can identify curricular elements most important to their learning. Through careful analysis of longitudinal interviews, the research and evaluation staff identified three major components that describe the development of self-sustaining learning or "learning to learn" (Mentkowski and Doherty, 1984; Mentkowski, 1988).

Components of Self-Sustained Learning (Student Outcomes)	Student-Attributed Cause
Taking responsibility for learning	Instructor attention and empathy, feedback, self-assessment
Making relationships between abilities and their use	Experiential validation, instructor coaching, professional application, integration of abilities
Using different ways of learning	Practice, feedback, modeling, and peer learning

The conclusion that students believed that using different approaches contributed to their ability to learn was strengthened by another finding. Student learning styles changed dramatically—from a clear preference for a single mode (that of taking in information from concrete experience and processing it through reflective observation) to a more balanced pattern (showing flexibility in choosing approaches, and relying equally on concrete and abstract modes, on reflective and active ones) (Mentkowski and Doherty, 1983; Mentkowski, 1988).

Another set of related findings came from the analysis of essays developed in response to the Knefelkamp and Widick Measure of Intellectual Development (Knefelkamp, 1974; Mines, 1982). Using the Alverno Criteria for the Perry Scheme (Mentkowski, Moeser, and Strait, 1983), the researchers found that older students started at the same place as younger students when they entered. But after two years, older students had made more progress in constructing classroom learning: now they saw it as more active and made up of multiple approaches. Younger students did, however, catch up during the last two years, when they made a leap in development.

Confirming what was previously more a tentative suggestion than an assumption, these findings encouraged the faculty to build more systematically into the curriculum learning experiences that would enable students to develop varied perspectives and approaches. The faculty changed the entry reading-performance test, which formerly involved analyzing a single extended article, to a group of three articles, all making contradictory responses to the same question. The arts and humanities faculty more explicitly made the acquisition of multiple perspectives part of its expected outcomes for students.

Gradually, the Global Perspectives Department more clearly determined the ability for which it is responsible as "the developing of global perspectives." Formerly, it was "taking responsibility toward the global environment." At the early levels, students must now demonstrate the ability to "analyze global issues from multiple perspectives" (level two) and to "apply frameworks in formulating a response to global concerns and local issues" (level four). These statements have helped the faculty to provide students with more opportunities to develop different ways of thinking and learning (Alverno College faculty, 1992).

Contextual Validity

The entire process of faculty design and implementation in a framework of continuous improvement is part of how the Office of Research and Evaluation is defining contextual validity — inclusion of a multiplicity of individual faculty and departmental perspectives on ability definition and instrument design and use (Mentkowski, 1989; Mentkowski and Rogers, 1985, 1988; Rogers, 1988). The process complements another important component of contextual validity: students' current performance should mirror as closely as possible the performance that will be expected of them in roles after college, so that students can transfer their performance to a range of other settings. This and other extensions of definitions of validity have been necessary because some traditional concepts and strategies proved not congruent with the underlying assumptions and principles of our assessment system.

Validation of Instruments

In addition to depending on the Office of Research and Evaluation to rethink the meaning of validity and to articulate a framework for it that would preserve the integrity of our system, the faculty turn to that office to assist in the validation of individual instruments. In collaboration with the faculty members that make up the Assessment Council, the research and evaluation staff has developed a series of strategies for the faculty to apply to instruments (Alverno College Office of Research and Evaluation, and Assessment Committee, 1989; Mentkowski and Rogers, 1988; Rogers, 1988).

For developing design-based validity, strategies include evaluating components in relation to guidelines for instrument design formulated by the Assessment Council. For establishing performance-based validity, strategies include evaluating criteria based on student performance; finding agreement between assessors and reviewers; evaluating assessor training and use of criteria, judgment, and feedback; and establishing that assessment leads to student learning. The choice of strategy for an individual instrument depends on where the instrument is in its development, whether the instrument is used in or outside class, and whether it is used as a milestone measure to judge a student's development of abilities across the curriculum. At the time these strategies examine validity, they also assist the faculty to achieve improvement goals within the assessment process.

Self-Assessment as a Developing Student Ability: A Prototype of Ongoing Change as Improvement

From the beginning of our program, the faculty assumed some degree of importance for self-assessment. However, our practice and evaluation studies have established the centrality of self-assessment and the need to develop it through progressive learning experiences; performance assessment is part of that learning.

Since the program began, level one of communication has centered on self-assessment. Before students entered, we assessed varied modes of communication, including reading, writing, speaking, listening, and quantitative reasoning. For each of these modes, students had to produce a performance and then judge it themselves according to criteria expressed in concrete questions.

After the first administration of the assessment, we found that students were unable to assess their own performance in speaking and writing. Besides lacking distance, they needed some practice in finding evidence and making judgments on the basis of criteria. Accordingly, we stopped asking students to assess their own writing and speaking performances at the time they produced them. We initiated a half-day session during orientation week for input and practice after which they did a self-assessment. This resulted in significant improvement in their ability to assess their own writing and speaking.

When the Assessment Council was studying how the faculty elicits self-assessment from the students, it found multiple methods, some more effective than others, but no clear pattern to assist students in approaching self-assessment developmentally.

Since the research and evaluation staff was working on further analysis of the interview data it had collected, it collaborated with the Assessment Council to discern students' developing perspectives on self-assessment (Loacker, 1991; Much and Mentkowski, 1984). They found that beginning students looked at self-assessment as the imposition of the instructor's job upon the reluctant student. Intermediate students were more willing to cooperate and participate. Advanced students looked at self-assessment as an ability they exercise not only willingly but at their own initiative because it assists them to improve their performance and to establish growing confidence in their own judgment.

Subsequent communication of these findings to faculty members has led them to design stimuli for self-assessment that are aimed at encouraging further development, not too broad at an early stage or too narrowly restricted at an advanced stage. Student writing portfolios have built-in, progressively sophisticated self-assessments. Departments include comprehensive self-assessments at key points in the students' academic career as part of their cumulative record.

Lasting Impact and Contributing Factors

There is no question that assessment as an integral part of the students' learning process and as a means of evaluating programs and the institution will endure at Alverno. It may in the future be called something else. We hope it will take new, increasingly creative forms. But unless someone proves the unlikely hypothesis that knowing how well one is doing does not contribute to further improvement, assessment will always take place at Alverno; improvement for us is systematic rather than intermittent.

With administrative direction that fosters faculty responsibility and focuses on accountability to the student, the Alverno faculty has developed a coherent system of education that incorporates assessment as an integral part. That system has been put into place within a strong, supportive culture. The coherence of the system rests on articulating and interrelating educational mission, values, assumptions, principles, theory, and practice. It relies on the reconceptualization of the use of time, academic structures, and other resources to bring about increasingly effective learning for students.

The words of a student indicate the possible impact of assessment on an individual: "Assessing has become such a part of you that it's something you're going to do your whole life. Every time you do something, or when you're about to do something, you're going to think about it. And after it's done you'll say, 'Well, what did I do well? What did I do wrong?' You're going to use it everywhere—in your nursing, in your art, in your marriage. It will be integrated into your lives."

References

Alverno College Office of Research and Evaluation, and Assessment Committee. *Putting the Validation Process to Work: A Series of Strategies for Establishing the Validity of Faculty-Designed Performance Assessment Instruments.* Milwaukee, Wisc.: Alverno Productions, 1989.

Alverno College Faculty. *Assessment at Alverno College.* (Rev. ed.) Milwaukee, Wisc.: Alverno Productions, 1985.

Alverno College Faculty. *Advanced Outcomes in the Major and Support Areas.* Milwaukee, Wisc.: Alverno Productions, 1990.

Alverno College Faculty. *Liberal Learning at Alverno College.* (Rev. ed.) Milwaukee, Wisc.: Alverno Productions, 1992.

Alverno College Faculty. *Student Assessment as Learning.* Milwaukee, Wisc.: Alverno Productions, 1993.

DeBack, V., and Mentkowski, M. "Does the Baccalaureate Make a Difference: Differentiating Nurse Performance by Education and Experience." *Journal of Nursing Education,* 1986, *25*(7), 275–285.

Halonen, J. (ed.). *Teaching Social Interaction at Alverno.* Milwaukee, Wisc.: Alverno Productions, 1992.

Knefelkamp, L. "Developmental Instruction Fostering Intellectual and Personal Growth in College Students." Unpublished doctoral dissertation, University of Minnesota, 1974.

Loacker, G. "Faculty as a Force to Improve Instruction Through Assessment." In J. McMillan (ed.), *Assessing Students' Learning.* New Directions for Teaching and Learning, no. 34. San Francisco: Jossey-Bass, 1988.

Loacker, G. "Designing a National Assessment System: Alverno's Institutional Perspective." Paper commissioned by the

National Center for Education Statistics, U.S. Department
of Education (in response to the national education goals panel
America 2000: An Education Strategy). Milwaukee, Wisc.:
Alverno Productions, 1991. (ED 340 758)

Loacker, G., Cromwell, L., Fey, J., and Rutherford, D. *Analysis and Communication at Alverno: An Approach to Critical Thinking.* Milwaukee, Wisc.: Alverno Productions, 1984.

Loacker, G., Cromwell, L., and O'Brien, K. "Assessment in
Higher Education: To Serve the Learner." In C. Adelman
(ed.), *Assessment in Higher Education: Issues and Contexts.* Report
no. OR 86-301. Washington, D.C.: U.S. Department of Education, 1986.

Loacker, G., and Jensen, P. "The Power of Performance in Developing Problem Solving and Self Assessment Abilities." *Assessment and Evaluation in Higher Education,* 1988, *13*(2), 128–150.

Mentkowski, M. "Paths to Integrity: Educating for Personal
Growth and Professional Performance." In S. Srivastva and
Associates (eds.), *Executive Integrity: The Search for High Human Values in Organizational Life.* San Francisco: Jossey-Bass,
1988.

Mentkowski, M. "Establishing the Validity and Integrity of
Higher Education Assessment: Some Issues for Discussion."
Paper presented at the 4th National Conference on Assessment in Higher Education, Atlanta, Ga., 1989.

Mentkowski, M. "Creating a Context Where Institutional Assessment Yields Educational Improvement." *Journal of General Education,* 1991a, *40,* 255–283.

Mentkowski, M. "Designing a National Assessment System: Assessing Abilities That Connect Education and Work." Paper
commissioned by the National Center for Education Statistics, U.S. Department of Education (in response to the national education goals panel America 2000: An Education
Strategy). Milwaukee, Wisc.: Alverno Productions, 1991b.
(ED 340 759)

Mentkowski, M. "Higher Education Assessment and National
Goals for Education: Some Issues, Assumptions, and Principles for Discussion." In B. L. McCombs and N. Lambert

(eds.), *Issues in School Reform: A Sampler of Psychological Perspectives.* Washington, D.C.: American Psychological Association, in press.

Mentkowski, M., and Associates. "Understanding Abilities, Learning, and Development Through College Outcomes Studies: What Can We Expect from Higher Education Assessment?" Symposium presented at the annual meeting of the American Educational Research Association, Chicago, Ill., 1991. (ED 342 296)

Mentkowski, M., and Doherty, A. *Careering After College: Establishing the Validity of Abilities Learned in College for Later Careering and Professional Performance.* (Rev. ed.) Final Report to the National Institute of Education. Milwaukee, Wisc.: Alverno Productions, 1983. (ED 239 556 to ED 239 566)

Mentkowski, M., and Doherty, A. "Abilities That Last a Lifetime: Outcomes of the Alverno Experience." *AAHE Bulletin,* 1984, *36*(6), 5–6, 11–14.

Mentkowski, M., and Loacker, G. "Assessing and Validating the Outcomes of College." In P. T. Ewell (ed.), *Assessing Educational Outcomes.* New Directions for Institutional Research, no. 47. San Francisco: Jossey-Bass, 1985.

Mentkowski, M., Moeser, M., and Strait, M. *Using the Perry Scheme of Intellectual and Ethical Development as a College Outcomes Measure: A Process and Criteria for Judging Student Performance,* Vols. 1 and 2. Milwaukee, Wisc.: Alverno Productions, 1983.

Mentkowski, M., and Rogers, G. *Longitudinal Assessment of Critical Thinking in College: What Measures Assess Curricular Impact?* Milwaukee, Wisc.: Alverno Productions, 1985.

Mentkowski, M., and Rogers, G. *Establishing the Validity of Measures of College Student Outcomes.* Milwaukee, Wisc.: Alverno Productions, 1988.

Mentkowski, M., and Rogers, G. "Connecting Education, Work, and Citizenship." *Metropolitan Universities: An International Forum,* 1993, *4*(1), 34–46.

Mines, R. "Student Development Assessment Techniques." In G. R. Hanson (ed.), *Measuring Student Development.* New Directions for Student Services, no. 20. San Francisco: Jossey-Bass, 1982.

Much, N., and Mentkowski, M. *Student Perspectives on Learning and Development in College.* Milwaukee, Wisc.: Alverno Productions, 1984.

O'Brien, K. *Portfolio Assessment at Alverno College.* Milwaukee, Wisc.: Alverno Productions, 1990.

O'Brien, K., Matlock, M. G., Loacker, G., and Wutzdorff, A. "Problem Solving at Alverno College." In D. Boud and G. Feletti (eds.), *The Challenge of Problem Based Learning.* London, England: Kogan Page, 1991.

Rogers, G. "Validating College Outcomes with Institutionally Developed Instruments: Issues in Maximizing Contextual Validity." Paper presented at the annual meeting of the American Educational Research Association, New Orleans, Louisiana, Apr. 1988. Milwaukee, Wisc.: Alverno Productions, 1988.

2

Providing
Leadership for
Organizational Change

Candace Cartwright Young
Michael E. Knight

Through a combination of a consistent vision, outstanding
leadership, and an innovative assessment program, presidents
at two universities transformed campus cultures and brought
about higher levels of student learning. During the 1980s, Northeast Missouri State University (NMSU) and Kean College of
New Jersey, once typical regional comprehensive state universities, became public universities that attracted national praise
and attention. Each president used assessment to draw attention to the importance of student learning, to help identify
campus strengths and weaknesses, to encourage program and
teaching improvements, and to monitor the success of new initiatives. Perhaps even more important, the presidents accomplished the rare feat of focusing faculty discussion and energy
on the improvement of student learning in and out of the classroom. Innovative cultures evolved. The stories of two institutions that made dramatic institutional changes with the assistance
of assessment follow.

25

Northeast Missouri State University

Charles J. McClain became the tenth president of NMSU in 1970. Upon assuming office, he faced significant challenges, such as preparing for accrediting self-studies under tight time constraints, guiding the school's transition from a teachers college to a regional comprehensive university, unifying a divided faculty and board, and maintaining stable enrollments despite a declining population in the service region of NMSU. It would have been exceedingly difficult to predict that McClain's concern with academic quality would be more than standard presidential rhetoric. Looking beyond the immediate deadlines and routine pressures, Charles McClain, his new dean, Darrell Krueger, and the faculty developed an assessment program that cultivated and reinforced a shared value system centered on student learning.

President McClain believed that as a teachers college, NMSU had a well-established direction: "Faculty and staff could verify how well they were doing by the placement of graduates, and by the intimate working relationship that the college had developed with the public schools and regional superintendents" (McClain and Krueger, 1985, pp. 33–34). However, with the regional *comprehensive* university mission implemented in 1972, Northeast Missouri needed to establish confidence in its new academic programs.

Quality measures in education are difficult to agree upon. Yet people do make judgments about institutional quality. Early in his administration, President McClain made it clear that he did not think NMSU should rely on traditional input methods of assessing quality, such as reputation and resources. Instead, the emphasis should be placed on the learning outcomes and value-added models of measuring quality. McClain and Krueger (1985) wanted the university to be able to demonstrate that it graduated students who were nationally competitive in their chosen fields of study and that it had made a difference in students' knowledge, skills, and attitudes. Thus, the university came to refer to its program as value-added assessment even though only a portion of the data collected accurately fit the paradigm.

Leadership for the Assessment Initiative

Critical to the success of the effort was McClain and Krueger's incremental and low-key manner of implementation. The administration repeatedly assured the faculty that the data would be used to help strengthen programs, not to eliminate either programs or individual faculty members. Faculty received annual and historical data on their student majors along with university averages and national norms when available; however, they did not receive comparative cross-campus data. Assessment became the vital linking mechanism of the university that allowed everyone to communicate using a common vocabulary and organizational focus. The president and the dean of instruction chose not to create a central assessment office. They feared that such an office would reduce faculty interaction with and analysis of the data, thus relegating assessment to an auxiliary exercise.

The president and the dean of instruction became the critical catalysts for faculty to consider the data. Each routinely used university data in conversations about the strengths and weaknesses of the campus, future goals for the university, and new program initiatives. In addition to demonstrating themselves how the data could be used, McClain and Krueger employed other strategies. These included committee work that required the faculty to review data on selected topics; informal inquiries in the hall (for example, "What do you think happened to Jane Smith? She has a 3.8 GPA in the major but only scored at the 20th percentile on her senior exam."); and assigned presentations on various topics at faculty workshops, planning retreats, or governing board meetings. Through these and other strategies, a significant percentage of faculty members interacted with the data. Similarly, the president and dean "planted" numerous seeds to suggest possible improvement initiatives, many of which faculty adopted.

Methods Employed

By 1981, the university had a relatively comprehensive system that required all students to take a nationally normed test upon

entry to and completion of the general education program, successfully complete the writing assessment, take a nationally
normed examination in the major, and complete a student survey. In the mid 1980s, faculty initiated additional programs that
complemented the standardized testing and survey assessments
with more qualitative ones and more student self-evaluation.
In 1986, the Faculty Senate adopted a requirement for capstone
experiences in the major and in 1989 added portfolio assessment of the liberal arts and sciences. Under NMSU's new president, Russell Warren, annual interview-based studies and an
oral communication assessment were initiated in 1992.

In addition, the university encourages faculty to create
program-level assessments for their majors and classroom evaluations in their courses. For example, a major requirement may
be a thesis, which is then formally presented before external examiners. Other majors may require students to give a presentation at an organized forum outside class, sit for a local comprehensive examination, prepare a discipline portfolio, or have
an interview with faculty from the discipline.

One commitment that Northeast Missouri has made over
the last twenty years is that every student should participate in
assessment. The university encourages students to use the information for self-assessment, and each adviser receives data
reports for students for which he or she is responsible. Another
area where NMSU remains atypical is that assessment continues
to be an activity of division heads and faculty. Two staff assis-
tants administer tests and facilitate information flow to faculty,
and these administrators are critical to the enterprise. However,
they remain backstage; they are facilitators, not directors of the
assessment effort. It is largely because of faculty involvement
and the extensive use of data by the president and chief academic officer that assessment findings have become an important part of campus decision making.

Assessment Findings and Resultant Change

Opinions about the significance of decades of assessment at
Northeast Missouri vary. Different academic divisions have their

own ways of using assessment and analyzing data, but all faculty
are aware of the existence of the assessment data and have access to them. In a faculty survey for our last accrediting self-
study, 69 percent of the faculty agreed with the statement "The
program of assessment developed by the University to measure
student achievement fosters curriculum evaluation and development." Only 11 percent disagreed. The same percentages of
faculty members agreed and disagreed that "NMSU's assessment system fosters discussions on the effectiveness of individual academic programs." Though not unanimous, the faculty's
support for and interest in assessment is unusually strong. One
indicator of this fact is that over the last ten years more than
20 percent of faculty members have participated in briefing visitors on Northeast Missouri's assessment program. Without the
sincere commitment of university leaders to academic excellence — as demonstrated by their speeches, conversations, and
disproportionate allocation of resources to academics and the
development of an intellectual environment — the faculty's will-
ingness to accept assessment and to support and implement
change probably would have been far less.

One of the most important benefits of assessment is the
data's ability to raise the critical questions, thereby setting the
institutional discussion and decision agenda. The data can assist
an institution in identifying problem areas and in monitoring
programmatic change. However, faculty-administrative conversations, grounded in the data, provide the primary opportunities
for university leadership to effect positive change. Concomi-
tantly, by combining multiple pieces of assessment information
with informed faculty and staff analysis, institution decision making gains legitimacy and focus.

President McClain and Dean Krueger were particularly
adept at suggesting program innovations that increased faculty-
student interaction, conveyed higher expectations for the academic development of students, and heightened students' involvement in learning. These initiatives included

- Increasing time on tasks and standards for student achievement

- Limiting the size of most introductory courses to forty or fewer students
- Requiring more writing across the curriculum
- Revising courses to teach the breadth of the discipline
- Developing a sequence rationale to coursework in the major
- Introducing a freshman week and freshman seminar experience
- Creating residential colleges, additional speaker series, an undergraduate research program, and learning communities

By the time the *Nation at Risk Report* (National Commission on Excellence in Education, 1983) and *Involvement in Learning* (National Institute of Education, 1984) were published, Northeast Missouri was already well advanced in implementing many of the reports' proposals. As Darrell Krueger (1992) recently asserted, it was only by linking assessment to causal models of educational quality that improvement at Northeast occurred.

Curricular change has occurred throughout the university. The key, according to one professor, "is whether the numbers shake you out of your complacency. We all thought we were good before, but the numbers convinced us that we needed to make changes in the curriculum and in the way we designed student questions and assignments" (Ordovensky, 1989, p. D1). Without assessment, the faculty might have reached similar conclusions, but probably not, and certainly not so swiftly. Although the data helped to raise questions, analysis by faculty of what students needed to know and be able to do upon graduation determined decisions. Across the campus, disciplines can now point to better writing and increased library use by students, improved performance by students on senior exams, and greater student satisfaction. The campus portfolio assessment furthers faculty understanding of student learning and will assist the campus (along with the testing, survey, and interview data) in restructuring its core curriculum and refining its liberal arts and sciences outcomes objectives.

Lasting Impact of Assessment

Changes that were made resulted from more than the data alone. The data cannot and should not be the sole determinant of decisions. The faculty, staff, and administrators must have the integrity to interpret information in a larger context of values and evidence. Individual members of the university community are really the ones responsible for change. The leadership of many brought the university to a higher order of excellence and to its current statewide designation as the premier liberal arts and sciences institution.

According to Peter Ewell (1984), self-definition and self-examination constituted the first and most important steps in the institutional improvement of NMSU. Through internal standards and evaluation, institutions help chart their course to better quality. Without a doubt, the assessment culture at Northeast Missouri causes the campus community to think more clearly about the desired outcomes of a college degree and as a result to analyze which methods, processes, and curricula are most likely to achieve the desired results.

Today, students attend Northeast Missouri because of the quality of the academic program, whereas fifteen years ago students reported choosing the university because of its low cost. Today, 30 percent of students pursue a graduate or professional degree; fifteen years ago, approximately 10 percent did so. In addition, graduates are attending a much more diverse and prestigious group of graduate schools.

When NMSU assumed its new mission, the faculty prepared an extensive five-year plan for implementation, complete with data projections for students' intellectual, personal, and social growth. Each year, the faculty reviews the data and updates the plan. In short, the culture embraces and creates the expectation that the faculty will specify objectives, create multiple methods for assessing them, and then review and analyze the information.

Symbolically, a campus indicates to the faculty, students, and others what is important by what it chooses to monitor. At Northeast Missouri, two decades of focusing on student learning in and out of the classroom has produced an institution with unusually high interest in teaching and learning. Over the last twenty years, the administration has spoken with a single voice regarding institutional priorities. Thus, NMSU has come to resemble Peters and Waterman's recommended "loose-tight" management practice (1982), whereby a set of shared values emphasizing student learning and the creation of an intellectual, academic environment provide the common framework for decentralized innovation and use. The faculty, staff, and students realize that there are stable expectations about what really counts. The culture that has evolved centers on the university's dedication to academic excellence, combined with an encouragement of faculty and staff exploration of better ways to accomplish the goal.

Will the impact be lasting? Organizational cultures, once transformed, continue to evolve. As in the past, the future of assessment depends on the university leadership's continued emphasis on high academic standards and continuous improvement, frequent use of assessment information, and creation of vehicles for faculty-administrative conversations grounded in the data.

Kean College of New Jersey

In 1985, Nathan Weiss, president of Kean College, initiated assessment by communicating the following vision: "We are committed to serving the students in our region, to making sure that they achieve the level of academic success we think they should achieve, and to providing developmental course work and special learning-assistance programs to make sure our students have opportunities to succeed. Our focus therefore has been not to increase standards for admission, but to increase standards for graduation" (Boyer, 1989, p. 3). It has been the responsibility of the assessment effort to support this focus.

All significant organizational changes require broad-based support if they are to be successful and sustainable. The primary source of the leadership necessary to develop this support for assessment at Kean was the president, Nathan Weiss. His vision of the college has been fostered through an approach of planting many seeds—that is, making suggestions, providing materials on a new idea, waiting for the seeds to germinate, and providing the support and encouragement necessary for the ideas to be implemented.

In some areas, Weiss acted in a more directive manner. The following quotation best presents the level of commitment that he demonstrated: "Every crusade needs champions or inspired leaders who embody the vision. People like Nat Weiss of Kean College don't just say the right words; they live them; they feel them. Weiss saw himself as leading a crusade." (Seymour, 1992, p. 110).

A limited number of faculty responded enthusiastically to the call for demonstrating the effectiveness of academic programs at Kean, and pockets of interest developed in using assessment as a stimulus for improvement. Faculty indicated their interest through a self-nominating process, and a base level of support was established. Weiss recognized the need to involve faculty in providing leadership and carrying the responsibility for implementing the assessment project. He recruited two faculty members, gave them a high degree of responsibility and authority, and supported their efforts vigorously.

In August 1985, Kean College submitted a proposal responding to New Jersey governor Thomas Kean's challenge to the state colleges to develop a comprehensive plan that would "chart their own paths to greatness." The plan was to center on institutional mission and to document the efforts of each college "to strengthen, to modify, and to clarify the institution's mission and to make the college academically distinctive." The challenge grant provided the opportunity for a number of Kean faculty, professional staff, and administrators to coalesce around the idea of assessment. President Weiss said, "The need for participation arises especially when major policy must be made, and it requires that those who are substantially affected by a decision (or those who must implement that decision) be consulted by the decision makers. The process of participation thus entails consultation, the forging of consensus, the decision itself, and implementation" (Ross and Weiss, 1991, p. 21).

During both the development and the approval of the grant proposal, broad involvement was achieved. The approval process required the participation of significant numbers of the faculty, professional staff, and administrators and created opportunities for all those interested to present their views. As a result, the number of people supporting the assessment effort increased, and the design moved toward one that was acceptable to a broad constituency.

After the college made a commitment to assessment, the president appointed a task force to study possible approaches and to make recommendations for specific programs. The twenty-four-member group had wide representation from the faculty, students, administrators, and members of the local board of trustees. Some members of the group had participated in the discussions developing the assessment proposal, and some had attended the American Association for Higher Education's first national conference on assessment earlier in the term.

Methods Employed

The Proposal for Program Assessment at Kean College of New Jersey (1986) presented five methods from which programs could select in designing and implementing assessment plans: licensing or certifying examinations; faculty-developed, criterion-referenced tests; senior seminars; coherent clusters; and key courses. These methods were offered in the spirit of Robert Waterman's "congenial controls"—providing guidance without restrictions and help rather than a prescription (Lumsden, Knight, and Gallaro, 1989).

Every academic program established a program assessment committee with faculty and student representatives. A suggestion was made to include alumni and professionals practicing in the particular discipline. This committee has the responsibility of developing the assessment plans and recommending these for the approval of the entire program faculty. One or more faculty members of the committee are designated as assessment liaisons. These individuals have the responsibility of coordinating assessment activities, writing reports, and reporting at department meetings.

As expected, there is great variety in the data collected and use of data collection tools. Assessment activities include analyzing student information data and test scores, evaluating portfolios and senior projects, conducting surveys and exit interviews, organizing focus groups, and requiring a variety of performances specific to the major.

Assessment Findings and Resultant Change

When Kean College initiated its outcomes assessment process in 1985, the program was designed to promote improvement as well as academic and personal growth for its students. At this time, analysis of the effect of the assessment program indicates that there have been far-reaching outcomes for the faculty as well as for students.

A comparison of the impact on various programs is difficult because each has designed and implemented its own procedures. Programs are also at different stages of development since the entire process was launched in four waves. Certain trends in the effect of assessment, however, can be identified.

The responses of faculty to surveys and interviews indicate a high level of satisfaction because of faculty members' increased participation in the definition and evaluation of the goals and objectives for their individual programs. The consensus achieved in the goal-setting phases has led to a feeling of camaraderie among colleagues. Faculty confidence in programs has been reaffirmed. Awareness of curriculum articulation from course to course has been enhanced. Faculty have become acutely aware of the coordination required between teaching and learning. Perhaps more important, the assessment process has led to general faculty renewal.

There have been many improvements in student life since the inception of the assessment process at Kean. Faculty and program advising has been augmented to improve communication of program goals and objectives between students and faculty. Students have become part of the process, rather than merely the purpose of it.

In the area of the academic majors, the focus of many courses has been adjusted to emphasize application as well as theory. Unnecessary course material has been eliminated. Important topics that were previously untaught have been added to curricula. Senior seminars have been added to consolidate learning.

The assessment process has resulted in many program-specific changes that can be grouped under the general headings of classroom practices, curriculum, and student life. In the areas of curriculum and classroom practices, surveys indicate that a majority of the faculty members participating in assessment have reported experiencing a greater sense of influence in shaping the academic program, a better understanding of program strengths and weaknesses, an increased involvement with colleagues in the discipline, and an improved effort among colleagues to place emphasis on high-priority goals in more than one course.

Assessment has had significant campuswide impact. Some of the changes implemented by many programs are identified below:

- Modification or creation of senior seminars
- Distribution of program goals and course sequences to students
- Increased emphasis on writing, oral communication, application, performance, and integration of students' learning
- Incorporation of portfolios with program assessment
- Expanded opportunities for internships and clinical experiences
- Integration of computers throughout the curriculum
- Revision of advising practices
- Inclusion of affective goals as part of the curriculum

When so many innovations to improve student learning and satisfaction were implemented throughout the campus, a change in campus culture occurred. One testament to the impact of assessment is that many of these changes are described as being built into the program and are no longer perceived as assessment activities.

Studying these two examples of leadership, assessment, and organizational change, one can observe many similarities between the two institutional leaders' visions and styles. As a crucial beginning point, each president served the institution for many years — enough time to build a clear vision and to persist in multiple efforts to realize it. Each continually brought attention to his educational vision and applied it to campus issues. As a critical part of the vision, each sought increases in the standards for student learning. These presidents expected the university to make a difference and to be able to *demonstrate* that it had done so.

Both emphasized the importance of the faculty's role in what they defined as the institution's primary enterprises: teaching and learning. Each sought faculty involvement in goal setting for student learning and in assessment development and analysis. The opportunities created for faculty to discuss desired student outcomes increased the commitment of faculty to outcome objectives and enhanced their common sense of purpose. The leadership team of each institution provided important support and encouragement for initiatives that furthered these objectives.

President McClain and President Weiss used assessment to focus attention on lofty goals for student learning. By making this their top priority, these leaders placed the faculty, their students, and the learning process at the center of the institution. Elevating the importance of teaching and learning enhanced faculty morale, the university community's sense of purpose, and the faculty's commitment to student learning.

According to Waterman (1988, p. 21), "Entropy says that everything that is organized will break down or run down unless it is maintained." One of a leader's responsibilities is therefore the need to inject energy into the system to fight this natural tendency of organizations.

Max DePree, chairman of Herman Miller, a Fortune 500 company, provides an interesting perspective on leadership from the corporate world. His reflective questions, such as "Can I be somebody here? Is there for me any rhyme or reason here? Can I 'own' this place?" (1989, p. 10), bring attention to the nexus between organizational culture and the individual's sense of belonging and importance. Leaders need to provide meaning to organizational members and encourage improvement or else accept unmotivated employees, stagnation, and mediocrity. Leaders at Kean and Northeast Missouri crafted environments that encourage innovation. Numerous teaching and learning initiatives were adopted and implemented. It was this focused, innovative organizational culture, grounded in assessment, that caused cross-campus learning initiatives to flourish. Today, assessment validates progress, continues to identify strengths and weaknesses, and helps to maintain what Ewell (1984) has called a "self-regarding" culture. Used effectively, it also can bring focus, direction, and improvement to the university. The alignment of leadership vision, leadership style, and assessment practice makes the difference between assessment for improvement and its use as an auxiliary reporting exercise. Through a synergistic combination of leadership, programmatic change, and assessment, organizations can fight off mediocrity and entropy. Witness Northeast Missouri State University and Kean College of New Jersey.

References

Boyer, C. *Improving Student Learning: The Outcomes Assessment Program.* Union, N.J.: Kean College Press, 1989.

DePree, M. *Leadership Is an Art.* New York: Doubleday, 1989.

Ewell, P. *The Self-Regarding Institution: Information for Excellence.* Boulder, Colo.: National Center for Higher Education Management Systems, 1984.

Krueger, D. "A Return to Excellence." *Assessment Update,* 1992, *4,* 1–4.

Lumsden, D., Knight, M., and Gallaro, D. "Assessing Learning Outcomes: Opportunities for Institutional Renewal." *Journal of Staff, Program and Organizational Development,* 1989, *7,* 181–185.

McClain, C., and Krueger, D. "Using Outcomes Assessment: A Case Study in Institutional Change." In P. T. Ewell (ed.), *Assessing Educational Outcomes.* New Directions for Institutional Research, no. 47. San Francisco: Jossey-Bass, 1985.

National Commission on Excellence in Education. *A Nation at Risk.* Washington, D.C.: U.S. Government Printing Office, 1983.

National Institute of Education. *Involvement in Learning: Realiz-*

ing the Potential of American Higher Education. Washington, D.C.: U.S. Department of Education, 1984.

Ordovensky, P. "Special Tests Give Students an Edge." *USA Today,* Feb. 2, 1989, p. D1.

Peters, T., and Waterman, R. *In Search of Excellence: Lessons from America's Best-Run Companies.* New York: Warner Books, 1982.

Ross, H., and Weiss, N. "Accountability and Autonomy: Achieving Institutional Change Through Shared Governance." In P. Van Dyke (ed.), *Keeping the Promise: Achieving and Maintaining Quality in Undergraduate Education.* Washington, D.C.: American Association of State Colleges and Universities, 1991.

Seymour, D. *On Q: Causing Quality in Higher Education.* New York: American Council on Education, Macmillan, 1992.

Waterman, R. *The Renewal Factor: How the Best Act and Keep the Competitive Edge.* New York: Bantam Books, 1988.

3

Using Assessment to Enhance Quality

A. Michael Williford
Gary O. Moden

The state of Ohio does not currently mandate student evaluation in any form, but for more than a decade Ohio University has committed itself to assessing its students. This commitment was developed as a result of President Charles J. Ping's 1980 state-of-the-university address, titled "Quality Dependent on the Making of Judgments," which called for the university to make a commitment to improved quality. In this address, President Ping (1980, p. 9) stated, "The conclusion too often drawn is that state officials must design and supervise the processes of program review and ultimately make determinations. . . . If it comes to Ohio, it will be because we bring it on ourselves by our failure to define and measure the quality of our own programs or because we refuse to act on judgments emerging from internal reviews."

In making this commitment, Ohio University assumed responsibility for defining and examining its growth in quality as a part of a ten-year plan adopted in 1978. President Ping also stated in his address that the assessment must have consequences and offer direction for decision making and action if it was to be of value. The focus of the effort was communicated by the statement "The key issue is whether we can use the [assessment] process of defining and examining to enhance quality" (1980, p. 6).

In 1980, an institutional-impact task force of faculty and staff was appointed to spend a year developing (with the assistance of the director of institutional research) a coherent, systematic, and ongoing program of assessing institutional quality and its impact on students. The objective was to enable the university, *within five to ten years,* to describe systematically through its students what was happening in its life as an educational institution and to evaluate improvement of the performance of individuals and programs.

The program designed by the task force addresses goals from the university's ten-year educational plan, including "providing our students with the knowledge and skills which are the essence of a solid liberal education" (Ohio University, 1977, p. 18) and "encouraging the development of an environment on the residential campus that reflects a vital commitment to learning and provides a community life for students" (p. 38). The assessment program takes into account the whole collegiate experience, not merely the specific knowledge and skills gained from a major field of study. It includes a diverse set of measures, allowing for the addition of new instruments or measures as they become available and the rejection of instruments as they become dated.

Ohio University's program — the Institutional Impact Project — has helped the university define its mission, judge its quality, and enhance its stature and effectiveness. The assessment program has provided useful information that has helped guide the development of the university as it approaches its third century of operation.

Program Description

The Institutional Impact Project uses both nationally developed and locally designed instruments. Five dimensions are included. First, the American College Testing (ACT) College Outcome

Measures Program (ACT-COMP) is employed to assess the impact of Ohio University's general education program on its students. A longitudinal design is used as an indicator of value-added learning gain in generic knowledge and skills from the freshman to the senior year.

Second, the student involvement study, originally designed by the Center for Helping Organizations Improve Choice in Education (Project CHOICE) and modified locally, collects information on three areas of involvement: academic involvement, social involvement and activities, and students' commitment to and satisfaction with the institution. A longitudinal design is used as an indicator of change in involvement patterns from the freshman to the senior year. Individual freshman responses are also used to identify potential (voluntary) dropouts each year so that residence life and other support staff can intervene to improve student retention.

Third, assessment related to retention and success is collected in the university's student-tracking system, which utilizes a longitudinal cohort survival method of tracking all freshmen until they either graduate or drop out. The purpose is to identify groups with the potential for high attrition, monitor progress within retention programs from year to year, and document progress in graduation rates.

Fourth, a student treatment study is used to measure satisfaction in all areas of university life. This study collects information on the attitudes and perceptions of new freshmen (after one quarter of enrollment) about the campus and its environment: treatment received from other people, quality of information received, and processes like academic advising.

Fifth, two follow-up studies of graduates, a short-term placement survey and a long-term alumni survey, are made. The placement survey is designed to collect basic placement and satisfaction information on graduates within one year of graduation. A more detailed alumni survey has been developed to survey graduates after they are away from the university for at least five years. The questionnaires address job placement information; employment status, satisfaction, and responsibilities; relevance of educational experience to employment; problems in seeking employment; competencies needed and developed; additional degrees received; and changes that graduates would make in their education. In the alumni questionnaire, each of the eight academic colleges at Ohio University asks questions specific to its program.

These five components—ACT-COMP test, student involvement surveys, student-tracking system, student treatment survey, and follow-up studies of graduates—compose the Institutional Impact Project. The system is evaluated regularly to ensure that it is meeting the needs of the campus community. Instruments are modified to respond to changes and areas that require further attention. From time to time, ad hoc assessments are included. For example, characteristics of entering freshmen and results from the freshman marketing and image study have provided valuable information during the university's transition from open to selective admissions.

Uses of Assessment Information
Linked to Quality Enhancement

The Institutional Impact Project is integrated into the planning processes of Ohio University. According to President Ping in his 1980 state-of-the-university address, "The measure of impact is an imperative both of integrity and of thoughtful planning. The value added to people's lives is, to use a very worn phrase, 'the bottom line,' in the success or failure of an institution. It would be as senseless for a business firm to ignore whether or not it is making a profit as it is senseless for a university to assume blindly that it cannot, or need not, understand its impact on students" (1980, p. 7).

The theme of quality enhancement has been continued in Ohio University's 1988 planning document, "Toward the Third Century." To provide direction for maintaining high standards of performance for faculty and high expectations for effective teaching and learning, the document recommends the use of student assessment information.

Campus Uses of Assessment Information

One purpose of student assessment in the planning processes of Ohio University is to assist in improving the performance of programs and individuals. To this end, planning units are provided with regular updates on the progress of students and an assessment of university programs. The University Planning Advisory Council, charged with setting the "action agenda" and allocating new resources for each academic year, receives student assessment information as a part of its annual allocation process. All other planning groups at Ohio University also receive the information. The Dean's Council is furnished with reports on general education, student involvement, retention, and placement and alumni survey results. Each academic college gets data on its own students and graduates appropriate to its specific planning needs. Other campus groups, including the Faculty Senate, the University Curriculum Council, and the University Advising Council, are regularly supplied with both oral and written reports on student outcomes.

The governance groups of the university must also be made aware of the evaluation of growth in quality. The Ohio University Board of Trustees meets only quarterly, but the president has determined that its fall meeting should be entirely devoted to evaluation. Reports are given on student quality, assessment, retention, program evaluation, and affirmative action programs. Trustees make personal judgments about improvements in areas such as academic advising, student retention, evaluation of general education reform, student satisfaction with campus services, and perceptions of graduates on the competencies they developed at Ohio University. These judgments influence trustees' decisions about institutional management, budget approval, and institutional goals.

The National Alumni Board of the university is briefed on a dimension of the Institutional Impact Project each year. The alumni relations director forwards to all members of the board the reports produced by the Institutional Impact Project. This dissemination of information to alumni allows them to evaluate efforts at programmatic improvement. Influential alumni often encourage this process. For example, a member of the National Alumni Board, a graduate of the College of Engineering and Technology, heard a presentation of study results on engineering alumni. On the basis of the presentation, he noted that although engineering graduates evaluated their program positively, they reported inadequate training in broad interpersonal skills at the undergraduate level. Using information from these results, he met with the engineering college dean and helped increase the amount of oral and written communication training in the engineering curriculum.

Individual administrative departments (career planning and placement, alumni relations, admissions, student affairs, residence life, and university news services) use results according to their own needs for program refinement or development. The placement survey assists in the evaluation of the Career Planning and Placement Office and provides practical information to incoming and current students. For example, lower-than-expected utilization of career services prompted the office to improve its outreach efforts. Also, the staff uses information on reported "best" sources of job leads to promote those sources most likely to result in employment. The Admissions Office and individual colleges draw on this information for advising prospective and current students. The alumni survey results assist in the long-term evaluation of academic programs and the identification of competency areas important to Ohio University graduates. Because the study has been conducted over a span of fifteen years, changes in patterns of responses over time are noted and are related to specific program developments to provide a historical context. Admissions personnel use information on alumni to identify characteristics of students likely to complete their academic programs.

The treatment study, in which students — the major clients of the university — assess the services provided, is used most comprehensively by individual campus departments. Information from this study is used to evaluate students' treatment by department staff, the sources and types of information provided by departments to students, and the departmental processes that students experience. All departments with which undergraduates come in contact are included. Benchmark data for each department were collected in 1979 to assist in measuring departmental progress in subsequent years.

This information is used for continuous program improvement. Where problems are identified, programs are revised or new ones implemented. For example, information from the treatment study was used to establish a new advising system for undecided students in the University College. Treatment study results on the advising of undergraduates who were undecided about their majors showed that the advising process was unsatisfactory, frustrating, complicated, and inefficient and that the information about advising that students received was inadequate. As a consequence of these findings, a faculty training program for undecided students was developed, advising manuals were created, new advisers were recruited, and funds were provided for advisers and students to meet in informal luncheon gatherings.

Treatment study results have also led to revisions in procedures during the first week of classes. In 1978, students reported that university personnel could show greater courtesy, accessibility, friendliness, and sympathy during that week. As a result, the dean of students initiated a training program for all relevant staff members. Subsequent treatment study results showed improvements in the ratings of the behavior of these individuals. Since then, the training program has been conducted on a permanent basis.

The treatment study also revealed that the student registration process at Ohio University was regarded as slow, inefficient, and frustrating to students. As a result, a new system, featuring on-line touchtone registration, is being implemented.

At the student health center and the student union, receptionists and front-desk staff were perceived as treating students poorly. Health center receptionists subsequently were trained in customer relations techniques. The student union front-desk staffing was reorganized to focus on improving student services and direct contact.

The assessment of treatment of minority students has had two important results. The student counseling center staff learned that information about getting help with personal problems was not effectively reaching minority students. Therefore, a counselor position with responsibility for conducting outreach programs across campus was created. A minority student programs office was also created within the dean of students area to provide specialized services to minorities and to involve them more in programs and activities.

Retention information is used at the department level. Data on attrition help colleges and departments in developing retention programs, such as an early intervention program for female potential dropouts. The student involvement study has been used to develop a system to identify individual potential dropouts. Retention-related advising and intervention programs have been developed based on needs identified through this system.

All academic programs at Ohio University are required to undergo an internal program review every five years. The University Curriculum Council has developed a comprehensive instrument to collect detailed information on each program's quality. The Institutional Research Office provides detailed student assessment information to the fifteen programs under review each year. This information is provided in a format that is consistent from program to program, an approach that facilitates comparisons and judgments about program strengths and weaknesses. University faculty doing the review use the information to prepare a descriptive evaluation of each program: enrollment patterns, quality and mix of students, and success of graduates. In their evaluation, reviewers make specific recommendations in areas such as curriculum, admissions and recruiting, and safety and quality of facilities. The internal judgments about program quality take into account student outcomes directly resulting from faculty efforts and academic program attributes. Recommendations are expected to be implemented before the next scheduled review.

President Ping recently initiated an ad hoc review of the general education program. Following a yearlong study by a group of faculty members appointed to evaluate general education, recommendations for improvement, based on assessment information, were advanced. The alumni survey, ACT-COMP test, and a review of general education enrollment patterns have assisted in this purpose. Alumni survey information on different competencies of graduates has helped to document the areas that graduates value in their current endeavors (five years after graduating) and areas that they consider strongly or weakly developed. Availability of several years of ACT-COMP data makes possible the evaluation of the current general education program and the performance of Ohio University's students compared to students nationally. The six subscores provided by COMP have yielded basic performance information. This information has been supplemented with an ad hoc item analysis of COMP questions that furnish specific information about performance strengths and weaknesses in twenty-two general education competencies.

The information from the alumni survey and COMP results has helped to place enrollment patterns into a meaningful context for discussion and review. For example, in its ongoing general education debate, the faculty has access to information on enrollment patterns, perceived need and effectiveness ratings, and competency strengths and weaknesses.

External Uses of Assessment Information

Public opinion of quality can be enhanced by an effective assessment program. By reporting the impact of the college experience, a college can increase applications for admission and improve popular rankings of the campus. The editor of the *Columbus Dispatch* learned of the assessment program at Ohio University and wrote an editorial ("OU: Testing, Testing," 1987) that praised the university and encouraged other institutions to follow its example: "Long before U.S. Education Secretary William Bennett made assessment of effectiveness of education an issue, O.U. was beginning to grade itself in that area. . . . O.U. deserves high marks for its insistence on finding out whether it is really providing the kind of higher education that the university says it is" (p. 14A).

The institutional impact information has been instrumental in the decision by the Ohio Board of Regents to grant numerous program excellence awards to Ohio University. Over the past eight years, the institution has received over $16 million from this source. Three "eminent scholars," in history, film, and zoology, have been awarded $1.5 million. Academic challenge and program excellence awards for $13.5 million have been given to the Honors Tutorial College and to programs in telecommunications, visual communications, journalism, computer systems in business, molecular and cellular biology, avionics, condensed matter, creative writing, film, health psychology, electrical and computer engineering, zoology-neurobiology, applied and professional ethics, and general education. In the applications for these awards, student assessment and success information was a critical component.

The most recent external application of assessment information at Ohio University came about as a result of a statewide mandate that the public colleges and universities of Ohio appoint task forces to study how the institutions were managed. The Ohio University task force, called "Managing for the Third Century," included university trustees and business leaders. It was charged with evaluating productivity and effectiveness. The task force was given assessment information from the Institutional Impact Project, that enabled it to document growth in quality and productivity over a ten-year period. The task force recommended implementing a universitywide continuous quality improvement program that would be evaluated in a number of ways. Standards for evaluation were of three types: they were based on the product, as evaluated by students, alumni, and employers; on certain criteria, as reflected in specific measures or indices (for example, retention, graduation, and placement rates); and on value, as recorded in data from marketing, image, and alumni surveys. The program was incorporated into a process of ongoing reform and improvement that will be implemented at Ohio University.

Institutional impact information is used in regional and specialized accreditation reviews. Assessment information was a vital component of the comprehensive review by the North Central Association in 1983. In 1993, the report for the association's visit began with the idea that assessment information would be an integral part of that review.

Institutionwide Transformation
and Quality Enhancement

Ohio University's Institutional Impact Project has provided
evaluative information in a continuous performance review over
the last decade. It has provided useful information about the
university's standing among its students during a change in its
admissions policy from open to selective admissions. The project
is an evaluative tool for assessing the university's goal of enhancing quality. Specific assessment components have provided
information about the various aspects of the academic program.
The following examples furnish evidence of how the quality
indicators in the Institutional Impact Project have been implemented and interpreted.

The COMP has provided useful evaluative information
during the implementation of a three-tier general education program (basic quantitative and communication skills, breadth/dis-
tribution, and senior synthesis). In addition, information about
the general education outcomes of students admitted under selective admissions is becoming available. Eight classes of freshmen and seniors admitted under open admissions were compared in this study. Seniors who took the COMP before the
three-tier general education requirement was implemented scored
lower than students who took the COMP during and after the
new requirements were implemented. Evidence indicated that
students who completed the revised general education program
scored higher than similar-ability students who completed the
former program. It should be noted that these selective-admis-
sions students also scored higher as freshmen than former open-
admissions freshmen. Seniors scored below the 50th percentile
nationally before the three-tier general education program was
implemented and at about the 60th percentile nationally afterwards. The most recent COMP seniors, admitted under selective admissions, have increased their scores to the 73rd percentile. COMP results, alumni survey information, and enrollment
pattern data are being used to help guide a current review of
general education.

Results from annual freshman and longitudinal freshman-to-senior involvement studies have shown increases in student involvement patterns. The increases are apparent from year to year, as well as in freshman-to-senior comparisons. The number of formal contacts (such as advising) and informal contacts (such as dinner with a faculty member) that seniors have with faculty is greater than the number of contacts they had as freshmen. Seniors report greater satisfaction with the faculty and Ohio University in general. The number of weekends freshmen spend on campus has increased, as has frequency of participation in extracurricular activities. Seniors report greater involvement in student organizations than they did as freshmen and more interaction with their peers. Involvement has also been found to change depending on students' entering academic ability. Students of lower academic ability decrease their social involvement and devote more time to their studies by the time they are seniors. Students of higher academic ability expand their social involvement by the time they are seniors.

Freshman retention has improved steadily since 1977. In 1978, 67 percent of the freshmen returned to Ohio University as sophomores. Under open admissions, the retention rate increased to 78 percent in 1986. By 1990, 85 percent of the freshmen returned under selective admissions, a retention rate that is higher than rates of peer institutions. The retention rate of students in the top quintile of their high school class improved from 81 percent in 1978 to 87 percent in 1990; similarly, the retention rate of students with a college grade-point average of 2.5 and above also rose.

In freshman surveys about the quality of treatment offered by the faculty and various campus offices, most areas improved between 1978 and 1991. But the greatest gains were in the academic sphere: advising, treatment by faculty, information about what to expect in the classroom, and information about the process of getting help with academic problems. These improvements resulted from training programs for faculty advisers and new initiatives in student advising.

Recent placement studies have revealed that about 93 percent of Ohio University graduates are employed or enrolled in graduate study within one year of graduating, and most graduates stay in Ohio. Most alumni reported being satisfied with the academic preparation they received at Ohio University for their first job, for additional academic work, and for establishment of career goals (about 95 percent). Graduate salaries were higher than national and state averages.

From a list of fifteen competencies, graduates selected those that were most needed and best developed at Ohio University. These included the ability to communicate orally, acquire new skills and understanding on one's own, evaluate and choose between alternative courses of action, think analytically, and apply knowledge from one's major field to one's current endeavors. The ability to write well has increased both in reported importance and in rating of development at Ohio University over the several years of this study.

The Institutional Impact Project at Ohio University has helped the institution document its progress in enhancing quality over the last decade. Various indicators of quality at different levels of the student experience gauge separate but often overlapping areas. These measures help demonstrate improvements and provide evaluative information in relation to the university's goals and planning processes.

The project has allowed Ohio University to respond to demands for change. These demands are internal, as the institution strives to improve its quality and increase its stature and strength. They are also external; calls for accountability and efficiency require public documentation of quality indicators. Assessment information at Ohio University documents improvement of programs without equivalent increases in resource allocation.

The university has gained statewide recognition for the project; in 1989, the Ohio Board of Regents turned to Ohio University as an example in making recommendations on assessment for the state. If other Ohio institutions follow Ohio University's example, statewide comparative information will provide a set of useful reference points.

The Institutional Impact Project must remain flexible as different assessment needs become apparent, both for internal and external purposes. Maintaining the involvement of the university community is a vital part of this process. Yet the primary goal remains to use assessment information at Ohio University constantly to define and examine growth in quality. As quality is measured in a number of dimensions related to academic and nonacademic programs, assessment fosters the participation of the faculty and staff in improving their programs.

References

Ohio University. "Ohio University Educational Plan: 1977–1987." Unpublished manuscript, Office of the President, Ohio University, 1977.

Ohio University. "Toward the Third Century: Issues and Choices for Ohio University." Unpublished manuscript, Office of the President, Ohio University, 1988.

"OU: Testing, Testing." *Columbus Dispatch,* Apr. 10, 1987, p. 14A.

Ping, C. J. "Quality Dependent on the Making of Judgments." Unpublished manuscript, Office of the President, Ohio University, 1980.

4

Helping a Campus
in Transition

Albert M. Katz

Experience at the University of Wisconsin, Superior (UWS) indicates that the greatest potential benefit of an assessment plan
is the process by which it is created and approved and the behavioral pattern with which it is sustained. A well-planted and
well-nurtured assessment program functions like an angioplasty
procedure on an arteriosclerotic patient. It clears the accumulated products of a rich or careless diet and a sedentary life-style
from the pathways to the heart. It sends fresh blood coursing
through the arteries to the heart, the muscles, and the mind.

From 1985 to 1992, UWS went through a major shift from
stagnation to vitality, from close to "lethally" low enrollment and
questionable public image to a position of rising enrollments
and high public regard in its region. After a decade of defensive lethargy, our curricular, cocurricular, and service functions
all evolved and grew significantly. This expansion was accomplished with essentially the same student population base and
the same faculty and staff at both ends of the seven-year span.

The driving forces during this period at our institution
were both negative and positive. The negative one was the stress

of our situation; the positive one was the leadership, from both the administration and the faculty, on our campus. The vehicle that allowed the changes at UWS to occur has been the assessment process.

Background

UWS, which is part of the University of Wisconsin system, followed the route of many state institutions of higher learning from a normal school, to a teachers college, to a comprehensive university. With the explosive enrollment growth of the 1950s and 1960s, our major plan seemed to involve constant growth. We wanted (and we got) more students, more buildings, more programs. We were so busy digesting new people and new resources that thoughtful, long-range planning was more a goal than a reality.

We are a small school, serving a very large but thinly populated geographical region. Our small size allows the faculty and staff to be easily accessible to each other and to deal with students in a personal way. It also presents significant difficulties relating to economy of scale. These have plagued us during each phase of our progression through growth, decline, and recovery.

In 1968–69, UWS peaked at 3,118 full-time-equivalent (FTE) students. At that moment, political, geographic, and local economic factors all collided, and we began a precipitous slide into greater and greater difficulty. For political reasons, the legislature raised out-of-state tuition. Since UWS is on the border of Minnesota and not far from the border of Michigan, many of our students came from out of state. The population of our geographical area declined as a failing economy caused families to leave the area. For 1969–70, we were budgeted and staffed for about 3,300 students, but we had a shortfall. We continued a slow steady enrollment decline until 1984–85, when we hit the bottom: 1,777 FTE students.

We fought a rearguard action until 1981–82, when we finally got our financial house in order by reducing faculty and staff positions and class offerings to bring them into line with

enrollments. From 1970 to 1982, we were in a state of constant
anxiety about the survival of individual faculty positions, major
programs, and at times the institution itself. By 1984, we had
come through the worst, both in enrollment and in financial
and programmatic stress, and had finally achieved some stabil-
ity. We were ready for positive change; what we were seeking
was a way to bring it about.

Leadership for the Assessment Initiative

The turnaround in our fortunes coincided with the beginnings
of assessment planning on our campus. In 1986, the University of Wisconsin System received a small grant from the Fund
for the Improvement of Postsecondary Education to explore
aspects of assessment. Three campuses took part in the research
and exploration; the other two campuses decided to study a single
aspect of the process. UWS chose to investigate the potential
for a comprehensive program.

Perhaps because UWS was, and still is, such a small
campus, its governance system is grounded in consultation and
consensus building. The Academic Affairs Council and our
University Senate represent the faculty, academic staff, and students, all of whom are voting members. There was already a
predisposition to involve the entire UWS community in planning significant policy changes.

We began our formal exploration in 1986–87. Each college of the university elected a faculty representative to the Assessment Committee. We then added representatives from Continuing Education, the academic staff, and the undergraduate
and graduate student body. I was elected from the College of
Fine and Applied Arts, where I teach in the Communicating Arts
Department, specializing in conflict management. I had already
attended several conferences on assessment; I was elected by
the committee to serve as chair.

We developed a plan for gradual and phased implementation. Committee members took the plan to each of their constituencies. As chair, I went to each college, department, and
office. I answered questions and took note of concerns and ob-

jections. The committee wrote a second draft and repeated the consulting process. Then the committee composed a third draft and sent it around again. Only then was the final product presented to the Academic Affairs Council and the University Senate. After a year of planning and consultation, the committee submitted what had become the university community's plan, to be phased in over four years. In spring 1987, it passed without a dissenting vote.

The plan contains the following explicit assurances to the university community. First, the purpose of our program is to repair deficiencies, not to create comparison with others. Second, data gathered for assessment will *never* be used to harm a student, faculty member, or program. Their only application is to improve the teaching and learning environment. Last, but by no means least in importance, the faculty is sovereign in the articulation of goals and objectives, the selection of instruments for assessing their achievement, and the interpretation of the data collected.

Methods Employed

Different methods are used in different parts of the assessment program at the University of Wisconsin, Superior. Our assessment program has three components:

1. *Assessment of general education:* for this purpose, we have selected the ACT-COMP exam, an instrument that appears best suited to our particular student population (which includes about 40 percent nontraditional-age students).

2. *Assessment of major programs:* we evaluate each major program listed in the catalogue. Each program has articulated its own goals and objectives and selected the instruments best serving its needs. We phased this process in over three years. Every program had to be in place by year three, but we sought volunteers in years one and two, and we found them.

3. *Assessment of nonacademic areas:* we borrowed, adapted, and developed a series of survey instruments that would help us assess all nonacademic areas of the university.

Faculty assumed ownership of the major program assessment processes because they developed and selected the goals and objectives and the instruments to measure them. Support staff went through the same process to assess the nonacademic areas. All survey instruments are also subjected to this process of examination by all affected constituencies, and multiple revisions are made until all are satisfied. All the people affected have input and take ownership.

Assessment Findings

Most people involved in assessment will say that the *process* is at least as important as the outcome data. In the process of selecting and validating the choice of an instrument, an academic department actually puts its objectives, then its curriculum, under a high-powered microscope. What it sees may be comforting; more often it is not. Sometimes it is downright frightening! In any event, the department looks at its curriculum carefully — often for the first time in a number of years.

The Educational Testing Service (ETS) Major Field Achievement Tests (MFAT) have provided both the occasion and the vehicle for curricular review in a dozen departments. The ETS takes its standards for breadth of content and depth of competence in each discipline from the standards promulgated by the relevant professional organizations and associations. When a department seeks to match its goals and objectives against the content of the ETS-MFAT, this fact is necessarily part of its thinking. These exercises in validation have been the occasion for considerable soul-searching on our campus.

Our chemistry department, for example, is certified by the American Chemical Society (ACS). Following normal practices, ETS used ACS guidelines as part of the design of the MFAT. Not surprisingly, our examination of the MFAT in chemistry revealed a substantial fit between what the chemistry department offered and what the MFAT examined. Faculty were pleased with both the reliability and validity of the chemistry MFAT. They were also pleased with their senior students' scores: one student was at the 40th percentile but all the rest were between the 66th and the 99th percentile of a national sample.

A number of our other departments also found a good fit between their offerings and the subject matter examined. Several departments did not find a good fit, however. In each case, the discovery led to an extensive debate about the meaning of the lack of fit and about the implications for future curricular decisions. For example, the political science department (which uses MFAT) continues to have extensive discussions about curriculum as a result of its participation.

The faculty members of each department began with the assumption that they were doing a responsible job and that they were covering as much of their discipline as their human resources would allow. My own view is that they were accurate in their analysis or at least honest in their belief. Most often, gaps in a "traditional" coverage of the curriculum resulted from a decision to provide depth in some specialty at the expense of breadth.

Regardless of *how* a lack of fit came about, each department had to decide what to do about it. Much of the benefit of assessment occurred in the debate leading to that conclusion.

Some departments decided that their current choices about curricula were the best ones available under the circumstances of budget and personnel. Some decided to revise their curriculum to develop a more traditional set of course offerings. Once they have done so and their students have a chance to absorb that new curriculum, these departments will use the MFAT for evaluation of student achievement.

As of spring 1992, ten departments were using the ETS-MFAT to test their majors. Others have sought or developed other kinds of examinations or assessment tools.

Changes Made on the Basis of Assessment Findings

The profile of our fall 1987 class of entering freshmen afforded by the ACT-COMP gave us some insight into the strengths and weaknesses of that cohort. The faculty had felt for some time that our entering students were not prepared to create patterns of thought from disparate bits of information. We believed they were ready to learn and repeat cognitive material but were not prepared to do the type of thinking required to solve problems.

To that point, our evidence was either visceral or anecdotal. With the scores of the 1987 administration of the ACT-COMP in front of us, it was evident that this freshman class fulfilled our preconceptions. Their scores were lower on the problem-solving segment of the COMP than on any other section. The class of freshmen entering in 1988 scored similarly on the ACT-COMP.

Using this information, we have attempted to introduce work in critical thinking and increased writing activities into as many of our general education courses as possible. We are striving to include these elements in our major courses as well.

Those departments that have used nationally normed tests (MFATs, the ETS-Dantes exam for criminal justice majors, or the certified public accountant exam) for two or three years are also receiving outcome data that assist them in validating and improving their curricula. For instance, outcome data from the psychology MFAT showed that senior students were performing quite inconsistently on portions of the MFAT dealing with experimentally based research competencies. This finding was puzzling to the faculty, as they were teaching those skills and were receiving very positive feedback from the classes (both in the form of students' performances in the classes and from course evaluations).

The faculty analyzed student transcripts and found that those students who were performing well on the sections of the MFAT dealing with experimental research had taken the elective experimental research courses; those who did poorly had not. The correlation between course selection and MFAT scores made perfect sense: the psychology major consisted of one required course and a wide variety of electives. The revelation to the psychology department faculty was the number of majors who had elected not to take the experimental research courses. To the dismay of the faculty, too many students, including many of the most skilled, simply chose other courses to fill out their major. As a direct result of MFAT outcome data, the psychology faculty revised course requirements, and new and more stringent requirements appeared in the next catalogue. Good advising ensured that current juniors and seniors elected the appropriate research courses. The next year's MFAT scores showed much more satisfying and appropriate data in all areas examined. Assessment data thus had a direct role in creating a significant change in the major course requirements.

Another example of the impact of the assessment program comes from the elementary education department. Richard Hanson, professor of elementary education, notes that his colleagues had initially dragged their feet about assessment (personal interview, April 1992). They assumed that evaluation in their field inevitably would be in the form of standardized examination, and that approach did not please them. The approach was philosophically incompatible with their beliefs about the teaching-learning experience. In addition, they believed the activities would simply provide accountability data to administrators while producing little if any benefits for either faculty or students.

The certification process, mandated by the state Department of Public Instruction, already included student teaching, and the education faculty simply selected that experience as its instrument of assessment while contemplating its next move. Student teaching as a capstone was satisfactory, but not completely so; an additional procedure or instrument was required.

UWS gently encouraged exploration of assessment options. The value system of our university allowed the elementary education department to go through a slow, laborious process that has now evolved into the adoption of a carefully considered portfolio system of assessment. Resistance has vanished with the realization that this form of assessment will assist both faculty and students to achieve their goals.

Each student works with an adviser to design and fill out the portfolio. One of the assets of this form of assessment is that it encourages *shared* responsibility between faculty and students. Each portfolio is a joint venture. It also puts the student in the role of active self-evaluator.

Each portfolio can be located on a disk in a reserved space in the Education Library. Materials that do not conveniently go on a disk, such as videotaped materials, will be preserved in the student's individual portfolio file. The portfolio is always available to the student for the purpose of contemplation and self-appraisal and also for job hunting, as portions of it can be submitted to potential employers.

The benefits of the portfolio assessment system flow in all directions. A new committee in the College of Education is now working on a proposal to encourage faculty to develop and file teaching portfolios analogous to those of the students. In elementary education, we have a mini–case study of the process at work and the positive outcomes that can result from time, patience, and collegiality.

Factors That Make Assessment Last

In 1989, UWS chancellor Terrence MacTaggert began to seek ways to articulate and sustain the progress the campus had achieved in the previous five years. The results of this exploration were embodied in the Superior Plan.

The process by which consensus was reached about the Superior Plan repeated the earlier process considering assessment objectives. Once again, there was a lengthy consultative exploration with the faculty, staff, and students. In May 1990, a plan of action was completed and presented to the academic community. The data collected through assessment provide the means by which we will gauge our progress toward the plan's goals.

There are strong analogies between the Superior Plan and the concept of total quality improvement (TQI). The plan has been described as the UW, Superior, manifestation of TQI. The plan focuses on the campus procedures that can be identified and improved in a communal fashion by the people most centrally involved and affected by them.

The Superior Plan has three goals, each with specific objectives. The first is to seek alternative teaching and learning strategies in the classroom. The core idea is for faculty to learn from each other as well as from their professional literature. The second goal is to strengthen affective support for learning in the classroom and in the overall environment. The third is gradually and steadily to raise the levels of expectation and performance of students. These three objectives are interdependent. All are built upon a foundation of assessment procedures and outcomes that provides both the incentive to seek new behaviors and validation of their outcome.

The Superior Plan Committee continuously seeks and receives feedback from its constituencies. It then makes recommendations to the administration and to relevant faculty committees for actions that may be beneficial. The committee's endeavors have produced an ongoing series of both convocations exploring current topics and concepts and in-service learning sessions to implement items identified as areas for continuing attention. In part, these sessions motivated the development of a working day each spring — a day set aside for the administration of the ACT-COMP exam for general education, the ETS-MFAT, and other senior assessment examinations. To avoid time conflicts, no classes are scheduled on this day. While the seniors take the assessment tests, the rest of the campus community is engaged in other activities, such as convocations and in-service sessions.

A number of faculty and administrators have testified to the positive impact of the assessment endeavor on the UWS community. For instance, Nancy Minahan (who came to UWS in 1967 as a junior faculty member, subsequently served as dean of humanities and social sciences, and is now the dean of the Graduate School) comments:

> [The process of developing the assessment program contained] the best strategized moves that I've seen on our campus. From my point of view, it worked because you were careful to involve all the relevant constituencies in the development process over and over again — and because you moved fairly slowly. There was time for piloting, revision, and a slow phasing in of different portions. People had time to have their say, and to get used to the concepts, before they were implemented. There was a great deal of resistance against the concept of assessment, so the final relative success of the model is especially noteworthy [personal communication, March 1992].

Chancellor MacTaggart, who left UWS to become the chancellor of the Minnesota State University System in 1991, states:

Assessment played an essential role in what I will call the UW–Superior renaissance. This rebirth in learning, in reputation, in institutional energy, and self-confidence . . . I believe, will continue for a long time. . . . The assessment program . . . became one of the distinguishing characteristics of the university. Assessment provided the cornerstone for a second initiative, the Superior Plan, which encouraged all academic programs to set higher expectations for student performance. Without assessment, there would be no adequate way to benchmark the points of departure or the higher expectations. General Education reform redefined the "what" of much of the curriculum, the Superior Plan redefined "how far" the new curriculum would go, and assessment provided a means of evaluating the achievement. In sum, the Superior renaissance was registered in the public mind as swift and positive improvements in the reputation of the university [personal communication, May 1992].

A survey by a UWS public relations class in fall 1992 revealed that attitudes toward the university have improved since the assessment program and the Superior Plan have been in effect. Nearly 63 percent of faculty members feel that university administrators are doing a good job, up 40 percent from 1986. Nearly 93 percent of staff members would encourage friends and family members to attend UWS. Forty percent of the students feel that the Superior Plan has made their classes more challenging. In addition, the students have a more positive initial impression of the university than did students surveyed in 1986 ("Public Relations Class Studies UWS Attitudes," 1992).

Assessment has provided the vehicle by which UWS has recovered from a very difficult and dangerous situation. I am convinced that even if we had chosen different people to act for us, different instruments to measure our progress, and other pathways to carry us forward, we still would have prospered so long as we engaged in the assessment process. The required constant for growth has been the *process* itself.

Assessment—planted in the faculty, nourished with administrative support, and given sufficient time to grow in whatever direction consensus-based decision making takes it—will be worthwhile. With evaluation systems in place, we will know where we seek to go (goals and objectives), we will know where we are (by means of instrumentation), and we will be in a solid and stable position to decide where we wish to go next.

We are a healthy institution. We are well regarded in our service region and in our system. We have every reason to expect that situation to continue for the foreseeable future.

Reference

"Public Relations Class Studies UWS Attitudes." *Superior Evening Telegram,* Mar. 23, 1992, p. 3.

Part Two

Adapting
Assessment to
Diverse Settings
and Populations

Transformation of the culture of an entire college or university is rare because it requires a combination of propitious circumstances, strong leadership, and sustained effort on the part of many, if not most, of the people associated with the institution. Across the country, there are many comprehensive—that is, campuswide and multifaceted—assessment programs that cannot be said to have caused a fundamental change in the way faculty and students think about their work and about their institution but that are making a difference nevertheless.

Persuading faculty to examine curricula and teaching for evidence of their effectiveness is not easy. The four chapters in Part Two illustrate the struggle involved in adapting assessment approaches to diverse settings and student groups. Each group of authors explains the difficulty of planning a meaningful assessment program in a particular setting, be it a liberal arts college, a community college, a research university, or an institution that serves a substantial proportion of adult students. Indeed, in Chapter Five, MindaRae Amiran and Karen and Karl Schilling tell us that it is not just a matter of finding what is right for each institution but also of determining what is right for a given institution at different stages in its experience with assessment.

Amiran, Schilling, and Schilling recount their joint experience in administering a faculty-designed general education assessment instrument to their students. At Amiran's institution, the State University of New York, Fredonia, where the instrument was developed, the experience of reviewing students' scores led the faculty to plan and implement a number of workshops that could help them improve various weaknesses they saw in their students. Three departments also added portfolios to their traditional ways of assessing student progress.

At Western College of Miami University, where the Schillings teach, the experience of giving the Fredonia test to students led to a very different set of outcomes. Faculty were frustrated by the lack of specificity in the student performance data that the test yielded. They could not tell how to improve the student experience. Thus, they decided to seek information from other sources — portfolios and studies of student time usage, student expectations, and the institutional environment. These data have prompted improvement initiatives in student recruitment, orientation, and advising procedures.

R. Dan Walleri and Jeffrey Seybert conducted a national survey on the use of assessment data in community colleges; this study forms the basis for Chapter Six. These authors cite multiple examples of uses made of data derived from transcript analysis, student tracking, program review, and student and employer surveys. Following the progress of students through monitoring their records has directed greater attention to placement testing, intensified work in basic skills, and more focused advising. Results of faculty efforts in these areas include higher passing rates in some courses and increased persistence rates. Program reviews and employer surveys have led faculty to update existing courses and to add new programs to meet employers' needs.

Chapter Seven is the tale of two research universities and their forays into assessment. James Watt of the University of Connecticut, Raymond Rodrigues, formerly at Colorado State

University, and their colleagues tell similar stories of faculty members' reluctance to become involved in assessment until it was clear that they could use it for their own ends. They could design their own instruments and make assessment a series of research activities. Student testing, focus-group interviews, and surveys for students and faculty have produced changes in the undergraduate curricula at both institutions, from the addition of a cultural diversity requirement for students at Connecticut to improvements in advising, field placement, and course and curriculum goals at Colorado State.

Like Walleri and Seybert, Carol Kasworm and Catherine Marienau undertook a national canvass of their colleagues in assembling the material for their contribution to this volume. Thomas Edison State College, Empire State College, and the University of Phoenix were found to be leaders in using assessment results to improve programs for adult learners. Chapter Eight contains evidence that surveys, interviews, and portfolio assessment have produced more helpful printed information about campus programs and services, more customer-oriented admissions procedures, specific improvements in writing instruction, and new faculty development programs. Empire State's studies of the effectiveness of its writing program, which have been undertaken periodically since 1978, have shown that the program does produce gains.

5

Assessing Outcomes
of General Education

MindaRae Amiran
Karen Maitland Schilling
Karl L. Schilling

Does a senior majoring in physics know more about the field than a beginning freshman? And if so, is it the result of the physics department's teaching? The answers to these questions are obvious, and, indeed, it is hard to imagine anyone worrying about them. The physics department is far more likely to be asking about its preparation of students on specific topics and equipment or to be concerned with its students' success in graduate school. But consider the dilemma of general education programs whose aim is to develop student proficiency in such skills as critical thinking, general problem solving, reading, writing, and scientific and ethical reasoning. Unless there is a core of general education courses that everyone must take, it is far from certain that students will show themselves more proficient in these areas as seniors than they were as freshmen. Moreover, even if the students do appear to be more proficient, it may be due to excellent teaching in other courses, experiences abroad, challenging summer jobs, time spent talking with their roommates, or the simple fact that they are older. Teachers of general education courses need to know whether their program is making a difference; if it is not, they need some idea as to what they should change in their curriculum or teaching.

Western College of Miami University and the State University of New York (SUNY), Fredonia—two rather different institutions whose general education programs strive to develop student skills and understanding—found themselves grappling with this problem in 1988, and joined forces in an effort to demonstrate student growth. This chapter sets forth the findings and the different uses these institutions have made of them: whereas Fredonia has stayed with its approach in difficult times, Western has struck out in new and promising directions. We speak first for Fredonia and then for Western.

The Story at Fredonia

When we on the faculty of the College at Fredonia decided to assess our general education program in 1986, problems of identifying effects were very much in our minds. We were aware of research suggesting that young adults mature more rapidly in college than out. Since our General College Program (GCP) focuses on broadly defined intellectual skills to be developed through any of a variety of courses, we also thought that our findings would have little impact on our colleagues unless we could show that whatever improvement we found was attributable to our particular GCP, rather than to a generic college experience. Impact on our colleagues was indeed our main concern: we were under no mandate to prove ourselves to any external public; happily, even today our only external public is the SUNY administration.

Our solution to the issue of "generic growth" was to seek a college with students similar to ours whose general education requirements made no mention of skills but were simply distributional by fields of study and to compare responses of our students and theirs to the series of paper-and-pencil tasks we had developed. Of course, we hoped that our students would prove more proficient than theirs, but we certainly wanted to know if they were not. Unfortunately for us, it chanced that our sister SUNY colleges, which would have been excellent comparison schools, were in various stages of installing ambitious new general education programs; any that had had simple distribution requirements were abandoning them. However, by chance, Karl Schilling was assessing his Western College Program at Miami University of Ohio and comparing the performance of Western students enrolled in an interdisciplinary core curriculum with that of Miami students enrolled in the universitywide general education program. At that time, Miami had only distributional general education requirements (the liberal education program at Miami was undergoing a reform process during the time this study was undertaken) and seemed a reasonable partner for us, although we later realized that Miami's admissions were somewhat more selective than ours. (At both institutions, students are almost uniformly of traditional college age, white, and middle class. However, Fredonia's mean Scholastic Aptitude Test (SAT) score for entering students at that time was about 1,000; Miami's, approximately, 1,115.) In any event, we gratefully entered upon a three-way comparison of the skills of students from Western College, Miami, and Fredonia.

The paper-and-pencil tasks we had developed with help from a grant from the Fund for the Improvement of Postsecondary Education (FIPSE) gave students the chance to demonstrate the skills that are the main target of our General College Program: reading, writing, metacognition, mathematical problem solving, scientific reasoning, and a construct we called socioethical understanding. The tasks were open ended, all were scored analytically and some also globally, and the same skills were called for in different contexts. We took the usual and proper precautions to assure such things as random samples, blind scoring, and interrater reliability and have reason to believe the students took the tasks seriously.

These were the results. Fredonia upperclassmen performed significantly better than our incoming freshmen in composition, reading, metacognition, one of two tests of scientific reasoning, and two of three tests of socioethical understanding. Upperclassmen at Miami were significantly better than freshmen at mathematical problem solving, the same test of scientific reasoning, and two of the tests of socioethical understanding (including one on which the Fredonia students showed no gains). Upperclassmen in the Western Program outperformed freshmen on the same test of scientific reasoning and on one of the tests of socioethical understanding, the one on which Miami students did well. (Neither Miami nor Western used our test of composition, since they already had information on this skill.) Although gain scores themselves are suspect — even *gain* is a suspect term in this context — the differences between mean scores of Fredonia freshman and upperclassman were larger than those between the comparable Miami and Western groups. Since the difference between Fredonia freshmen and upperclassmen was greater on more tests of skills, we had therefore succeeded in showing that our GCP was indeed doing something for our students, beyond the generic effects attributable to attending any good college.

Yet our findings had much broader implications. To begin with, the mean score of our upperclassmen on almost all of our tests and subtests was similar to (or lower than) the comparable scores of Miami and Western freshmen, sometimes not exceeding half of the possible points for the test. Moreover, certain skills were consistently weak, whatever the kind of subtask requiring them and even if the students' total scores for the entire task in question were adequate. Because of these findings, our assessment committee made a series of recommendations to the campus: that all classes emphasize assumptions and biases, that all make some effort to improve student reading, that students be given more practice in problem solving in different contexts, that science and social science courses give more attention to methodology, that all courses give more attention to historical contexts, that the college require a general education portfolio to stimulate metacognition, and that there be administrative support for faculty workshops and small classes.

A number of these recommendations have begun to be followed. A grant funded a faculty workshop on multiculturalism and bias; two faculty working groups published bibliographies, recommendations, and model assignments directed at improving targeted skills in sciences and humanities; the mathematics department held a workshop on problem solving for adjunct faculty; and although there was insufficient faculty support for a collegewide requirement for portfolios, three academic departments now require them. The completion of these steps seemed to justify reassessing our program. In summer of 1991, we gave incoming freshmen our battery of tests and plan to test the same students in their junior year; this will be a genuine longitudinal study, as opposed to a study based on matched samples.

However, the horizon for this reassessment is not unclouded. On the one hand, it is not at all certain that we have really improved our instruction in the skills we found weak in our first assessment; on the other hand, it is not at all certain that our tests will reveal improvements that may actually have come about. To begin with the first problem, many factors have inhibited our faculty from experimenting with new methods of helping students improve their intellectual skills. New York's ongoing budget crisis — the steady drain of funds from SUNY — has been a continual discouragement as untenured faculty struggle to lengthen their publication lists in preparation for possible job hunting while tenured faculty scheme and struggle to retain their younger colleagues. Meanwhile, class size has increased, funds for faculty development are disappearing, and faculty worked without contract for a critical year.

During the initial malaise, some faculty members simplified the results of our first assessment and concluded that with such a poor report card, the program should be flunked out. Most faculty members were much better readers, but even their days had only twenty-four hours; attendance at meetings on the improvement of teaching grew sparse, and visible administrative support for the assessment recommendations was buried under budget preoccupations. Of course, many faculty members continued to experiment with better ways of helping students in their classes, and it may well be that the GCP has at least held its own, possibly even improved, as the targeted skills receive more attention. Still, there is room for doubt. It will be a great pity if the fruits of assessment are destroyed, in SUNY and elsewhere, by the plague of underfunding in the public sector.

The second problem may actually be more troublesome in the long run, though at least it is much more interesting, namely, our ignorance of basic facts about adult development of complex skills and our consequent difficulties in interpreting our assessment findings. First, we are not at all sure how dependent on context a given complex skill is. Research on reading and problem solving at least holds out the hope that general ability factors can be detected, though they will always interact with specific knowledge of content in the problem area or reading material. Our work on socioethical understanding, however, suggests a bewildering number of factors to consider, with no immediately identifiable general ability.

We divided this construct into subsets including such things as awareness of mainstream American values, ability to avoid ethnocentrism, and recognition of multiple causes in human events. We devised three different tasks to demonstrate student socioethical ability: one was to list ten of the most important events in human history, one was to answer rather negative questions about this country from a European exchange student, and one was to analyze problems in a mythical developing Third World country (Malbavia). Students in the three colleges responded differently to these tasks and showed more understanding in one situation than another. For example, Western College upperclassmen were significantly less ethnocentric than the freshmen in listing the ten historical events, and Fredonia's upperclassmen in analyzing Malbavia. All the responses to the exchange student were less ethnocentric than answers on the other tests — perhaps students were imagining themselves as hosts in a social situation. If we had used only one of the tasks, we would have come to conclusions very different from those we actually drew. It seems undeniable that if we had used other tasks we would have come to still different conclusions. Are we succeeding in developing our students' socioethical understanding? This question, *mutatis mutandis,* haunts our assessment of other skills as well. And it leads us to wonder whether we may possibly be fostering student improvement that our choice of tasks simply does not reveal.

Another aspect of our ignorance about basic facts of development emerges from comparisons of students from the three colleges. Some of these comparisons make a great deal of sense. For example, Miami upperclassmen did much better than freshmen in mathematical problem solving, while Western and Fredonia upperclassmen did not. Moreover, the mean scores of Western and Fredonia students were almost identical. Western attracts students with humanistic interests, and Fredonia's sample for the math tests excluded math and science majors, so these results could have been anticipated. Neither school had in fact given sufficient attention to problem solving in its general education program. But it is surprising that upperclassmen at Fredonia outperformed freshmen in such skills as reading, metacognition, and socioethical understanding (in the history and Malbavia tests), whereas upperclassmen at Western did not. To our way of thinking, the small classes; frequent, serious assignments; and close faculty-student interactions at Western supply ideal conditions for learning. Is it possible that Western (and Miami) students' higher freshman scores on our tests imply some kind of learning curve, whereby students starting at the levels of our students can advance considerably in some skills in three or four years but students starting at the Western-Miami levels cannot? Are there unavoidable plateaus in the learning of certain skills?

Moreover, since we know perfectly well that most of our freshmen are generally different from our upperclassmen in their academic abilities (teaching a freshman general education class is obviously quite different from teaching a class of juniors and seniors), why are we (and most other researchers) not able to demonstrate more dramatic changes than any that appeared in our measurements? If we understood adult skill development better, would we see that there are certain catalyzing skills, or certain intellectual components of complex skills, that we are overlooking? In short, if the results of Fredonia's GCP reassessment in 1994 are not better than our results in 1989, will it be true that the program has not improved? Or is it that students starting where ours do can improve no further in three years, having reached an invisible plateau? Or have they perhaps improved in ways they could have shown if our choice of tasks had been different? The answers to these questions, if we had them, would considerably affect our use of our assessment results.

The Western Program Story

Starting with funding provided by the state of Ohio in 1987 and FIPSE, 1988–1991, the Western Program undertook a comprehensive assessment project designed to explore the impact of two different approaches to general education: discipline-based distribution and interdisciplinary core curriculum. The project utilized a number of the existing commercial assessment instruments—ACT-COMP, ETS Academic Profile, McBer-Test of Thematic Analysis and Analysis of Argument, ACT Activity Inventory, ACT Alumni Survey, College Student Experiences Questionnaire (CSEQ), College and University Environment Scales (CUES), College Characteristics Index (CCI), Cooperative Institutional Research Program Survey—as well as noncommercial instruments (SUNY-Fredonia faculty-developed general education assessment instruments, Baxter-Magolda's Measure of Epistemological Reflection, Pettit's Alumni Survey, a locally developed structured interview, free-writing assignments).

The project resulted in a considerable amount of interesting statistical data about the relative performance of students in the Western Program compared to students from elsewhere in the university and at other universities. The commercially available instruments demonstrated ceiling effects when used with this sample. The Academic Profile in particular showed a ceiling—with first-year students as a group scoring near the 99th percentile on senior norms—leaving little room for growth. Other commercially available instruments appeared to punish bright students as their thinking became less strictly linear and more complex.

The information collected from the FIPSE project has proven useful for research purposes and in the preparation of grants and reports, but it has not had much impact on the curriculum. The failure of the project really to influence the curriculum is related to two factors: first, faculty mistrust of the American testing movement; second, the lack of direct connection between the measures and what we were actually trying to achieve in the classroom. Probably like at most liberal arts colleges, the faculty at Western have a deep suspicion about the utility of standardized testing as well as concerns about the ethics of using such information. When the data from the project were presented to the Western faculty, they routinely began an extended discourse on the many problems associated with this approach to assessment — the inherent value bias, the tendency to favor certain perspectives, and so forth. After this discussion, faculty members were willing to look at the information and were generally pleased with what they saw in terms of student performance. When test results suggested potential deficiencies in the program, however, these deficiencies were difficult to address because the items contained on the scales rarely connected very directly to the skills or content being taught in an interdisciplinary, liberal arts core curriculum. This situation was true even for the noncommercial Fredonia instrument; though they were designed by liberal arts faculty, the instruments were related to the specific goals of Fredonia and to its faculty's understanding of the appropriate curricular experiences for a liberal arts education.

The absence of obvious connection between the curriculum and the testing was clearly the major impediment to using the assessment results in the classes being taught. There was not enough solid documentation about what actually occurred in the classroom, let alone in the student's (or for that matter, the faculty member's) head. Therefore, it was difficult to know what to do with the information. Gains were clearly evident in both the cross-sectional and longitudinal studies, but the linkages of outcomes to causes were not obvious except in insights provided through student interviews and free writing.

At the end of the project, we thus had a rich collection of nationally normed data on student performance. We could easily compare our students to students elsewhere on the dimensions purported to be measured by the various instruments, but we had little sense of how they got there — wherever "there" was.

At this point, we became involved in an Exxon-funded project on portfolio assessment of general education. Because of this project and our previous experience, our first tendency was to develop rating scales to be used in scoring the portfolios and to do comparative scoring with other programs. However,

once we began collecting portfolios at the end of the first semester, we put aside that approach in favor of one that has
proven very useful. Since the portfolios were comprehensive (that
is, the students put all work developed for classes into them),
we realized that for the first time it would be possible to describe
in concrete terms what students actually did in their classes —
at least in terms of assignments completed. The value of better
understanding *what* our students were doing before exploring
how well they were doing was apparent. Also, because the obviously evaluative and comparative focus was removed, discussions among faculty became less defensive, and faculty were
more open to serious exploration of our students' work. Indeed,
in their reviews of portfolios, faculty quickly moved from using
the term *my* students to using *our* students. Individual faculty
members began to see their own classroom activity more clearly
in the context of their colleagues' work. Suddenly, it was clearer
to all faculty members that students did not take just their individual courses but that they were part of a larger curriculum.
Through the portfolios, it became possible to see what the curriculum is — to actually describe it.

Our first attempt at description involved some fairly mechanical approaches. We summarized portfolios by categoriz-
ing assignments by types: papers, lab reports, projects, in-class
writing, exams, quizzes, and computer exercises. Each of these
categories was broken down further (for example, the category
"papers" was broken down into research, reaction, essay, creative, and journal components). The percentage of each type
of assignment in relation to the total work was calculated using
the number of pages in the portfolio and the number of discrete
assignments. We were able to calculate the number of pages
in the average portfolio. In addition, we were able to produce
vignettes, based upon individual cases, that displayed the range
of materials within students' portfolios. In this way, data reported
on "average" students did not obscure the range and diversity
of experiences.

After sharing this information, we asked the faculty to
review the portfolios in a workshop setting, taking into account
the various goals and curricular expectations of the program.

We asked them not to assess how well we had met the goals, but rather where they saw evidence of an assignment that required skills or abilities that the program faculty viewed as important, for example, assignments that gave evidence of emphasis on critical thinking or that reflected our effort to improve quantitative reasoning across the curriculum. In describing what we were doing, rather than how well we were doing, we fostered discussion that took on a less defensive tone. As we proceeded through our course development process in 1992, faculty made reference to insights they had gained through the initial portfolio review session. A number of faculty members identified things they saw as missing in the portfolios. For example, the Western Program requires all students to complete yearlong senior projects. However, the portfolios showed that (at least in the first year) we did not systematically teach research paper–writing or library skills. We were also engaged in revising our divisional five-year plan, and many of the "missing" areas were designated as goals that we needed to work toward.

The most important aspect of the portfolio is that the faculty is always reviewing the actual products of the Western Program curriculum — not some abstract or generic indices of performance on objectives we may or may not be trying to achieve. Because the assessment is based upon the actual products generated for that curriculum (acknowledging, of course, that there are many aspects of the curriculum and the students' experience of teaching and learning that are not reflected in the portfolios), the feedback necessary for curricular reform is immediate; little translation is necessary. In addition, faculty members have been able to view the products of the program through the lens of their own goals. Faculty have been forced to take ownership of the curriculum and either change it or their goals if they are not content with the products generated. They control the agenda.

In the summer of 1992, the Western Program graduates who serve on the Dean's Advisory Council were asked to review course syllabi and work in the student portfolios. They then gave their feedback on the portfolios in light of programmatic objectives and compared the materials to their own experiences at

Western. Later, we will be asking educational, political, and business leaders to review the portfolios and to make observations about them in relation to both the program's curricular goals and their own agendas. The experience with the Dean's Advisory Council taught us that we need to allow more time — probably a minimum of two days for this activity. The afternoon given to the Dean's Advisory Council proved insufficient time to allow for more than cursory reading and reflection. However, even this brief time gave some confirmation that the increased emphasis we have given to the teaching of scientific methods and quantitative reasoning is showing up in the work contained in the portfolios.

The Western Program has also been involved in three other assessment activities of a descriptive nature: studies of student time, student expectations, and institutional environment. Each of these relates to Western's mission as a residential, student-centered program. In supporting our claims to be a twenty-four-hour educational institution, our assessment work has focused not only on the classroom aspect of students' education but also on the nonclassroom, "lived" experiences of the students. Again, descriptive approaches appear to offer the most value. Indeed, we have made a number of significant changes in the program as a result of this information.

The goal of the student time-use study was to better understand the way students spend their time. Michael Moffat (1989) from Rutgers and David Kalsbeek (1989) from Saint Louis University both used anthropological approaches to study student use of time (among other things). Each reported that students spend little more than an hour a day on academic work outside the classroom. Using a diary approach (students filled in what they were doing throughout the day in an hour-by-hour diary), Richard Light and his colleagues in the Harvard Assessment Seminars found greater amounts of time devoted to academic work (Light, 1990). We, however, were interested in more precise and concrete accounts of what students were doing.

First-year students were given beepers to carry around for one week in the middle of the semester. They were asked to write in their logs very precisely what they were doing at the point the beeper sounded. Beepers sounded on a random basis throughout the week according to a predetermined schedule. Logs revealed that approximately 40 percent of students' waking time (students logged off the beepers when they went to bed) was devoted to academic matters (being in class, reading assignments, studying, receiving academic advising, and the like). An unexpected 10 percent of the recorded beeps were related to moving throughout campus. Perhaps this should not have been a surprise to us, since Miami is a residential campus spread over a sizable rural physical plant. However, none of the previous studies had noted so much time devoted to walking. Indeed, this information has had the biggest impact to date. We now make it a point to talk with students about how they spend their time; we assist them in understanding that walking time can be used in a number of ways: as social time, as exercise, as reflective time, as "zone-out" time, or as a moment to organize a paper or the daily "to do" list. The beeper material has been used during summer orientation to help students begin thinking about time as a resource and to make them more conscious of how they are investing it.

Several years ago during summer orientation, we started a project in which students (and their parents) were asked to write freely for five minutes about their hopes, dreams, and fears about college. The results provided such interesting information about our students that we asked that group of students to repeat the task (now changed to read "about the coming semester") at the start of every semester throughout their four years in college. The writing demonstrated very vividly a sophomore "slump" at the beginning of the second year. Formerly confident students were concerned about a lack of direction and about the choice of their upper-level program of study. These students were certain that their peers did not have their same insecurities. This finding led us to shift our career-development, upper-level support program from the spring semester, when students are actually asked to create their upper-level program, to the fall semester. The free-writing responses made it clear that students were anxious about this issue and needed support earlier than we had thought. Many students noted in their free writing that they appreciated the career workshops and speakers on various educational opportunities. Indeed, more students wrote of their appreciation for the sense of support that these programs provided than actually attended them! This fact suggests that symbolic support may be more important than actual programs in helping student morale.

We have made extensive use of campus environment questionnaires that describe student values and perceptions of various aspects of campus life, along with behavioral self-report items (use of the library, various support services, and so forth). The UCLA Cooperative Institutional Research Program Freshman Survey (CIRP) has proved to be one of the most useful instruments of this type. This information gives a base-line picture of who students are before they have had extensive contact with the institution. It has been very useful in designing brochures and developing student recruitment strategies because it provides a profile of student values and reasons for attending college as well as documenting high school activities of students. This information has provided a basis from which to evaluate the data collected on the CSEQ, CUES, and CCI. We started with the CUES results and initially thought that the Western experience had clearly shifted the values of students toward the importance of knowledge for its own sake and toward a community orientation. However, when we obtained the CIRP data for our students, it was clear that they entered already predisposed toward this orientation. This finding tempered our ability to claim program impact too boldly.

Alumni surveys (the ACT Alumni Survey and a survey developed by a group of institutions led by Joseph Pettit, 1990, at Georgetown University) also have been quite useful in providing descriptive information about institutional impact, particularly as they reinforce information gathered through other sources. For the Western Program, these surveys have provided consistent feedback that our students felt insufficiently prepared to deal with quantitative information (an outcome the Fredonia findings corroborated). This information led the faculty to emphasize a quantitative reasoning across the curriculum to match our highly successful effort on writing.

Thus far, descriptive and self-report materials have proven to be more effective in creating an impetus for curricular and program change than more evaluative or normative approaches. Part of the reason may be the fact that descriptive approaches, in trying to present what *is,* avoid a defensive response because they invite the faculty and staff to ask themselves whether the effects they are observing as a result of their programs are what they want to see. The descriptive approach also avoids some of the problems in outcomes assessment that Fredonia has identified. To date, this approach has provided many small changes that have resulted in improvements in the educational program at Western. In the long run, descriptive approaches to assessment hold the potential to transform programs because of their ability to engage faculty and staff in feeling responsible for the results.

And in the End

What have we learned at Fredonia and at Western through our collaboration as we assessed our general or liberal education programs? For one thing, our stories reveal the complexity of such programs and their assessment. Complicated, incompletely understood outcomes; multiple measures; and the changing process of assessment in different institutional contexts are all involved. Fredonia began with a focus on locally constructed assessment for an internal audience but found it needed a comparative study with an external institution. Western College started with an external focus on nationally normed means of assessment; moved through its collaboration with Fredonia; and then went on to a purely local, internally oriented descriptive approach.

It is not simply a matter of finding what is right for each institution but also of understanding that different emphases are right for the same institution at different stages in its assessment process. If Western had not begun with normed instruments, it would not have appreciated its need for descriptive measures. If Fredonia had not undertaken its comparative study, it would not have been so cautious in interpreting its local results. Comparative and local factors; external and internal foci; outcomes and activities; judgments by others and oneself—these alternate as figure and ground in the assessment picture; it may be important to retain one's ability to keep reversing them. It is also important to affirm the value of the very complexity that baffles us in assessing liberal education: we cannot draw Leviathan with a hook.

References

Kalsbeek, D. "What Really Happens: Rhetoric and Reality of Students' Non-Classroom Experiences." Workshop presented at the 4th annual American Association of Higher Education Assessment Conference, Atlanta, June 24, 1989.

Light, R. *The Harvard Assessment Seminars: Explorations with Students and Faculty About Teaching, Learning, and Student Life.* Cambridge, Mass.: Harvard University Press, 1990.

Moffat, M. *Coming of Age in New Jersey.* New Brunswick, N.J.: Rutgers University Press, 1989.

Pettit, J. "Do Your Graduates Have Worthwhile Ideas for Your Curriculum?" Paper presented at the 5th Annual American Association of Higher Education Assessment Conference, Washington, D.C., June 30, 1990.

6

Demonstrating and Enhancing Community College Effectiveness

R. Dan Walleri
Jeffrey A. Seybert

Community colleges serve more students than any other provider of U.S. higher education. Created to provide broader access, community colleges have consistently expanded their missions in an effort to be all things to all people. Yet the phenomenal growth of these colleges has not come without criticism. Concern has been raised about the success rate of students entering community colleges, as well as the ability of the colleges to move students on to the bachelor's degree. As a consequence, assessment and accountability have become an increasingly central focus, with "institutional effectiveness" now a major part of the community college lexicon.

Demonstrating institutional effectiveness presents a special set of problems for community colleges (Calhoun, 1991).

Note: The authors wish to express appreciation to the following colleagues who provided the material for the case studies discussed in this chapter: David Hanson, Virginia Western Community College; Julie Aspinwall-Lamberts, Lane Community College; Tim Griffin, Community College of Denver; Janice Friedel, Eastern Iowa Community College District; and Jack Bautsch, Seattle Central Community College.

They typically have a much broader teaching mission than four-year colleges and universities. In addition to traditional freshman and sophomore coursework, community colleges provide career training, occupational retraining, developmental coursework, community and continuing education programs, contract training for business and industry, courses for special populations, and a variety of other educational offerings. Moreover, community college students often differ dramatically from traditional college students. The former are much more diverse in age, background, employment status, preparation, and educational objectives than their four-year-college counterparts. Thus, measures of institutional effectiveness common to four-year colleges and universities (for example, number of graduates or proportion of graduates to students admitted) are in most cases not applicable to community colleges. As a result, assessment in two-year colleges should involve a broad-based approach to evaluation of overall institutional effectiveness.

The importance of evaluating student learning remains, of course. Yet outcomes assessment should be one of a number of crucial components in a larger effort to examine all facets of the two-year college and its diverse mission. Other important components include, for example, systematic program reviews, follow-up surveys of former vocational students and their employers, follow-up surveys and senior institution transcript analyses of former transfer students, periodic evaluation surveys of college offices and services, and analyses of course retention and attrition rates and grading patterns. This chapter describes the ways some of these assessment strategies have been implemented in two-year colleges, the results of those strategies, and the changes that have occurred as a consequence. In particular, many institutional examples (using the methods of transcript analysis, student tracking, systematic program review, and career-vocational student and employer follow-up surveys) are provided.

Transcript Analysis

The following discussion focuses on transcript analysis at two western institutions: Seattle Central Community College (SCCC) in Seattle, Washington, and Mt. Hood Community College (MHCC) in Gresham, Oregon.

Institutional Setting — Seattle Central Community College

SCCC is one of three institutions within the Seattle Community College District. The comprehensive college serves about nine thousand students per term, the equivalent of approximately five thousand full-time students annually. Of these students, 40 percent are minorities; Asians account for the largest minority group.

Assessment Strategy and Findings. For several years, it has been observed that students at SCCC and across the nation have a difficult time with college-level mathematics courses. At SCCC, data collected on student performance showed that only about one-half of the students who enrolled in intermediate algebra courses from 1987 through 1990 received a C grade or better. Results were similar for students who continue on to the next level of math studies: about one-half of them will fail their next math course. Administrators and faculty sought to determine the conditions or factors that influenced the achievement of students in math courses and to see whether these factors could be manipulated to help improve student performance.

As a beginning, the math faculty examined information on the skill levels that students brought into the algebra course as well as their other characteristics. It was determined that (1) the students were being properly assessed and placed, (2) performance in developmental math correlated positively with grades in the algebra course, (3) a student's total credit load was not associated with performance in the course, and (4) repeating the course did not result in an improved grade. These findings led the faculty to examine the curriculum and teaching approach as possible sources of the deficiencies in student performance. It was concluded that the standard algebra course consisted of a sequence of disconnected manipulative skills taught in isolation and that major revisions would be necessary if student performance was to be improved.

Improvements Undertaken. The faculty revised the intermediate algebra course to focus on graphing functions. Students examined, discussed, and became familiar with graphs based on real-world situations. In the process of learning about graphing functions, students also acquired algebraic skills. Working in groups, students learned to solve linear equations, then quadratic equations, and eventually exponential equations. Following implementation of these changes, the percentage of students receiving a C or better in the course increased from 53 to 71 percent.

Future Developments. The improvements in student performance achieved through transcript analysis and subsequent curriculum revision led to further changes, emphasizing technology, throughout the math program. Courses are now linked, and students are provided with a Texas Instruments graphing calculator. The plan is to continue this process with the aim of expanding computer-assisted instruction.

Institutional Setting — Mt. Hood Community College

MHCC is a comprehensive institution serving a mostly white, middle-class suburban district of 220,000 people, just east of Portland. The college enrolls almost 30,000 different students on an annual basis (the equivalent of approximately 6,500 full-time students). Between 40 and 50 percent of all students entering test below standards set for college-level studies.

Assessment Strategy and Findings. In the early 1980s, the Student Success Task Force was established at MHCC to conduct a systematic review of college policies and practices with the aim of initiating changes to promote student success. The plight of underprepared students was of particular concern, given the growing perception that the community college "open door" had become a "revolving door." The college had an assessment and placement program for entering students, but it was strictly voluntary on the students' part. Perceptions of the problem, even if one was admitted, varied widely among administrators and faculty. To develop an empirical base upon which to address this issue, a random selection of transcripts of students testing below college standards was made. The purpose of the analysis was to determine if students were (1) following advice with regard to enrollment in developmental education courses, (2) successful in remediation, and (3) subsequently successful in college-level courses.

Although transcripts revealed that the vast majority of the students were enrolling in appropriate developmental education courses as advised, most were concurrently enrolled in other courses requiring the very skills for which they had been referred for remediation. It was also found that some students were spending an extended period of time in developmental education (four to six quarters). Overall, the persistence and academic performance of these students were far below college norms for students not requiring remediation.

Improvements Undertaken. As a result of the transcript analysis, a decision was made to implement a mandatory testing and placement program for all entering students seeking to enroll for nine or more quarter hours or for any enrolling in a writing or mathematics course (Japely, Kennedy, and Walleri, 1987). The college's computer registration system was modified to match course requirements with the deficiencies of students so that students were not able to register concurrently for developmental courses and college-level courses for which they were not prepared. In addition to remediation, students were provided with a structured sequence of coursework. Every effort was made to present the program as nonpunitive, a fact reflected even in its name (Guided Studies).

Since the inception of the program, the persistence rate and grade-point average of underprepared students have been slightly lower than for prepared students, but the differences have not been statistically significant. The only major difference between the two groups is that the underprepared students normally require about two to four quarters longer to complete a program than those who are prepared.

Benefits and Problems of Transcript Analysis

Although transcript analysis can be revealing, as shown in the case of MHCC, the process is usually manual and thus very time-consuming. To date, relatively few community colleges or state systems have developed computerized transcript analysis systems. Manual approaches are subject to numerous pitfalls, including the lack of consistent coding and suspect reliability. Yet transcript analysis can be an objective, reliable way of producing a realistic picture of students' academic performance and progress that supplements — even corrects in some cases — information reported by students. Although it may be low tech, transcript analysis remains a valuable tool in an institution's repertoire of assessment strategies.

This approach has many applications beyond the cases described here. Performance in sequential courses and transfer success are two such examples. Adelman (1992) demonstrates the use of transcript analysis, taken from a national sample of community college students, in describing a variety of student outcomes. Johnson County Community College has implemented a comprehensive follow-up tracking system for former students who transferred to four-year colleges and universities (Seybert and Soltz, 1992). This system includes analysis of both the students' community college and university transcripts in addition to data collected from surveys. This approach provides a more complete assessment of the outcomes of transfer students' experiences at both the community college and the four-year college or university and of the role played by the community college in those ultimate outcomes. Institutions and state systems could significantly enhance their assessment activities through the development of computerized transcript analysis systems.

Student Tracking

Our discussion next focuses on how three institutions — the Community College of Denver (CCD), Colorado, Lane Community College in Eugene, Oregon, and Virginia Western Community College (VWCC) in Roanoke, Virginia — have used student tracking to improve their programs.

Institutional Setting — Community College of Denver

CCD serves the city and county of Denver, which have a population of approximately one-half million. The college enrolls almost twelve thousand (the equivalent of nearly four thousand five hundred full-time students annually). Of these, 40 percent are minorities, with Hispanics accounting for the largest minority group. Established as a separate entity from a larger metropolitan district in 1985, CCD has struggled to survive as a consequence of severe funding restrictions. Defining its mission in terms of serving the needs of the city, CCD has experienced a 50 percent increase in enrollment since 1989.

Assessment Strategy and Findings. CCD first implemented its student-tracking system in 1989. Within two years, the system had evolved to include retention analysis by instructional program and the ability to partition the cohorts to produce special studies on at-risk students, among other groups. Initial findings revealed that attrition was primarily the result of students' withdrawing from college, especially during the first semester. The typical at-risk student was young (twenty-five years of age or less), a minority group member, and enrolled in a transfer degree program.

Subsequent refinement of the tracking system identified particular problem areas: a gap between the time of students' entry to the college and matriculation into a specific program, the failure of developmental education students to move on and enroll in higher-level courses, and a relatively high attrition rate among non-native English speakers. Level of academic skills upon entry was found to be the single most important determinant of success.

Improvements Undertaken. These findings, along with analysis of testing data, contributed to a successful application for a Title III grant to establish an academic early-warning system and basic skills labs in English and mathematics. Efforts to reinforce basic skills throughout the curriculum were initiated through scholarships for faculty projects granted by the CCD Teaching and Learning Center.

In addition to (and perhaps more important than) specific program changes, the student-tracking system has had an impact on the culture of the organization. Tracking results have been integrated within ongoing institutional processes, beginning with program review and unit plans. Student entry procedures have been developed for every degree program. Collaboration has increased between the instructional and student services branches as the different units attempt to eliminate barriers to and enhance prospects for student success.

Future Developments. The student-tracking system is being modified to include a classification structure for program majors that will allow for the delineation of the period when a student is between entering college and actually beginning a program of study. In combination with the new entry procedures, it will be possible to identify student movement toward and between majors. This information will in turn assist in faculty advising, the early-warning system, and efforts to monitor student progress.

Institutional Setting — Lane Community College

Founded in 1964, Lane serves a population of over 282,000 in a district of five thousand square miles ranging from the Oregon Cascade mountains to the Pacific Ocean. Lane provides comprehensive services to more than 32,000 people each year.

The state has been plagued by layoffs in key industries such as timber and lumber, fishing, and agriculture. Many of the recently unemployed workers struggle with limited educational backgrounds, low skills, and low self-esteem. Because of the district's heavy dependence on timber, Lane Community College attracts a significant number of these dislocated workers.

Assessment Strategy and Findings. Lane's student-tracking system relies on microcomputers for flexible analysis of student cohorts. The system contains over fifty elements of data from admissions, testing, and academic records. It is used to identify new students who could be at risk for retention and goal achievement. Two primary at-risk predictors were found: low reading and writing skills and uncertainty regarding major area of study.

Improvements Undertaken. Information from the tracking system resulted in new advising procedures, improved advising recommendation forms, and the creation of two successful intervention strategies: a college success course and counselor intervention with at-risk students.

The college success course teaches essential personal skills, such as learning to be proactive, recognizing and using personal resources, and objectively evaluating personal situations. The course provides a broad array of tools to assist at-risk students in achieving their objectives. Students who complete the course are significantly more likely to complete credits attempted than other at-risk students.

The college's advising function has been reorganized to provide more direct, personal services to students who have low reading scores or who have not declared a major. Counselors recommend coursework based on test scores and conversations with the student. Follow-up data reveal that 80 to 90 percent of the students take the courses recommended by the counselors. At-risk students involved in the special advising procedures have improved their course completion rates to equal those of the general student population.

Future Developments. The current challenge is to integrate student tracking within ongoing institutional processes, especially at the program level. Individual departments can use tracking system data to design intervention activities. For example, the counselor for the mechanical technologies department works directly with students with low reading and mathematics scores regarding appropriate course placement, and instructors reinforce the need for competence in reading and mathematics and the availability of assistance. The department has increased its retention of at-risk students. Program curricula are being restructured to include clear identification of prerequisite reading and mathematics skills.

Institutional Setting—
Virginia Western Community College

VWCC serves a diverse urban, suburban, and rural population of about 220,000. Annually the college enrolls more than 12,000 students (the equivalent of about 3,500 full-time students).

Assessment Strategy and Findings. As an important part of its comprehensive student outcomes assessment program, VWCC has been developing and implementing an automated student-tracking system since 1987. There are several components that make up the system, each in a different stage of development. The ultimate goal is to provide the necessary information for entry-level placement, advising, the auditing of degrees, and follow-up after students leave the institution. At each stage, data can be collected for institutional assessment, feedback to area high schools, and program improvement.

Each summer, data from transcripts for all new high school graduates who apply to the college are entered into the college's data base. Currently, these data are entered manually, but a dialogue is under way to explore the feasibility of loading computer tapes from the high schools directly into the college's computing system. This system enables VWCC counselors to examine each student's high school record when making recommendations for entry-level assessment and course placement. This information is vitally important because college policies rely heavily upon prior academic achievement. For example, a student who did not do well in high school English submits a writing sample, which is then analyzed to determine whether the student is ready for college composition or should first take a developmental writing course. Informal observations, combined with basic statistical analyses, have determined that type of high school diploma, GPA, and standardized test scores all have value as indicators of readiness for college-level coursework.

Each year, VWCC officials meet with area high school administrators and counselors to discuss these data. A service-area composite summary and individual summaries are provided for each high school, with individual student records also available. This feedback is especially helpful to high school counselors.

Curriculum-progress tracking is the part of the system that follows students through their program of study and that is used for academic advising and certifying students for graduation. A curriculum progress report is available on-line or as an unofficial in-house transcript, listing each student's completed courses and unfulfilled program requirements.

Improvements Undertaken. As a result of the high school transcript system, placement criteria and procedures have been modified to enhance the efficiency and appropriateness of student support services. Improvements in the academic retention and mean GPA of new freshmen have been noted (fall to spring enrollment has increased by four percentage points while the proportion of students entering with a 2.00 GPA or higher has increased by six percentage points). The dialogue with staff from the high schools has led to cooperative arrangements to help improve students' preparation for college.

The automated advising system enables counselors and faculty advisers to help students make informed decisions about curriculum changes and course selections. It virtually eliminates the guesswork for students working toward graduation by displaying all their course credits, including substitutions, course equivalents, transfer credit, the way these credits fit in their curriculum, and remaining requirements. The program calculates an overall cumulative GPA and also a curriculum GPA (for just those courses that apply toward a student's program of study).

Future Developments. A follow-up tracking system has been designed to integrate postcollege data on students who leave the college for the work force or to attend another institution. Employment and transfer data for noncompleters and graduates are maintained on personal computers. A standard reporting format has been developed to enable four-year colleges to share complete academic records on all community college transfer students. This should permit the data to be merged with the mainframe student information system and the tracking subsystem. Employment information will be the last component to be integrated. Results from follow-up tracking will be incorporated within the ongoing program review and improvement process at VWCC.

Systematic Program Review

Systematic program review has been a major assessment tool in the Eastern Iowa Community College District (EICCD).

Institutional Setting — Eastern Iowa Community College District

EICCD is a comprehensive, multicampus district in east-central Iowa serving a four-county area with a population of roughly 290,000. Approximately fifteen thousand credit students enroll annually at Clinton, Scott, and Muscatine community colleges (the equivalent of nearly ten thousand full-time students).

Assessment Strategy. As part of its effort to assess institutional effectiveness, EICCD utilizes a systematic program evaluation process. The process was developed in 1985, was tested on thirty-eight vocational and technical programs, and has subsequently been revised and implemented on a three-year cycle. It is an evaluation process by which timely and accurate data are provided to both faculty and administrators regarding the health and viability of college programs; program recommendations are formulated and validated; and decisions are made regarding resource allocations and the maintenance, revision, or termination of programs. In addition, the process provides opportunities to compare business and industrial standards with those of occupational programs; inform former students, employers, and the business community of the institution's commitment to self-improvement and excellence; utilize the expertise of representatives from related businesses and industries; and identify needed modifications in program outcomes, curriculum, physical facilities, and instructional equipment.

The process consists of two phases. Phase one is an annual review, which includes the collection and analysis of ten discrete program data elements. These data are compared year to year over a three-year period. Phase two is an in-depth program evaluation, also conducted on a three-year cycle, and consists of five major components: a series of constituent surveys, a local labor market assessment, a program self-study, an internal review-team report, and the college response to that report.

Improvements Undertaken. The results of the program evaluation are used to make decisions about program outcomes, curricular changes, the acquisition of new equipment, facilities requirements, and faculty development activities. District policy dictates that one-third of its annual equipment acquisition budget be tied to equipment approved for purchase through the program evaluation process. Funds for faculty development are also allocated based on needs identified in the evaluations.

The information gained through the evaluations has provided direction to the development of competency-based curricula in the EICCD's vocational-technical programs. All programs have been modified based on the information obtained through the evaluations, a few have been terminated, others shortened or lengthened, and six new programs have been developed.

In addition, numerous specific programmatic changes have been implemented as a consequence of the results of the process:

- Incorporation of computer-aided design into the drafting program
- Major revision of the building maintenance program into two programs: industrial electricity (with an electronics option) and manufacturing maintenance
- Revision of the automotive technology program into a ladder structure that awards a certificate after the first semester, a diploma after one year, and an associate degree after completion of the two-year program
- Development of customized and contracted programs for local business and industry in computerized numerical controls, statistical process controls, just-in-time management, and total quality management

Future Developments. The ultimate goal of any component of an assessment process is to improve teaching, learning, and delivery of services to students. Thus, programmatic enhancements based on assessment results are only an interim step. Ultimately, the effects of such changes should be translated into enhanced student outcomes. Efforts to measure student outcomes related to the program modifications just outlined are currently under way.

Career and Vocational Student
and Employer Follow-Up Surveys

Career and employer surveys have affected a range of programs at Johnson County Community College (JCCC) in Overland Park, Kansas.

Institutional Setting — Johnson County Community College

JCCC is a comprehensive community college serving a middle- and upper-middle-class Kansas suburban county of approximately 350,000 residents. Credit enrollments total roughly thirty-two thousand annually (or about sixteen thousand FTE students).

Assessment Strategy and Findings. For several years, as a part of its overall institutional effectiveness program, JCCC has annually surveyed former students who complete a career program. Both graduates (certificate and degree recipients) and students who leave with marketable skills (those who have taken sufficient courses in a program to obtain employment in that field) are surveyed. Survey items deal with a variety of demographic and other topics and the respondents' ratings of achievement of their educational objectives, evaluation of the instructional and other experiences at the college, ratings of characteristics of their current position, and estimation of gains on a number of cognitive and affective dimensions of attending the college.

The survey methodology utilizes two mailings, followed by telephone interviews of those former students who did not respond to either mailing. This procedure has generally produced response rates between 80 and 90 percent. One item on the survey asks for the name and address of the former student's employer. These employers are then surveyed by mail regarding their evaluation of the job preparation and training provided by the college. Response rates on this employer survey generally fall in the 75 to 80 percent range.

Improvements Undertaken. Results of both follow-up surveys are reported to career program administrators and faculty annually. The results are used to inform decisions regarding career program staffing, equipment and facilities, and curriculum. Examples of these program modifications and enhancements include

- Revision of the curriculum in the heating, ventilation, and air-conditioning program to include advanced controls, sheet metal, and electronic applications
- Addition of courses in computer-assisted design, textiles, graphic communications, upholstery, and drapery to the interior merchandising curriculum
- Modifications in the paralegal program, including upgraded qualifications for adjunct faculty, addition of courses in computer-assisted legal research and computer applications in the law office, and incorporation of job-search skills into several paralegal courses

Future Developments. As was the case for the EICCD program review process, the purpose of each component of the JCCC institutional effectiveness program (including the career student and employer follow-up surveys) is improvement of instruction and services to students. It is assumed that program changes based on results of these assessment processes will lead to those improvements. The college is now assessing the effects of those changes on student outcomes.

Implications for Community Colleges

One of the major features of the contemporary community college movement is the effort to enhance and demonstrate institutional effectiveness, including a strong outcomes assessment component. As a consequence, the need for and appreciation of advanced information systems, especially for student tracking, have become more pronounced. The development and utilization of information systems to enhance institutional effectiveness marks a major turning point in the evolution of community colleges.

As is evident from the case studies offered in this chapter, student-tracking systems can have a significant impact, both in sustaining student success and in transforming the organizational culture. The systems also play an integral role in the larger assessment agenda, as seen in the cases of Eastern Iowa and Johnson County.

Community colleges are increasingly acting as "brokering" agents for access to education and training services. Linkages are being extended both down and up the educational ladder, facilitating the transition from high school through attainment of the bachelor's degree. Concurrently, local and statewide economic development strategies have come to rely heavily on community colleges, especially for quality gains within the work force. Within such a context, assessment programs must have a broad scope and employ multiple indicators of effectiveness.

References

Adelman, C. *The Way We Are: The Community College as American Thermometer.* Washington, D.C.: U.S. Government Printing Office, 1992.

Calhoun, H. D. "Implementing Institutional Effectiveness at Two-Year Colleges." In J. O. Nichols, *A Practitioner's Handbook for Institutional Effectiveness and Student Outcomes Assessment Implementation.* New York: Agathon Press, 1991.

Japely, S. M., Kennedy, M. J., and Walleri, R. D. "Assisting Success Through an Improved Student Information System." *College & University,* 1987, *62,* 117–125.

Seybert, J. A., and Soltz, D. F. *JCCC Transfer Students: Their Destinations and Achievements.* Overland Park, Kans.: Office of Institutional Research, Johnson County Community College, 1992.

Building Assessment Programs in Large Institutions

James H. Watt
Nancy Hungerford Drennen
Raymond J. Rodrigues
Nancy Menelly
Erica K. Wiegel

The establishment of assessment programs at large state-assisted research institutions is no small task. These institutions frequently have highly decentralized academic programs with powerful departments and colleges. The departments and colleges may disagree strongly in some very basic ways about the nature and goals of undergraduate education. As a result, they also disagree about the kinds of evaluation that are appropriate and may have quite divergent views of the usefulness of assessment information. One college may see assessment as a tool for improving individual courses or curricular areas, whereas another sees it as a way of evaluating success in fostering general high-level thinking skills. Throw into this mix the separate agendas of academic administrators who may regard assessment as a tool for resource allocation and of academic regulatory agencies and legislatures who want broad-based assessment for accountability and the problem becomes even more complex. This chapter will summarize the experiences of two state-assisted research institutions that have completed the first phases of introducing assessment into their normal operations.

University of Connecticut

The University of Connecticut (UConn) is a Tier I land-grant research university with approximately ten thousand undergraduate and five thousand graduate students and 1,100 faculty in eleven colleges and 106 departments. The university has traditionally placed emphasis on graduate education and research rather than on undergraduate education. Only in recent years have serious thought and debate been directed to articulating the goals of general education and to implementing a curriculum that achieves them. However, even with five years of experience with a formal general education curriculum, it is still a somewhat fragmented process. Courses are still developed and staffed within departments and are then presented for approval for the general education curriculum by a Faculty Senate committee. There is minimal cross-disciplinary discussion about their impact on the general education of undergraduates, and most of this is in the form of casual conversations with colleagues in other departments.

Colorado State University

Colorado State University (CSU) is also a Carnegie I research university, with approximately 18,600 full-time students (or a head count of about twenty-two thousand) in eight colleges and fifty-seven departments, taught by approximately 1,200 faculty. As a land-grant university, CSU is committed to research, teaching, and service on behalf of the state, region, and nation. In an environment of diminishing state resources, the university has had to rely increasingly upon tuition, contracts, grants, and donations to support its work. State funds now constitute less than 30 percent of the university's available moneys.

Colleges and departments have always developed their academic programs in an atmosphere of relative autonomy. In the mid 1980s, the faculty implemented the university's first broad-ranging general education program for all students. No sooner had the faculty accomplished the extensive deliberations needed to create this new program than the state moved to require assessments of both general education and education within the majors. This timing led to a series of strained attempts to implement the new program while also having to begin thinking of what it meant to assess it.

UConn Approach to Assessment

In 1986, the Faculty Senate of the University of Connecticut made sweeping changes in undergraduate education, identifying six academic areas and two skills (writing and quantitative reasoning) to guide curriculum change. As a response to faculty questions about the likely effectiveness of the new curriculum, the Ad Hoc Committee to Evaluate the General Education Curriculum was created. This committee was charged with identifying appropriate methodologies and conducting research to answer a fundamental question: does the general education curriculum work?

The question of the nature of assessment and its purpose was made even more salient by rumblings within the state board of governors about the imposition of state mandates for assessment activities. The faculty reaction to the possibility of widespread assessment activity imposed from above by either the university academic administration or the state educational bureaucracy was not favorable, to put it mildly. The specter of assessment testing's being used to evaluate courses or punish instructors whose classes performed poorly was raised, as was the fear that a single standardized test would be used as an (invalid) indicator of success in achieving a very diverse set of goals.

The skepticism about the merits of assessment and its potential outcomes sparked heated debates among members of the Faculty Senate. There were distinctly opposing opinions about whether assessment should be undertaken at all and about what, if anything, should be done with the results. The nature of these debates clearly indicated that if the General Education Assessment Project was to succeed, it would not only require faculty involvement but would also have to be viewed as faculty-directed activity (see Ewell, 1988).

In this atmosphere, a three-year research program to evaluate student advancement toward the general education goals was proposed by the Ad Hoc Assessment Committee in 1987 and begun in 1988 with support from both the UConn provost's office and a Fund for the Improvement of Postsecondary Education grant. Several critical decisions were made at this point, decisions that have shaped the perceptions and practice of assessment at UConn.

First, the faculty was involved on a very large scale. Over seventy-five faculty members from eleven different colleges were involved in the first phase of the project. Second, the assumption was made that assessing different academic areas would require various measurement techniques and tools and that faculty members were the best judges of the appropriateness of both. Third, it was judged that the approach to undergraduate education at the University of Connecticut was sufficiently different from that of other colleges and universities that the school could not import an intact assessment program; one would have to be developed that would fit the view of general education articulated in the statement of goals. The importance of tailoring assessment to institutions has been noted elsewhere (Hexter and Lippincott, 1990). Finally, the people involved saw assessment not as a single activity, but rather as the conjunction of a number of related research projects aimed at answering different questions about student education and experiences. Although assessment is often equated with simple evaluation, we wished to use the results for curriculum improvement, as suggested by our faculty and others (Pine, 1989; Wright, 1990).

The research program included multiyear testing of students, focus-group interviews, and surveys of faculty and student groups. In the initial phase, completed during the 1988–89 academic year, a faculty subcommittee for each of the general education areas was established. Each faculty group examined the goals for its respective area and debated the best type of test instrument for measuring performance on the individual goals. The subcommittee then developed sixteen original instruments and specified one standardized test to measure student advancement toward each of the specified goals. During this initial phase, faculty members were also surveyed concerning their agreement with the general education goals established for their areas.

Forty-seven percent of the faculty members (316 individuals) responded to the survey.

The second research phase (1989–90) involved the pilot testing of the original instruments created by the area subcommittees on 1,148 incoming freshmen and on a convenience sample of 342 advanced (junior and senior) students who were "volunteered" by their course instructors. Statistical analyses of the pilot-test results were conducted to determine predictive and discriminative validity of test items. Instrument instructions and grading protocols for essay questions were also modified as an outcome of the pilot test.

Complementing this research on student performance were two studies of student reaction to general education. A number of focus-group interviews and a survey on students' own perceived competence in each of the six general education areas were conducted. In the interviews, conducted by trained student moderators, 44 students openly discussed their impressions of general education and their experiences with its course requirements. In the survey, 724 students were asked to rate their abilities to execute the skills implicit in the goals specified for the individual areas of general education. Although both the interviews and the surveys were conducted on convenience samples, an effort was made to arrive at a sample of students that included a wide diversity of academic majors and interests.

The final phase of the project included testing the revised performance instruments on two distinct student groups. During the 1990 freshman summer orientation program, 1,694 incoming students were tested. A tightly controlled sampling and recruiting procedure also yielded a sample of 601 junior and senior students that was representative of the university population by school and major. These students were tested with the revised instruments during the fall 1990 and spring 1991 semesters. With few exceptions, each student took two tests from different areas in a single testing session and received $15 for participation. Compensating students was crucial, as the Faculty Senate had made clear that any instructional time devoted to assessment was to be at the discretion of the instructor. As the willingness of instructors to participate in assessment varied widely, testing was done outside the classroom, and compensation appeared to be the only way to assure participation of a reliable sample of motivated students. By combining compensation with multiple telephone contacts, postcards, and considerable interpersonal persuasion, 76 percent of the sampled students were convinced to participate in the assessment activities.

CSU Approach to Assessment

Unlike the University of Connecticut, CSU, along with all other public institutions of higher education in Colorado, was required by the legislature and the Colorado Commission on Higher Education (CCHE) to implement an assessment program. In 1985, Colorado House Bill 1187 (in addition to redefining the missions of state universities and colleges) required institutions to submit goals and plans for an accountability program by 1988. As defined by the CCHE, the regulations forced institutions to demonstrate improvements in student knowledge and skills, disseminate results publicly, and express clearly to students expectations for their performance. Improvements in performance were to be achieved through effective use of time, effort, and money. If a state university or college failed to meet all requirements, 2 percent of its budget could be withheld. Further, the legislation stipulated assessment of general education, discipline-specific education, retention and completion of students, alumni and student satisfaction, after-graduation performance, costs of implementing the assessment program, and minority student performance. To the advantage of the universities and colleges, the CCHE left it up to them to determine which evaluation procedures worked best.

Because CSU had only recently revised its general education program but had done so without assessment in mind, the university used goals approved in 1981 for the undergraduate education program as the focus of its two-phase accountability program. In the first phase, the university developed plans for general education assessment in 1988 and reported the first results in 1989. During the second phase, departments developed plans for discipline-specific assessments, submitted them to CCHE for approval in 1990, and reported the first results in 1991. Thus, although assessment of general education was begun almost immediately, discipline-based assessment was gradually developed and implemented.

Administrators at CSU took advantage of an opportunity to acquire an excellence grant from the CCHE to implement the assessment process by using the ACT-COMP examination for five years. At the time, the ACT-COMP was the only available nationally normed examination of general education. To guide the assessment process, the Office of the Provost created the Student-Outcomes Steering Committee, composed of staff with technical expertise and some faculty. Composition faculty in the English department experimented with the written form of the ACT-COMP and found that it did not meet their standards for assessment and for reliability, so that form of the test was dropped. To determine constituent goals for undergraduate education, a student outcomes assessment survey was created and administered periodically to legislators, faculty, students, parents, and recruiters, beginning in 1988. Alumni surveys focusing upon satisfaction with undergraduate education were developed and administered in 1990 and 1991. Retention and completion data were compiled by the institutional research office of the university.

After acquiring the CCHE grant, the university set about developing an in-depth plan for assessment, which was reviewed by appropriate Faculty Council committees and extensively revised. At the same time, the university began to hold a variety of workshops for faculty: bringing in external consultants, having faculty take the ACT-COMP and report their responses to it, and reviewing the results with the University Curriculum Committee, the Committee on Instructional Development, and a committee of external advisers (consisting of business, corporate, and community representatives).

Despite the workshops, discussions in Faculty Council and administrative committees, and public releases of results, faculty awareness of the purposes and plans for the standardized testing and goals surely remained relatively low. The initial impression of many faculty members was that accountability was merely a mandate to be fulfilled.

It was not until the individual departments were required to submit plans for discipline-based assessment and to begin implementing these plans that the faculty truly became engaged with the process. In many departments, faculty thought that they had to use standardized tests. In part, this was the result of their observing the university using a standardized examination for general education. Many hesitated to report results honestly for fear that the CCHE would impose more penalties. The 2 percent recision threat loomed large in their minds. Eventually, through extensive discussions and revisions of their plans, the departments developed a wide variety of assessment procedures that they believed would best assess their disciplines and provide them the most meaningful data. Assessment procedures now include portfolio evaluations, student interviews, focus groups, and even a few standardized tests.

When the CCHE grant ran out, CSU rapidly moved to eliminate the ACT-COMP because it had not provided data that faculty could meaningfully translate into curriculum revisions. Since that time, CSU has developed focus groups to concentrate upon specific areas—such as advising, selective testing in composition and mathematics, a variety of student development instruments, and the progress of the Colorado State 100: a group of one hundred freshmen that the university is tracking using focus groups and data collection throughout their undergraduate years. Each year, refining its procedures through experience, CSU will create a new Colorado State 100 group.

Assessment Findings at UConn

The first conclusion produced by this project came before any data were collected from students: the faculty's direction of and direct involvement in the assessment project is a good thing. There are three specific benefits. The first is political. Faculty become less defensive when they feel that they are directing the project toward the end of improving instruction; in fact, some come to feel a real investment in the success of the process.

A second major benefit is in improved measurement. Faculty are likely to have good and often innovative ideas about ways that student performance can be observed. For example, one UConn instrument asked students to respond critically to themes of warfare in actual samples of music, painting, and drama. Another had students analyze the historical and political development of a hypothetical colonial society, while yet another tested their ability to comprehend and analyze critically articles about social issues that appeared in the popular press. Faculty development of assessment tools like these also assures that measurement will be strongly tied to the diverse missions and unique goals of a research university.

Third and most important, the act of designing assessment studies and creating instruments and procedures forces faculty to confront directly the goals and contradictions of general education for undergraduates. Faculty subcommittee members have reported intense and stimulating debates within the subcommittees. Furthermore, these discussions have continued with departmental colleagues not on the subcommittees. This is an important finding in a university in which curricular reform typically comes from the bottom up (individuals to departments to college) rather than being directed from above.

Aside from these procedural findings, the research addressed these fundamental questions:

1. Does the level of performance in these general education areas improve with increasing time in the university?
2. Does the number of courses taken in a general education area and performance in those courses predict improved performance in that area?
3. Do the faculty involved in general education courses agree with the goal statements for that area?
4. Do students feel that general education provides them with benefits?

Samples of upper-division students were compared with samples of incoming freshmen to determine if the level of performance in the general education areas improved with increasing time at the university. The better performance of upper-division students appeared in all but one of the general education areas and in the majority of the goals in each area. This finding gives some comforting evidence of the positive impact of the university experience; however, attrition of less-well-prepared students (as indicated by lower entering SAT scores) during the freshman and sophomore years accounts for some (but not all) of this gain.

To determine whether the number of courses taken in a general education area and the quality of performance in these courses were associated with improved performance on the area test instruments, statistical tests controlling for confounding factors like differential SAT scores, semester standing, and performance in other courses were conducted. The results showed clear evidence for a moderate positive association between performance in the general education curriculum and performance on assessment instruments, when other relevant variables were held constant statistically.

Were faculty members sympathetic to the goals of general education? The answer was an unequivocal yes. Survey responses showed a very strong and consistent agreement among faculty members on the basic goals of general education that fell within their area. There was no controversy about what the university should be achieving, only about methods of achieving it and ways of measuring that accomplishment.

In-depth focus-group interviews conducted during the second phase of the project revealed that students believe the general education curriculum is beneficial. In particular, students recognized that the goal of the general education requirements was to give them a broad education and that this breadth was beneficial. Overall, although there was much discussion over the value and execution of particular courses, the students generally accepted the abstract principle of general education, even when it meant taking courses that they felt were less personally relevant and that might steal time from studies in their major.

Students also felt fairly competent that they could personally achieve the goals of general education. Students felt most confident in the social sciences area and least confident in philosophy. Interestingly, perceptions of self-efficacy seemed to decrease over time in some general education areas (foreign languages and arts and literature) and to increase in others. This finding was unexpected and will probably stimulate further research.

Assessment Findings at CSU

From 1986 to 1990, Colorado State students made improvements in each of the ACT-COMP test areas — functioning in society, using science, using the arts, communication, solving problems, and clarifying values. Seniors in 1990 were above national norms for the ACT-COMP in all areas except using the arts. Seniors had their strongest showing compared to national norms in the area of using science. This finding was encouraging to faculty because it is consistent with the mission of Colorado State in the area of science and technology. However, the faculty continues to struggle with the question of defining the role of the arts at this university and of determining if there was cause for concern about the score in the arts, which was slightly below the national norm.

The assessment that asked constituents to rank educational goals indicated agreement among the faculty, students, parents, legislators, and recruiters for the most important ones (the ability to write and speak clearly, to think, to analyze situations, and to solve problems) as well as for the least important goals (understanding and enjoying art, music, drama, and literature; becoming actively involved in contemporary political and social issues; and becoming actively involved in student life and campus activities).

Unfortunately, the faculty of CSU could not determine from the ACT-COMP results whether anything should be revised. CSU students entered the university strong in the sciences and left strong in that area. They entered weak in using the arts and left in the same condition. However, the student and parent priorities for general education goals did not indicate that such results were out of line. If anything, their attitudes justified not changing anything.

Motivated and valid student participation has always been problematic. Freshmen took the ACT-COMP and other assess-

ments because they were required to do so, but sophomores and
seniors were less willing to spend time seriously taking the tests.
(Juniors are not tested.) The university tried various incentive
systems — payments of $25 for taking the tests, free caps and
gowns for seniors — all to no avail. Only priority during registration worked for sophomores. As a result, the university uses
many approaches to increase the number of participants. Some
students are invited after random selection to do "walk-in" testing at two sites. The university uses follow-up letters and personal telephone calls to improve participation. Some students
are tested in their senior courses after their instructors volun-
teer to host the testing. The university continues to examine
freshmen in large groups when they arrive. Resident hall staff
members test both sophomores and seniors on a variety of student development measures.

Improvements Undertaken at UConn

As the research projects were completed in September 1991,
only the first steps toward using the results of the assessment
have been taken. Nonetheless, there are clear signs that assessment is being integrated into the process of designing and improving the undergraduate curriculum. One of the first uses
made of the research results was to propose and justify a cultural diversity curriculum requirement. Performance of students
on goals in the general area of recognition of ethnocentrism was
mediocre, and this fact was used (in conjunction with other arguments) to persuade the Faculty Senate to approve the curriculum change.

Assessment instruments and procedures are also central
to a proposed new program in teaching-assistant training. This
program, if funded, will use continuous assessment testing to
provide quality control information to a formal TA training and
mentoring program.

Some organizational change has also been produced by
the conjunction of the general education assessment project and
a state requirement for planning and reporting upon assessment
activity across the whole institution. A standing committee of

faculty, academic administrators, student services administrators, and students has been formed to initiate, direct, and monitor assessment activities. This crucial development provides the organizational mechanism for introducing assessment into a wide range of university activities.

Less quantifiable are the effects of the faculty discussion generated by the three-year project. There have been informal discussions about the creation of new cross-disciplinary courses that address weaknesses in goal achievement uncovered by the assessment process. But these are currently submerged in distractions and dislocations that have been introduced by two years of budget cuts at the university. In addition, some sentiment has been expressed for revising the general education goals. Some goals appear to be too abstract, some overlap, and a portion of the faculty has expressed the need for additional goals. It is probably safe to say that discussions of these topics would not have occurred had the assessment project not been carried out. But the ultimate effect of improved faculty discourse has yet to be determined.

Improvements Undertaken at CSU

Assessment at Colorado State can be best characterized as an evolutionary project. Currently, the project is comprehensive and multifaceted to encompass both general education and discipline-specific assessment. Mathematics and composition assessments compare sophomores and seniors to their placement test results in these areas. Data on goals for undergraduate education from students, faculty, parents, legislators, and recruiters are collected and compared. Student development is assessed in the areas of life-style, cognitive skill, moral reasoning, and identity development.

Attention to successful outcomes for undergraduates has increased the recognition that the 1981 goals for undergraduate education were too general to guide accountability efforts. This fact is not surprising since the goals had been developed long before anyone considered how to assess them. Consequently, a massive effort to restructure the goals and the framework for the undergraduate experience has begun. A key element will be the cogent design of assessment objectives that elaborate the goals and facilitate the choice of useful assessment mechanisms that will guide change. Faculty from across the campus are directly involved. CSU's experience supports the conclusion that the faculty's direction of and participation in assessment are crucial to success.

Discipline-specific assessments have resulted in changes ranging from adjustments in curriculum content and sequencing to changes in advising information and approach. The Department of English, for instance, has begun distributing a handout to new students that outlines their responsibilities for collection of material and participation in outcomes assessment activities. Several departments reported changes in field placement activities as a result of assessment findings. Finally, a number of departments discovered that their current goals for undergraduates were difficult to assess and have begun comprehensive revisions. For example, the Art department recently revised its procedures to reflect the twelve different concentrations within the major.

Overall, increased faculty engagement with assessment has occurred largely because of the discipline-based activities. To us, this involvement means that faculty members have more direct links to the students in their majors and a very strong commitment to students' education. The faculty's commitment to general education, on the other hand, is not so certain, for it is removed from faculty members' direct involvement in specific disciplines — both in teaching and in research. Now that faculty have experienced some success with evaluating student learning in their majors, have realized that the CCHE will not punish them if they find weaknesses, and have begun to use assessment to improve their curricula, they more fully understand its value.

A synthesis of the Colorado State accountability experience began to take shape with the first full (general education and discipline-specific) reporting of results in 1991. Action began immediately, as noted earlier, to thoroughly examine the goals for the undergraduate experience. Faculty development is a higher priority than ever before, particularly in the areas of assessment and teaching. Departmental involvement has stimulated interest, discussion, and engagement in many areas across the campus.

Results that left unanswered questions have stimulated more focused assessment activity in the area of advising and the arts. These activities involve separate task forces using a variety of approaches to answer basic questions of what things are valued and what recommendations can be made that can result in practical improvements.

Institutional commitment to accountability is more visible. Guidelines for six-year program reviews require reporting of assessment results and impacts. Some departments have also begun using assessment findings in their strategic planning efforts.

Strengths and Weaknesses of Methods at UConn

A major strength of the multimethod, multi-instrument approach based strongly on quantifiable measurement is that it fits the dominant paradigm of a research university. The faculty of a research university generally feel comfortable with an approach that views assessment as a research activity. Furthermore, since assessment measurement is clearly tied to curriculum goals, the results are much more likely to be useful for diagnostic and prescriptive purposes than are the results of general skills testing.

The research paradigm also encourages evolutionary studies, with the results of one project suggesting modifications to the research procedures, as well as entirely new questions. This process clearly occurred with the UConn project. The results have pointed to improvements that need to be made in measurement and have spawned one major study of the effects of particular "clusters" of courses and course sequencing on student performance.

There is a drawback with evolutionary, faculty-determined assessment, however. Since the test instruments and research designs change over time, long-term studies are not possible. The approach outlined here is more likely to be helpful in conjunction with general skills testing, which uses a stable instrument. The approaches are probably complementary, rather than alternatives.

Another weakness is the one endemic to all research: information costs money. A diverse approach with many projects is inherently expensive; it requires both faculty time and staff-support dollars. We estimate that if faculty time is taken into account, assessment of general education has cost UConn about $500,000 over the past four years.

Like all projects involving a large number of fairly independent faculty members, assessment projects such as that at UConn are difficult to coordinate and administer. The lines of authority are more informal than rigidly prescribed, and it is sometimes hard to find out who is doing what and when it will be finished. Though this is the normal way of doing business at our university, it can complicate the assessment project.

Strengths and Weaknesses of Methods at CSU

In many respects, the assessment experience at CSU resembles that at UConn. It was easy for our legislature and our regulatory agency, the CCHE, to mandate assessment, but implementing it in a research university has not been a simple, linear process. Research faculty have been trained to question procedures, to view research as something that may lead to dead ends and that may occasionally fail, and (most frustrating to those at the regulatory agency who had to evaluate our reports) to equivocate, that is, to question the validity and reliability of the findings and to be unwilling to arrive at exact conclusions that could be immediately translated into curricular or environmental changes.

Like the UConn experience, assessment at CSU has taken many years to mature. Even now, it is not a mature assessment program. Faculty quickly note that it takes four or five years before any change in the curriculum or environment can be evaluated. Considering that true results may not occur until our students have graduated and worked for a few years, it may take even longer to develop truly meaningful assessments of the education that our students receive. Can legislators wait that long or even understand the need for such a long wait?

We know that there can be no single assessment that will give us all the answers. We are convinced that the multifaceted approach, while extremely challenging to implement and monitor, has given us data that we find more reliable and has revealed newer directions for assessment. For such reasons, we believe that the long-term process, especially one that has permitted assessment to evolve, has been beneficial and will continue to be so.

In retrospect, having begun our assessment procedures without the full involvement of our faculty seems inappropriate. Yet a mistake early on meant that when faculty were fully involved in discipline-based assessments, they could proceed with greater security that they were on the right track and that honest intellectual inquiry was at the heart of assessment.

Lessons from Both Universities

In the long run, both assessment programs have worked well, although each has its share of false starts and changes. Although assessment should be directed by the faculty, a thorough program also requires a strong commitment of resources and leadership from the academic administration. The faculty members who direct the assessment projects need to work closely with the administrators who provide the resources so that each group understands the needs of the other. Administrators must be both managers of resources and teachers — teachers who help the faculty learn what is possible and who develop effective communication between various faculty groups and external constituencies.

Those who judge the effectiveness of university efforts to assess learning must also be aware of a number of considerations. Faculty whose teaching, research, and service demand heavy time commitments must be compensated in some fashion when they are asked to devote large amounts of time and effort to evaluation. Effective assessment takes a long while to implement, for the goal is to learn not simply what students know at any given moment, but also what they retain and use effectively over a longer period. Changes in curriculum and the university environment will also cost money and take time.

If anything, the experiences at both Colorado State University and the University of Connecticut reveal not only that faculty should be centrally involved in assessment but also that procedures must allow for flexibility and change over time, that communication with external constituencies is essential, and that all of the constituencies — legislators, parents, regulators, students, faculty — must have faith in their separate commitments to assessment.

Finally, the writers make one major recommendation: faculty effort on behalf of assessment must be recognized as scholarship. Just as teachers are rewarded when they think creatively, acquire grants, and publish results, so research in assessment should be documented and given weight equal to that accorded other forms of scholarship. When universities do that, they will have moved one giant step toward linking teaching and research, and assessment will become just as much a part of university culture and faculty expectations as journal articles, grants, and books now are.

References

Ewell, P. T. "Implementing Assessment: Some Organizational Issues." In T. W. Banta (ed.), *Implementing Outcomes Assessment: Promise and Perils.* New Directions for Institutional Research, no. 59. San Francisco: Jossey-Bass, 1988.

Hexter, H., and Lippincott, J. K. "Campus and Student Assessment." *Research Briefs, American Council on Education,* 1990, *1,* 1–18.

Pine, C. "Using Assessment to Improve Instruction: The New Jersey Algebra Project." In R. T. Alpert, W. P. Gorth, and R. G. Allan (eds.), *Assessing Basic Academic Skills in Higher Education.* Hillsdale, N.J.: Erlbaum, 1989.

Wright, B. "But How Do We Know It Will Work?" *American Association for Higher Education Bulletin,* 1990, *42*(8), 14–17.

8

Assessment Strategies for Adult Undergraduate Students

Carol E. Kasworm
Catherine Marienau

Assessment programs represent the nature of the institution in which they are conducted, the students, and the curricular educational process. Discussions of outcomes assessment in colleges and universities to date center primarily on the intellectual and developmental involvement in college of young adults. They are guided by the predominant assumptions that the students are typically eighteen to twenty-one years old and are educated within the boundaries of a traditional campus curriculum and extracurriculum. However, the vast majority of universities and colleges today have a more diverse student body. Specifically, 40 percent of undergraduates are adult learners, ranging in age from their mid twenties to their sixties and beyond (National Center for Education Statistics, 1991). Adult learners constitute an important but different type of student in the outcomes assessment program. For example, in institutions serving adults, one can hear comments such as these.

> We have mountains of information from our outcomes assessment program, but I still don't know

121

what impact we are having on the adult working
student at our institution! We just aren't asking the
right questions, and we aren't examining our data
for differences with this major student subculture.
— Faculty member at a public university

I am anonymous! I have no voice at this institution. I am not valued unless I can respond to programs, services and institutional questionnaires as
if I were an eighteen-year-old student.
— Adult student at a private liberal arts college

The adult degree program is housed in our Continuing Education Division, [is] offered in extension centers, features several distance education and
assessment for credit strategies, and uses few of the
traditional faculty resources. Institutional assessment has ignored our program because we don't
fit their conception of the academic programs for
full-time young adults residing on campus. We're
like strangers in a strange land, who speak a different language and view the academic process in fun-
damentally different ways from the traditional undergraduate baccalaureate program.
— Dean of continuing education at a four-year
       public college

These comments reflect some of the dilemmas in approaching program outcomes assessment with adult students. These
individuals are usually ignored in the strategies, outcomes measures, and underlying assumptions of most institutional assessment programs. The growth in numbers of adult undergraduates is heightening awareness of the differences of this population
and the impact of these differences upon the outcomes assessment process.

Among the numerous implications for outcomes assessment, we highlight four that are particularly relevant to adult
learners. First, adult-oriented institutions have found that they
must expand their focus for outcomes assessment beyond the

internal curricula and instructional efforts to include a connection to the broader community. This broader environment is the source of both support and the daily interaction between knowledge and application. As students, adults actively pursue their learning concerns at the university at the same time that they learn and work in their profession, their family, and their community.

Second, issues of design and implementation of the program are reexamined, often through the dynamic process of a "campus conversation." Institutions are finding that a dialogue among faculty, staff, and adult students can result in thoughtful and critical reassessments of the nature of the institutional mission as it can facilitate adult learning.

Third, institutions discover that alternative assessment mechanisms are needed to gain access to adults and to appropriate and relevant information. Many adult-oriented programs face serious difficulties in finding sufficient numbers of adult students for group testing, as well as in using traditional tests normed on younger students. They often must reexamine the necessity and appropriateness of many of the traditional student assessment strategies and mechanisms.

Fourth, adult-oriented assessment typically uses both the process evaluation strategies of formative assessment and outcomes assessment product evaluation. Adult-oriented programs value the formative process involving evaluation by students, faculty, mentors, external faculty experts, employers, and support staff. In particular, they view students as responsible agents to bring about changes that influence outcomes. They also believe that their programs are individualized to meet specific adult student's needs, with the subsequent effect of supporting student-defined (and in some programs employer-defined) outcomes. They also value the unique contributions of outcomes assessment for its key role in institutional improvement.

Impact of Outcomes Assessment: Three Profiles

This chapter describes three institutions that represent a commitment to the centrality of adult students and to the value of outcomes assessment: Thomas A. Edison College, a public institution in New Jersey; Empire State College, a public college in New York; and the University of Phoenix, a private college in Arizona with off-campus centers. The following three profiles present an in-progress status report on the impact and the differences that may be attributed to outcomes assessment.

Thomas A. Edison State College

Because of its unique mission and educational emphasis on access to learning without limits of time and place, Thomas Edison State College does not offer direct classroom instruction. Rather, this institution provides multiple mechanisms for students to participate in learning experiences that meet specific aspects of the curriculum. These mechanisms reflect alternative participation on other college campuses in classroom instruction, distance education learning (correspondence courses, telecourses), assessment for credit mechanisms (such as the College Level Examination Program), and other alternative learning and assessment strategies. The institution's self-study notes:

> As independent adults, students of Thomas Edison State College are expected to be self-directed and goal-oriented, and to be capable of making intelligent decisions regarding their educational careers. The College controls the parameters of the curriculum, but not the sequence, the method, nor the timing of credit acquisition. Given its student characteristics, it is inappropriate for the College to assume responsibility for their personal development. . . . In short the College has responsibility to empower students so that each student may make proper decisions regarding his or her academic career and to provide flexible, academically sound options tailored to the needs of adult, distant learners [Thomas A. Edison State College, 1988, pp. 3–4].

Within their outcomes assessment efforts, Edison faculty have established five mission-related priorities:

- *Student empowerment:* the quality and accessibility of information provided to current and prospective students. Achieved largely through publications and various levels of advising, this information enables the student to make accurate, informed decisions regarding academic pursuits.
- *Testing and assessment:* the process of reviewing credentials, creating and administering course-equivalent examinations, and evaluating portfolios that document out-of-class learning results in the award of credits.
- *Curricula and student learning outcomes:* the creation, structure, content, and periodic review of curricula for validity and currency. The assessment of learning outcomes determines the extent to which students who have satisfied curricular requirements are able to demonstrate desired levels of intellectual competencies.
- *Distance learning:* the effectiveness and quality of directed independent study.
- *System building:* examination of the effectiveness of a statewide testing and assessment center; the program on noncollegiate-sponsored instruction; 164 credit transfer articulation agreements; and relationships with a variety of educational government, military, corporate, and community services.

Thomas Edison State College faculty completed their first outcomes assessment report in 1988. Many of their assessment activities were based on a series of telephone surveys of six types of clientele: prospective students, people requesting information, applicants, enrolled students, inactive students, and graduates. The surveys were conducted by a contracted research firm utilizing a ten- to twelve-minute telephone interview. These surveys provided baseline information on (1) adults without degrees, (2) the value of marketing strategies to prospective students, (3) helpfulness, readability and clarity of college publications, and (4) knowledge of college policies and procedures (Streckewald, 1992).

What impact did these surveys have on the institution in relation to its five outcomes assessment priorities? Thomas Streckewald, director of Institutional Research and Outcomes Assessment, reports ten modifications or modifications in process (personal communication, 1992). One of the major changes was the reorganization of the admissions function, creating a more service-oriented and individualized information function. Thirty thousand people make inquiries each year; thus, the college needed to identify relevant and viable ways to provide more one-to-one service to students. Secondly, utilizing the survey data and other sources of input, the staff defined the concept of student empowerment as a key goal of the institutional mission. The survey findings, as examined and discussed by the staff, helped create understanding of this objective. The staff considered what it wanted to achieve to facilitate adult student action and to craft a notion of ideal student engagement with the institution.

Another use of the survey findings was to promote recognition of the need to restructure publications to support the major institutional goal. One objective became consistency: to present uniform images of the institution. Another was to manage better the information flow to prospective and enrolled students, to ensure they had appropriate information when they needed it. The staff therefore examined the specific concerns of students and people making inquiries regarding programs, policies, and services; with this information, the staff mapped appropriate sequencing of information throughout a student's program.

Thomas Edison also employed the survey results to help refine college data bases. These were rewritten to provide college staff with only necessary and relevant data, a process that enhanced efficiency. Results from telephone surveys also provided insights into improvement of other specific functions of the college: for example, modification of the organizational pattern of the Registrar's Office and of the way the college assesses personnel in that office. The office evaluates twenty thousand transcripts, a vital function in the student's life and progress at the institution. The performance of personnel needed to be directed toward realizing the goal of student empowerment.

One unusual result of the surveys and of monitoring the students through the data base was an assessment of fiscal outcomes. In examining both student input and participation patterns, Thomas Edison State College made a decision to "unbundle" its fee structures. The college now charges the use of specific services and activities on a pay-as-you-go basis. This modification has helped students better understand the fee structure and has increased the financial options of first-year students. At the same time, it has also placed the institution on a firmer financial footing.

The surveys also helped the college in examining its minority outreach effort through the five clientele groupings — from people making inquiries to graduated students. Faculty discovered that they needed to use different strategies to communicate with minority populations in the community and with minority leaders. Outcomes assessment identified that they had not followed their initial planning with sufficient action.

Beyond the use of telephone surveys, Thomas Edison also utilized external reviewers, as well as its own staff, to conduct degree-program reviews. This process has provided valuable information for revision of anticipated student outcomes for general education, as well as for particular majors. At this time, faculty are developing their own tests to assess learning outcomes in the major curricula.

Empire State College

In its distinctive mission and educational approach, Empire State College also serves the adult learner. The institution provides the following innovative elements (Empire State College, 1989, p. 2):

- Individualized education, carried out through a contract mode of learning
- An open format for access, placing minimal constraints on the time, place, residence, and manner of learning
- A degree program developed by the student in consultation with faculty mentors, joining the course of study to the student's educational goals
- A portfolio assessment process certifying prior college level learning
- A flexible curriculum, incorporating broad areas of multidisciplinary study and modes of inquiry

- Continuing development of learning resources using new pedagogies and technologies (most recently telecommunications)
- Highly dispersed and decentralized college organization, relying for its delivery on a unique mentor-student model

Marjorie Lavin, assistant vice president for academic affairs, reports that the outcomes assessment efforts of Empire State have focused upon three major strategies, including: (1) review of student degree portfolios, (2) assessment of student writing, and (3) student surveys and self-reports (personal communication, 1992). In particular, she notes that the college has turned to locally developed instruments after finding limited value in nationally normed tests. For example, the ACT-COMP exam did not work at Empire State. The college found it logistically difficult to give a mass-administered, three-hour exam, when its entire operation is based on a one-to-one relationship. In place of assessment testing with multiple-choice instruments, Empire State College faculty utilizes narrative evaluations, process evaluations, individualized instruments, and protocols for qualitative judgments for portfolios. Faculty use outcomes assessment data to enrich their own practice, and they consider the varied feedback from assessments of specific content areas as well as broader areas of knowledge, skills, and attitudes.

Perhaps the longest-running investment in outcomes assessment for Empire State College has been focused upon a series of studies of writing skills, achievement in the major, and related general education outcomes. Because students' involvement in learning is based on writing performance, Empire State focused its first study in 1978–79 on evaluation of brief essays. The faculty developed a holistic scoring protocol to evaluate writing. From this study of outcomes, the institution has made specific improvements in the writing program to include (1) development of a writing-skills handbook for faculty as a development tool, (2) development of a standard diagnostic procedure that features collection of writing samples at orientation (scoring these and providing student feedback at that time), and (3) creation of noncredit writing workshops.

In 1981–82, one of Empire State's regional centers reviewed the effectiveness of the writing program. Faculty identified students who were having writing difficulties and offered remediation in specially designed courses. This institutional study group tracked both the participants and a similar group of nonparticipants and examined writing performance two years later. Participating students reported improvement in writing, higher persistence in their academic programs, and better performance in learning contracts. This study confirmed the value of the writing-skills program. Further, the group found that greater competence in writing also reflected broader skills improvement, to include study skills and critical reasoning. The faculty thus extended assistance with writing skills to other support services at all centers. Within the last few years, the College Senate created the Basic Skills Committee. Through the actions of this faculty committee, a tracking system has been developed, and each center reports on improvement in basic skills.

Due to the individualized and experiential nature of the curriculum of Empire State, outcomes assessment has also concentrated upon the review of student portfolios by faculty panels and external validation groups for each major area. In their self-study in 1988, these external and faculty groups established an important agenda of academic program and policy issues. In particular, the Empire State faculty revised curricular guidelines and pointed to the need for greater clarity regarding general education. As a result, the college has offered faculty development seminars on liberal learning for adults. Faculty members have also conducted an in-depth examination of how they communicate their expectations of performance. They found that they were often clearer about their expectations with one another than with students. To remedy this situation, they have reexamined written materials and communication mechanisms and inaugurated learning contracts — the major learning tool in their curriculum — to provide clear and consistent communications of performance expectations.

Because of a major investment in portfolio development and assessment, Empire State College continues to examine and streamline procedures for evaluation of prior learning. Most recently, the faculty has looked at college expectations regarding quantitative, humanities, and social skills and has offered a number of faculty development activities. Although there is no agreement regarding requirements for quantitative skills, the faculty has come to a consensus about minimal expectations across degree programs.

University of Phoenix

The University of Phoenix offers yet another approach to the education of adults; it employs an educational model that unites a faculty of practicing professionals with a student body composed exclusively of working adults. The mission of the university is to serve students whose personal and professional obligations might otherwise rule out a continuing formal education. Curriculum content is developed by the practitioner-faculty with the technical guidance of instructional design specialists working under a centralized curriculum development and validation department. Instructional design incorporates both faculty-led and peer-learning groups. Classes are offered at times and places accessible to working professionals. The university's educational mission has shaped and focused its assessment efforts. Evaluation of customer service is a key aspect of outcomes assessment.

The University of Phoenix is perhaps the best current example of an institution making a significant investment in the development and implementation of an adult-centered, multitrait, multimeasure assessment program. Key to this program is equal emphasis on the measurement of both academic *process* and *outcomes*. Included in the measurement matrix are cognitive and affective outcomes. Measures are taken during five phases of the student's development cycle: at the time of registration, monthly (throughout the course work), upon graduation, and one and three years after graduation. Graduates' employers are also asked to evaluate the graduates.

Several measures are administered using a pretest and posttest design. Some measures have established control or contrast groups through cooperative efforts with other universities. Incoming groups form cohorts that are followed longitudinally to graduation. Students receive individualized, computer-genererated results of their comprehensive examinations. One of the university's more interesting process assessment systems is a computerized knowledge-based comment analysis system, which classifies and produces monthly reports for faculty and administrators based on more than 110,000 handwritten student comments yearly (over 350,000 total). The analysis, tracking, and reporting of student comments have proved to be an enormous benefit to the daily academic management of the institution (Tucker, 1992).

The university's process assessment system is called the Academic Quality Management System (AQMS). This system consists of a grouping of continuous measures of classroom activity and formative outcomes, including a student end-of-course survey system, a faculty end-of-course survey system, and the student comment analysis system. The university's outcomes assessment system is called Adult Learning Outcomes Assessment (ALOA). The ALOA project consists of eight primary domains:

1. Comprehensive evaluation of achievement in the major field, based on matriculation and graduation testing
2. Assessment of professional and citizenship values, based on matriculation and graduation testing
3. Assessment of alumni impact, using surveys and interviews with alumni
4. Evaluation of faculty involvement, based on surveys and interviews with practitioner faculty
5. Assessment of employer impact, drawing on surveys and interviews with supervisors, managers, and CEOs who employ graduates
6. Research project evaluation, arising from an independent panel's review of student projects
7. Assessment of study group process and outcome, based on surveys and interviews with student study groups
8. Longitudinal assessment of student needs, using meta-analysis of the thousands of data points collected annually for each of the university's students and instructors

The University of Phoenix began its full-scale assessment activities in 1988. According to Robert Tucker, senior vice president for institutional research and developer of the assessment research program, the university has continued to expand and refine its AQMS and is realizing daily benefits from the application of the information it produces. Both the process and outcomes assessments have led to significant changes within the institution (personal conversation, 1992).

Identifying faculty and staff training needs have been one example of the impact of the university's assessment system. In the past, identification of needs was based largely on anecdotal reports and subjective professional judgment. Today, adequate process and outcomes data reliably pinpoint training priorities. Early AQMS results, for example, indicated that instructors needed additional skills in guiding the formation and development of peer study groups. Subsequent ALOA information supported these findings. Since study groups are required to produce substantial projects (including written final reports in most courses), it was clear that successful efforts to improve the quality of study groups would contribute to overall academic performance. Accordingly, several new training programs have been developed for instructors, including a self-directed videotape training series.

Similar benefits have come in the form of identifying curricula in need of revision. A special report, based on analysis of student comment data and the student and faculty end-of-course systems, indicates curriculum strengths and weaknesses on a course-by-course, textbook-by-textbook basis. In another case, the outcomes research showed that faculty selection criteria for student-teaching project courses were too broad and not adequately focused on current professional experience in research design and analysis and interpretation of information. Due to these findings, faculty selection and assignment criteria have been redefined for the courses, and new faculty training activities in the project area have been developed.

From the employer impact assessment survey, the university learned that it was not effectively communicating with employers. Most of the employers interviewed lamented that it took several years of interaction with the university before they fully understood the advantages to their organizations of a university serving working adults. Several new programs of employer education and outreach have therefore been developed.

In the alumni survey, feedback on academic quality and standards was an important theme. These graduates reported their support for improving institutional grading standards: they wanted the university to make it tougher to get a high grade. Because of this finding, which was consistent in separate alumni studies over a three-year period, the university has studied the complex issue of grading adult students in criterion-referenced educational settings. The study has revealed that overall grade-point average is perhaps only a little high but the variance is excessively low—that is, the faculty tends not to make the full range of distinctions between levels of performance. The solution has been to measure and publish grading variance reports on a quarterly basis, to initiate training programs for instructors, and to hold colloquia on grading and student evaluation.

Tucker also noted improvement of the major student research project and study groups, revision of a number of assessment instruments and processes, and redefinition of the measures by which the work of academic staff is appraised and incentives are assigned. He states, "Five years ago, there were many differing opinions as to the value of the university's assessment program. Now, it has become an accepted and central component in the continuous assessment of the university's ability to meet the needs of its stakeholders" (personal conversation, 1992).

How Outcomes Assessment Has Made a Difference

Outcomes assessment has made a difference for these campuses. It has helped each to grapple with the question of what it is and what it is about. Each of these institutions has taken a unique stance in the education of adult students. Faculty and staff at each have raised appropriate questions about the educational process of adults in their institution, the use of normative and locally designed instruments for assessment, and desired outcomes for adult students.

Outcomes assessment has made possible a dialogue among faculty, staff, mentors, employers, community leaders, and students about the mission of the institution and the nature of teaching and learning experience. It has created multiple sources of information for contemplating and rethinking the nature of a high-quality academic experience and its improvement. At these universities, outcomes assessment has provided strategies for faculty to be coinvestigators with their adult students.

Each of these institutions has designed its own "rulers" for measuring the excellence of the academic experience and warranted improvements. For each, the impact has come from a consensus of the academic community about goals and the development of strategies to assess them.

References

Empire State College. *Assessment at Empire State College: A Strategic Plan and Position Statement for the Future.* Saratoga Springs, N.Y.: Office of Research and Evaluation, Empire State College, 1989.

National Center for Education Statistics. *Enrollment in Higher Education, Fall 1989.* (NCES 91-217.) Washington, D.C.: Office of Educational Research and Improvement, U.S. Department of Education, 1991.

Streckewald, T. C. *The Use of Survey Research in an Outcomes Assessment Program.* Unpublished manuscript, Thomas A. Edison State College, 1992.

Thomas A. Edison State College. "Outcomes Assessment at Thomas A. Edison State College." 1st annual report, July 1987–June 1988. Unpublished manuscript, Thomas A. Edison State College, Sept. 1988.

Tucker, R. W. *Assessment, Innovation, and Continuous Improvement: Measure Everything—Improve What You Can.* Phoenix, Ariz.: University of Phoenix Press, 1992.

Part Three

Outcomes Assessment Methods That Work

Some assessment techniques and approaches have attained sufficient credibility with faculty to induce improvement-oriented activity on a variety of campuses, regardless of institutional type or nature of student population. The chapters in Part Three describe the most productive of these methods: portfolios, major-field assessment instruments, surveys and other techniques for gathering perception data, affective measures, measures of student involvement, and classroom assessment techniques.

In Chapter Nine, Lendley Black demonstrates the use of student portfolios in evaluating the effectiveness of general education programs at several institutions. He asserts that portfolio assessment has helped faculty understand and become more committed to goals for student learning. The dialogue with colleagues and with students that accompanies portfolio assessment has led to more effective integration of knowledge across disciplines and thus to enriched course content. Portfolios help students understand what they have been taught; they also teach the valuable skill of self-assessment. Items in portfolios can also supplement students' employment résumés. Black concludes by urging that faculty develop methods of scoring portfolios that include a numerical rating to communicate to external audiences as well as a verbal description for use within the academy.

Reid Johnson and the coauthors of Chapter Ten have gathered information on assessment in academic majors from institutions across the country. Although some institutions have been engaged in evaluating major-field achievement for sufficient time to be able to demonstrate increases in student learning as a result of curricular and instructional improvements undertaken, these authors emphasize that to date the principal accomplishments of assessment accrue from the process of faculty collaboration on the establishment of goals, instrument selection or design, and review of student performance.

Faculty searching for an early victory in a fledgling assessment initiative should be encouraged to include a survey as one of their first data-gathering instruments. As John Muffo and Mary Anne Bunda point out in Chapter Eleven, information about the opinions and attitudes of students, graduates, and other stakeholders in the higher education enterprise can be powerfully persuasive in stimulating change. According to these authors, additional opportunities to apply mathematics in courses across the curriculum, improvements in career advising, and funding for library expansion are some of the specific actions undertaken on the basis of recommendations derived from questionnaires, telephone interviews, and focus groups.

In Chapter Twelve, R. Stephen RiCharde and T. Dary Erwin, campus assessment coordinators at Virginia Military Institute (VMI) and James Madison University (JMU) respectively, and Cynthia Olney, assistant assessment specialist at JMU, cite evidence that measures of students' affective development have made a difference at these two institutions. At VMI, profiles of entering students that include scores on the Myers-Briggs Type Indicator, the California Personality Inventory, a measure of locus of control, the Learning-Thinking Styles Inventory, and the Academic Anxiety Test have been employed to identify students at risk due to stress and academic failure. Changes made in new-student orientation, advising and other academic support services, and the writing program have apparently reduced freshman attrition and improved academic performance, especially among black students.

Erwin reports that at JMU students' scores on the Career Decision Scale (CDS) and the Student Developmental Task and Lifestyle Inventory have assisted the career services staff with design of a career-planning class for undeclared majors. Pretesting and posttesting with the CDS reveals that students become more decisive because of the class experience. A series of affective measures have helped document the value of a transition program for minority students and also have suggested the need for some program modifications.

C. Robert Pace has contributed more than any other scholar to our understanding of the links between the extent of time and effort students invest in the college experience and such important outcomes as persistence, academic achievement, personal development, and satisfaction with college. Jack Friedlander, Patricia Murrell, and Peter MacDougall report in Chapter Thirteen on the outcomes of using Pace's Community College Student Experiences Questionnaire (CCSEQ) at several two-year institutions in California and Tennessee. Students' CCSEQ responses have led faculty to undertake a variety of approaches to increasing student involvement—from adding features to freshman orientation, to awarding course credit for participation in related out-of-class activities, to providing students with maps of the steps required to achieve transfer or career goals.

Classroom assessment, a portfolio of active learning strategies that involve instructors and students in formal study of what happens daily in the classroom, is the subject of Susan Obler, Julie Slark, and Linda Umbdenstock in Chapter Fourteen. Involvement in classroom assessment makes students active participants in learning, rather than passive recipients. Students are more likely to complete courses in which this evaluation occurs. The authors present evidence that classroom assessment helps students improve their communication skills, become more competent and self-confident in their interactions with others, and develop their abilities to judge their own strengths and weaknesses.

9

Portfolio Assessment

Lendley C. Black

Institutions involved in portfolio assessment tend to have their own conceptions of what portfolios are and how they should be used. However, portfolios used by institutions often share many common characteristics. They are usually folders into which faculty or students put products of learning, such as tests, papers, and lab reports. These folders are often kept for a specified period of time. Material is added to the portfolios on a regular basis, and evaluators examine them for evidence of student achievement.

The faculty determine what student products are to be collected and how these products are to be evaluated. They make these decisions based upon the goals of student learning that have been agreed upon by the institution. Hence, one can place virtually *anything* in an assessment portfolio (audiotapes, videotapes, artwork) so long as the items are truly representative of student learning and they tell the faculty something meaningful about the success of academic programs. Both of these requisites are important, since the ultimate goal of assessment should be program improvement. Portfolios, perhaps more than any other type of assessment tool, provide very rich information that can lead directly to the betterment of academic programs.

Portfolios have been part of student outcomes assessment for a long time. English faculties have often required students to keep representative samples of their work over the course of a semester or longer in order to evaluate progress and development. Programs in the fine arts have used the portfolio for many years to demonstrate student skill and learning. There are many similarities between these discipline-specific portfolios and those employed now for assessment purposes by many institutions across the country.

In the early 1970s, some institutions, like Alverno College and Manhattanville College, began using portfolios to measure a wide range of student competencies. It was not until the late 1980s, however, that many institutions began to consider the portfolio as a viable evaluation tool for academic programs like general education. Hence, portfolio assessment of general education and academic majors is a relatively new phenomenon.

Institutional interest in portfolio program assessment was promoted by articles by Morris Keeton (1988), who suggested that the standards file (portfolio) was a useful tool for documenting an institution's educational outcomes, and by Pat Hutchings (1989), who recommended the portfolio as an effective means to get behind and beyond student learning outcomes. More recent studies (Forrest, 1990; Hutchings, 1990) have further explored the use of portfolios to assess academic programs, and the North Central Association of Colleges and Schools recognizes portfolios as one of six approaches in evaluation processes (Payne, Vowell, and Black, 1991).

A growing number of institutions use portfolios, and only a few can be used as examples here. Emporia State University (ESU) is a public comprehensive university in Kansas that has made portfolios a key part of its extensive, institutionwide assessment program. Indiana University–Purdue University, Indianapolis (IUPUI), is a larger doctorate-granting university that also uses portfolios. Miami University of Ohio's Western College Program has made portfolios part of the innovative evaluation of its interdisciplinary academic programs. Manhattanville College, a small private college in Purchase, New York, has employed portfolios since 1972 to measure several competencies of its undergraduate students. Alverno College in Milwaukee, Wisconsin, is a pioneer in this area; their portfolios help reveal how students are developing as learners. Additional institutions with excellent programs include the College of William and Mary, the Evergreen State College, Sonoma State University, and the State University of New York, Fredonia.

Colleges and universities with successful portfolio programs usually base this assessment technique on well-defined goals and learning outcomes. Clear goals stated in terms of student learning outcomes are important for any type of student or program assessment. However, they are even more crucial for the portfolio, a qualitative assessment tool that is usually criterion-referenced.

Most institutions have statements that articulate the objectives of their academic programs. Too often, however, these statements remain buried in university catalogues. One of the benefits of portfolio assessment is that it forces the faculty to pull these goal statements out of mothballs, refine them so that they really reflect the thrust of academic programs, and use the goals on a regular basis to help judge program effectiveness. The goals should be well publicized to faculty, students, and external agencies so that there is a clear understanding of what the general education program attempts to accomplish.

Once the goals are in place, the faculty can then decide what to include in the portfolios. To ensure that portfolios are productive and affordable, two principles should be kept in mind. The first principle is that most general education programs are best assessed with a variety of diverse assessment tools. For example, portfolios might be employed in conjunction with alumni surveys, standardized tests, or even beepers, an innovative assessment tool developed at Miami of Ohio.

We use portfolios at ESU primarily to evaluate two of our five general education goals. These goals deal with integration, critical thinking, analysis of issues, value clarification, and multicultural issues — learning that is difficult to assess through quantitative measures. At IUPUI, portfolios are used primarily to help in assessing student writing. One may thus wish to evaluate only part of the general education program with portfolios. An institution can be selective or all-inclusive with portfolio assessment, depending upon its needs and resources, but the full burden of assessment should not rest on portfolios alone.

The second principle to consider is that a great deal of useful information can be learned from relatively few items. Faculty may be leery of portfolios if they envision immense folders that are awkward to store and examine. One does not have to collect every important student product or even products from every class. With portfolios, the faculty can base valid and reliable general education program assessment on a relatively small, yet representative, sample of students.

The faculty should choose the smallest possible number of class products that provide adequate information about the goal being measured. At ESU, for example, we have decided upon nine products that will give us an adequate picture of student achievement toward our general education goals. Some excellent programs (for example, Miami of Ohio and Alverno) ask students to keep very large portfolios (virtually everything produced), but portfolios do not have to be voluminous to be effective.

One of the principal advantages of portfolio assessment is that it provides a detailed view of student learning over time. Hence, there are usually regularly scheduled reviews of the portfolios that correspond to key points in a student's academic career. Some universities will have the portfolios analyzed after the sophomore or senior years or both, whereas others examine them more often.

The faculty should play a key role in evaluating the portfolios. Who else is involved, and how this analysis is accomplished, will vary substantially from one institution to the next. Each school should develop a system that improves its general education experience and provides valid assessment results that are credible to outside constituencies.

What Does Portfolio Assessment Tell Us?

Portfolio assessment can reveal the essence of the academic program that is being evaluated. As previously stated, the process itself requires faculty to undergo a thorough self-examination of what they expect students to learn as a result of their academic programs. For example, when we first discussed assessing the general education program at ESU, we realized that there was little understanding of the program, even though we had a new core curriculum at the time. Many faculty members thought it was a good idea to have a general education program (though some hated it), but most had little idea of what the program was intended to accomplish. Hence, the process of developing portfolio assessment required faculty members to discuss with one another the potential goals of the program and to agree upon a statement of what students were to learn.

Once objectives and guidelines were agreed upon, the faculty and students who oversee the program decided to sponsor a meeting of the general education faculty and interested students for the purpose of communicating this information to the rest of the campus. During the meeting, strategies for achieving the goals were also discussed. A productive suggestion originating in this meeting was that each course instructor should explain to students at the beginning of the semester what the course was intended to do, how it fit into the general education program, and how it helped the program achieve its broad goals. Another result of this meeting was that it prompted the General Education Council to sponsor at least one meeting each subsequent semester that focused on some general education issue. These meetings stimulated productive discussions among faculty and students on such topics as multiculturalism and improvement of writing throughout the general education curriculum. It was the process of developing portfolio assessment that created the need for and interest in these meetings.

Once the faculty began looking at student course products in portfolios, its understanding of student learning increased tremendously. For example, our faculty had established the integration of knowledge as a component of its general education goals — one that was assumed to be fulfilled by our core curriculum courses. Almost from the beginning of our portfolio analysis, however, there was little evidence that this goal was being achieved. As a result of these findings, the content and teaching strategies of some key courses have been refined to increase the integrative learning within the program. For example, the course on analysis of fine arts now covers less historical material and involves our students in more active learning experiences. Students discuss more artworks and draw more conclusions about their individual responses to art, connections between the arts, and the integration of the arts with society.

Portfolios also indicated a lack of student understanding of diverse contemporary cultures, in spite of a multicultural category and goal in the core curriculum. We have therefore undertaken two initiatives: a new multicultural course is being considered, and all faculty who teach general education courses are asked to judge for themselves if they can improve the multicultural learning that occurs within their courses. If they can, multicultural learning will be increased throughout the curriculum, and many courses will contribute to the achievement of this objective.

Another improvement in the general education program prompted by portfolio assessment was a modification of the multicultural goal itself. The more we assessed related student learning, the more vague and elusive this goal appeared. As a result, the faculty and students on the General Education Council rewrote the goal to make it reflect more accurately the intended student learning. The process of refining goals is an important general benefit of assessment. An improved articulation of the goal makes it easier to make substantive changes in teaching that help ensure the achievement of the goal.

Improvements in curriculum and student learning as a result of assessment are also evident at Indiana University–Purdue University, Indianapolis. IUPUI faculty have established a comprehensive approach that provides appropriate documentation of student learning and emphasizes an interrelationship of curricular design, teaching, learning, and assessment. Portfolios are an important element of this process in the schools of nursing and education.

It is in the Department of English at IUPUI where portfolio assessment is most advanced and has had the most effect on student learning and curricular change. After examining its goals, the Department of English determined that a new assessment tool for student writing was needed. The faculty devoted a lot of time and resources to developing a program that includes portfolios for all students and for all writing courses. As a result, there is more collaborative teaching than before, and faculty have an improved understanding of their students' writing. Another product of portfolio assessment has been the creation of a capstone portfolio in which students integrate their learning and from which the English faculty learns more about its success.

Portfolio assessment at Miami University of Ohio has revealed that students have little instruction in how to use the library and conduct research, even though they are asked to undertake a yearlong research project. The faculty has therefore written a grant and made a commitment to increasing instruction in these areas.

At Manhattanville College, undergraduate students are asked at least twice during their academic career to submit class products in a portfolio (a large brown envelope) to demonstrate specified competencies. As a result of this ongoing process, faculty have made several modifications to these competencies and the ways that their academic programs attempt to achieve the competencies. In some cases, expectations have been made more specific. For example, faculty members shifted a broad quantitative competence to a particular mathematics requirement. They also added research as a key component. Students reflect on their accomplishments through a self-evaluation that becomes part of the portfolio.

The faculties of ESU, IUPUI, and Miami feel they are making a difference with the improvements and changes mentioned here as a result of portfolio assessment. Though there is little hard data available yet to substantiate their perception, all three institutions can confidently point to improved faculty understanding of, interest in, and commitment to established student learning goals. This is itself a significant accomplishment. Alverno and Manhattanville have many more years of experience with portfolio assessment, and the continued commitment of their faculty members to this technique testifies to their satisfaction with its results.

Even though we have advanced in portfolio assessment over the last few years, it is still a relatively young tool. It may be a few more years before we have data that are quantitative, as well as qualitative, and "prove" the positive effects of portfolios. Yet even if we never have hard evidence of the value of the changes this type of assessment brings about, many of us feel the improvements are still valid. They may have more important consequences for student learning and curricular change — especially in general education — than improvements that are easier to quantify.

Strengths and Weaknesses of Portfolio Assessment

Perhaps more than any other assessment technique, portfolios provide a detailed mosaic of student learning as it develops over time. False assumptions about what is taught and learned often stifle academic reform and progress. Portfolios provide good qualitative evidence that either affirms or challenges these assumptions and that makes improvements more likely.

Portfolio assessment also helps faculty remain in control of their academic programs and the assessment of them. As stated earlier, faculty should participate in each aspect of portfolio assessment. It is a tool that is essentially developed and supervised locally. Although colleges and universities borrow portfolio techniques from each other, the specifics of each assessment process evolve from unique circumstances. Portfolio assessment of general education is especially beneficial to those institutions that have a general education council or committee that governs the program. It helps these faculty committees understand the program and assists in their administration of it.

Portfolio assessment can provide direction for faculty development. Evidence from portfolios is extremely helpful to faculty who are interested in improving their teaching; it tells them much more about student learning than one can get from standardized test scores or surveys of student opinion. Faculty also improve their teaching effectiveness because of the dialogue with colleagues and students that is often produced as a result of portfolio assessment. This dialogue becomes even more meaningful when it involves faculty discussions across disciplines, and it can lead to better teaching and integration of knowledge that spans academic areas.

Portfolios contribute to student learning and help students prepare for careers after college. Many institutions require students to write reflective essays about the material in their portfolios from time to time. This process of self-examination helps students understand better what they have learned, and it allows them to see how they have progressed. Items collected in the portfolio can also become material to supplement the student's résumé. There may be senior seminars or capstone experiences where students work to review their materials and present them in a way to make their knowledge and skills clearer to graduate schools and employers.

Portfolio assessment is a good cornerstone for programs that employ multiple measures. Portfolios may be the best tool for evaluating the goals that faculty care about but find difficult to assess by other means. They can be used effectively to measure different types of student learning, such as basic skills, knowledge, generic abilities, and values. Portfolios are also a means of storing results from standardized tests and other assessment tools. They can be combined with advising folders (as they are at ESU) and other records to make better use of institutional resources.

Inevitably, there are some weaknesses in portfolio assessment. The process requires an institution to grapple with a number of key philosophical issues, such as defining program goals, faculty expectations, and academic freedom. There are also many practical questions: What is to be collected, by whom, and when? Where are the portfolios to be kept? Dealing with these issues is time-consuming and can involve heated debate among faculty members, especially when they place their vested interests above the good of the students and the institution.

Moreover, even though there are certain accepted practices in portfolio assessment, there are few prescriptions that can be transferred from one institution to the next. Refining a portfolio assessment program can take a long time, and the faculty, administrators, and outside governing bodies may become impatient.

Leaders should keep all concerned parties well informed about the process as it evolves and help to develop trust among those who may not be familiar with its potential. Since portfolios do not yet have the type of outside validity and credibility enjoyed by some other assessment measures, those in charge of assessment must continually talk about the validity, reliability, and benefits of this approach.

Some faculty members, especially those with highly quantitative research perspectives, may be suspicious of the portfolio and might question the validity and composition of a small sample. They may also be concerned with the appearance of a subjective evaluation method that places emphasis on individual assessments of student learning, even though multiple evaluators are involved. Portfolio assessment must be viewed differently than quantitative measures like standardized tests, and some people are uncomfortable with this difference.

Even with a relatively small student sample, portfolios involve a lot of material that must be collected and evaluated carefully. It is important that a system be used that ensures student privacy and protects the integrity of the exams and assignments being examined. These are hurdles that can be overcome, but they do require careful planning and appropriate resources.

Further Improvement of Portfolio Assessment

Portfolio assessment will be improved further if those institutions that use it in similar ways (for example, to assess general education) continue to share information and resources. Portfolio assessment can maintain its unique character on each campus and still gain greater external credibility. Campuses with compatible programs could exchange faculty evaluators or evaluators from outside academia, such as legislators and business leaders. The more public we make portfolio assessment, the more it will grow.

Unfortunately, some faculty members still see assessment as a means of punishing them and discovering what mistakes they are making. As a result, these people complain about violations of academic freedom, and they try to hide what happens in their classrooms. We will all be well served if we use assessment as a means to tell our university story better and to show off the good things that occur in our academic programs. There is tremendous potential for portfolios to do just that, as well as to gain more external credibility for assessment.

We also need to move further in the area of merging the quantitative assessment mandates that many of us face from governing bodies with the more academically useful qualitative information provided by portfolios. For example, we could score portfolios with numerical protocols that would provide the types of quantitative results some governing bodies seek. Of course, if we use only numerical scoring, we could lose one of the primary benefits of portfolio assessment. Faculty would not have the detailed information about student learning that is most useful in improving academic programs. Yet, if we score portfolios with only qualitative descriptions, governing bodies may reject the results or be suspicious of the conclusions drawn. I am now working with a faculty subcommittee of the General Education Council of ESU to develop scoring protocols that include both a numerical rating and a verbal description that will be useful for program improvement.

We need to continue examining new technologies that will allow us to create and evaluate electronic portfolios. It is now possible to store student products on disks, though this technology is still too expensive to be practical. Electronic portfolios, however, hold enormous potential, and are being examined at institutions like ESU and IUPUI. Much more information could be stored in a much smaller space, and students could take their disk or a copy of it with them when they graduate.

Perhaps the best way to make this kind of assessment a catalyst for positive campus change is to be sure that information gleaned from portfolios is communicated to the faculty, especially to those individuals who teach courses in the academic program being evaluated. It is easy to get so caught up in the mechanics of making assessments and communicating results to outside constituencies that not enough work is done with those faculty members who have the greatest influence over the learning that occurs.

Faculty may not always be receptive to the information discovered from portfolios. Nevertheless, if it is presented in a way that recognizes and values faculty opinion and input, it is likely to get results. Faculty can be informed of the conclusions of portfolio assessment and asked if they can make changes in their classrooms that will further improve student learning. They should also be reminded on a regular basis of the goals of the academic program and asked to refine their teaching to help the institution better achieve the goals. Often, faculty will be more cooperative if they feel their opinions are valued and if they are active participants in the program being assessed. Portfolios have the potential to encourage faculty dialogue and cooperation.

Portfolio assessment done well can take advantage of faculty collegiality. It can strengthen academic ties and help in working toward common institutional goals. Most important, it can help faculty members ascertain if they are making a real difference in the educational development of their students.

References

Forrest, A. *Time Will Tell: Portfolio-Assisted Assessment of General Education.* Washington, D.C.: American Association for Higher Education, 1990.

Hutchings, P. *Behind Outcomes: Contexts and Questions for Assessment.* Washington, D.C.: American Association for Higher Education, 1989.

Hutchings, P. "Learning Over Time: Portfolio Assessment." *AAHE Bulletin,* 1990, *42*(9), 6–8.

Keeton, M. "Thoughts on Documenting an Institution's Educational Outcomes." *CAEL News,* Jan.–Feb. 1988, pp. 4–5.

Payne, D. E., Vowell, F. N., and Black, L. C. "Assessment Approaches in Evaluation Processes." *North Central Association Quarterly,* 1991, *66*(2), 444–450.

10

Assessment Options for the College Major

Reid Johnson
Robert D. McCormick
Joseph S. Prus
Julia S. Rogers

According to the first in-depth national study of the higher education assessment (HEA) movement conducted in 1990, 63 percent of institutions engaged in comprehensive student assessment programs included the assessment of at least one of their majors (Johnson, Prus, Andersen, and El-Khawas, 1991). Since all six regional accrediting agencies now require comprehensive assessment in both public and private institutions, it seems reasonable to infer that the large majority of departments in this country are involved, or soon will be involved, in assessing the effectiveness of majors.

Many institutions just entering the HEA mainstream choose one or more majors as a place to start, and that is a logical decision. Especially when educators view the prospect of HEA with alarm or ambivalence — as most apparently do — majors seem to offer several advantages:

- A relatively well defined domain of knowledge and other potential student outcome objectives

- A relatively well organized, cohesive faculty group responsible for the academic program, its requirements, and implementation
- In some cases, learned societies, professional associations, and specialized accreditors that have already promulgated standards or even model programs for undergraduate majors
- A reasonable level of agreement among disciplinary faculty, administrators, and students about what the major program is supposed to accomplish (as compared to more-difficult-to-define objectives, such as for general education or students' personal-affective development)
- Available commercial tests and surveys that at least claim to assess student outcomes in a wide variety of majors

With easily defined objectives, quick access to reasonably priced assessment instruments, a department full of faculty to do the assessing, and a captive population of degree-seeking advanced students to be evaluated, "What could be simpler?" ask beginner evaluators.

One thing veterans in the field know and few novices appreciate is the implementation fact of life, which might be called Murphy's Law and HEA Corollary: "Whatever can go wrong, will. And everything you try to do will take longer, cost more, and be opposed by more important people than you think possible." Often, novices quickly find their apparently level playing field strewn with difficult, seemingly insurmountable, obstacles and pitfalls. For instance, too often departments do not agree with external standards or models for their majors but are then unable to reach consensus on their own program objectives either. Many faculty members see assessment as a diversion from their traditional roles as teachers and researchers and are concerned that the academic reward structure may not adequately recognize assessment-related efforts. Others simply feel too overloaded to take on more work. Even students frequently object to requests that they spend additional time on assessment activities. And when they comply, they may do so with a form of passive resistance. Those sophisticated commercial test and survey results packages are not nearly as impressive when the data are invalidated by inconsistent student efforts. At the departmental level, many disciplines have traditions opposed to specifying program objectives or quantifying outcomes. This opposition can be related to other concerns regarding how administrators and "outsiders" will use major assessment results, especially unfavorable results.

Thus, though assessing a major may be a simpler task than most other HEA programs, it is not a simple task! Considerable effort in planning, creative and critical thinking, consensus building, cooperation, and problem solving are going to be required for any successful effort. Yet despite all these obstacles, it can be done, and as the exemplary programs in this chapter show, it can be done *well*.

Some Core Concepts and Principles of Higher Education Assessment

Student assessment in the major is an integral part of any HEA effort. Now that at least forty states and (as previously stated, all regional accrediting agencies) require the evaluation of institutional effectiveness — although the exact language may vary somewhat — all institutions must assess their majors for two distinct but related purposes: internal program improvement and external accountability. These purposes, often portrayed as quality enhancement versus quality control, may be different, but the methods that work in assessing majors are almost always useful for both purposes, if proper planning and problem-solving skills are employed.

There is no more critical juncture in implementing a successful assessment of the major than the moment of methods selection. Although there are only three strategic alternatives (to adopt an existing measure, to adapt an existing measure to fit particular needs, or to develop a local measure), choosing the right combination of methods for a particular combination of program objectives, students, and assessment resources is still a challenging task. Most of the remainder of this chapter provides descriptions of methods that work for assessing majors and offers some specific examples from programs that have used them successfully.

Common Characteristics of Successful Methods

For an assessment method to work, it must help the assessor attain some important goals. In amplifying the major internal and external purposes for assessment just cited above, three critical dimensions of methodological validity may be identified: relevance, accuracy, and comprehensiveness. *Relevance* means that a method measures educational objectives that are appropriate to an institution and its curriculum and that it samples them as directly as possible. *Accuracy* is the detail and specificity of discrimination among different degrees of achievement the method affords. *Comprehensiveness* refers to the breadth and depth of the method's sample; the more objectives sampled and the more thoroughly, the better.

Other considerations are also important. It is obviously an advantage if assessment methods are of relatively low cost, easy to use, easy to analyze and interpret, and offer a quick turnaround. Methods are better when they afford good validity and still make relatively low demands on the faculty. These include initial time spent designing and preparing the method for use; administration effort to conduct the assessment method with students; subsequent time spent in scoring, analysis, and interpretation; or any other assessment-related tasks faculty would perceive as outside the boundaries of their usual duties. Extra student effort is also an important consideration. Like faculty, students do not respond well to assessment demands beyond those they perceive as their usual duties.

The Exemplar Pool of Major Assessment Methods

Evidence for the success of the methods that follow has come from a wide range of programs. In preparing to compile the material for this volume, Trudy Banta circulated assessment questionnaires to a variety of large and small, public and private, two- and four-year institutions of all levels of prestige. Responses from some of those schools are included here. Reid Johnson is coordinator of an assessment consortium that includes thirty-eight members, and examples also come from those institutions. But the primary sources of data and examples, the base institutions, are three universities chosen for their success in translating good assessment principles into meaningful practice, particularly in academic majors.

Although all three institutions share the mission of public comprehensive universities and are led by enterprising and conscientious evaluators, they also differ in some important respects. Montclair State College is a relatively large school (13,000 students in 73 degree programs) in northern New Jersey. Winthrop University is moderately sized (5,000 students, 91 degree programs) and located in South Carolina. The University of Montevallo is a smaller institution (3,250 students in 79 degree programs) in Alabama. One distinction they share is that of the combined 164 undergraduate degree programs they offer, over 80 percent have implemented efforts to assess student achievement in their majors. At these institutions, as with most others, the methods that are described have proven most successful for both internal program improvement and external accountability purposes.

Examples of Successful Methods

Norm-referenced, standardized multiple-choice tests are widely used to measure students' knowledge of content in their majors. The music program at Montevallo found a close match between its curriculum and that sampled by the relevant Educational Testing Service (ETS) Major Field Achievement Test (MFAT). By disaggregating the group results (Banta, 1988), the faculty discovered significant strengths and weaknesses in its program, including the fact that transfer students (most of whom entered the program at the junior level) scored substantially lower than nontransfer students in music theory, which was taught primarily at the sophomore level. By moving the required music theory course to the junior year and incorporating more theory in other courses throughout the program, this problem is being corrected.

At Winthrop, several majors are employing regionally or nationally standardized tests in a similar manner, including music education and all teacher preparation programs (using one of the National Teachers' Examinations or other ETS tests), psychology (using one of the Area Concentration Achievement Tests — ACATs — produced by Anthony Golden at Austin Peay State University in Tennessee), and chemistry (using an American Chemical Society test). In all cases, standardized testing is but one component of a multiple-measure approach to assessing student knowledge, but it can be a useful one, particularly in demonstrating external validity.

Probably the most widely used method for evaluating student progress is the locally developed test or exam. For assessing the internal validity of a program (relevance, accuracy, and comprehensiveness) a test designed by the same people who set the objectives and teach the courses is often the best approach. But since these measures are not standardized or objectively scored, considerable care must be taken to avoid bias in the test-item selection, administration, scoring, and interpretation processes. Objective administration and scoring remain significant advantages of standardized commercial tests, but many departments find the internal validity of local tests, as well as their cost, interpretation, and data turnaround factors, more than compensatory. A well-constructed, carefully administered, comprehensive examination that is scored double-blind (graded by two or more judges with no knowledge of each other's evaluation) is still one of the best methods for assessing virtually any major.

For example, a written exam produced by the physical education, recreation, and leisure studies department at Montclair State revealed unexpected inconsistencies in how faculty members were teaching core courses. As a result, each department meeting now allocates time for presentations on course objectives and content, greatly improving intradepartmental communication. The psychology major at Winthrop uses department-generated, short-essay exams based on major objectives both to help diagnose seniors' core content strengths and weaknesses and to evaluate efforts to remediate those weaknesses in the capstone course. Such uses of local tests are widespread among the three base institutions, including in the Spanish and psychology majors at Montclair State and in Winthrop's biology, history, modern and classical languages, music education, nutrition, physical education, and sociology majors.

Another method for assessing student knowledge and other competencies is the oral examination. Though not nearly as widely used as written tests, oral exams offer significant internal validity advantages, such as an unparalleled opportunity to probe breadth and depth of student knowledge, individualized administration and evaluation, and other process and formative evaluation techniques that no written test can match. External validity problems (such as lack of standardization in administration and scoring and various subjectivity biases) are potential concerns with oral examinations. Still, several majors are using them as primary or supplementary assessments, including political science at Montclair State and philosophy-religion and modern languages at Winthrop.

As those people assessing majors become more involved in the program evaluation process, many develop a great appreciation for student projects, papers, demonstrations, and other types of performance appraisal techniques. This category of methods encompasses a wide variety of specific tasks, all having in common that students are required to demonstrate their acquired competency level by actually performing the skill in question. The distinct advantage of performance appraisals over written tests is their directness and relevance; they measure what students can actually do, as opposed to what they "know should be done." Majors with applied-skills objectives usually emphasize this distinction in their curricula through methods courses, labs, practica, internships, and other field placements. The same principle applies in assessment. From specific skills (such as playing a musical instrument, dissecting a lab animal, teaching a class, designing a bridge, or running a computer program) to more general competencies (critical thinking, problem solving, or creativity), the best way to measure the progress of students is to have them perform a structured task requiring the systematic demonstration of those skills. Many programs in the performing arts, education, business, and other professional and preprofessional programs have incorporated performance appraisal techniques in their student evaluations for years, but these disciplines are not unique in their need for this valuable method. Any major that includes skill development in its program objectives — and virtually every major does — should consider using performance appraisal techniques.

Teacher preparation programs at our base institutions rely heavily on performance appraisal in such areas as student teaching, classroom management, computer applications, and internships, resulting in improved student and consumer satisfaction reports. In Winthrop's biology department, majors are assessed on nineteen operationalized laboratory skills in eight courses. The department is thus able to monitor progress and make needed corrections before skill development falls too far behind. Additionally, programs in music and music education, dance, theater, chemistry, physics, social work, psychology, and English incorporate both intermediate and outcomes performance appraisals. Alverno College, the acknowledged master of this approach, uses performance assessment in all majors.

With all its advantages in validity, performance appraisal has some practical drawbacks; there are some student skills that do not lend themselves readily to assessment within the normal campus curricular environment. It is obviously unfeasible to use performance appraisal to assess the ability of students to handle a person threatening suicide, to protect crops from locusts, to remove a suspected abused child from a parent, or to maintain order in the classroom despite threats from a substance-abusing teenager. Yet even in instances like these, major evaluators need not settle for highly inferential written tests just because full performance appraisals are impractical.

Performance simulations provide a reasonable compromise; they offer more validity than written tests and more practicality than performance appraisals. Simulations include a wide range of situational approximations requiring demonstration of student skills (from simple role playing to flight simulators and any points in between) that can elicit valuable evaluative data on major objectives. Along with traditional simulations like mock trials, in-box exercises, role playing for social work interviews, psychological counseling, and practice teaching, emerging technological developments in interactive computer programs offer great potential for breakthroughs in both the quality and quantity of simulation assessment techniques.

Another performance-based technique with considerably more authenticity than written tests is the use of portfolios of student work. Portfolios are samples of student performance products, usually collected over time and evaluated both for overall quality and for degree of improvement. Like the previous two methods, a portfolio can be used to assess virtually any skill but has the significant advantage of providing longitudinal data (changes over time related to instruction) with fewer practical problems than other performance-based methods. Disadvantages might involve the heavy investment of faculty time in careful review of substantial portfolios and security issues, such as ensuring that the student being evaluated did all the work within the time allotted. Still, portfolios of collected works in art, writing, research projects, and lessons plans are considered invaluable assessment components for many majors. At Montclair State, the fine arts and foreign languages programs utilize various types of portfolios, as do the art and design, teacher preparation, and writing programs at Winthrop.

All these performance-based assessment methods offer strong support for internally valid evaluation of student learning and program quality, but all likewise share a potential weakness: namely, questionable external validity. In all three cases, the design, administration, scoring, and interpretation of results are largely subjective and conducted by the same program faculty being indirectly evaluated. To be concerned about the validity of such a process is not mere cynicism. Though there is anecdotal evidence that most faculty members actually are harder on their own students and programs than are more objective assessors, prudent evaluators of majors always need to take steps to avoid the appearance of impropriety and demonstrate the external validity of their results.

In addition to the norm-referenced standardized tests already discussed, there are other alternatives to demonstrate external validity. One is the use of external examiners in student assessment activities. Examples of potential external examiners would include faculty from a "model" or peer program in the same discipline, representatives from the discipline's national association or learned society, prospective employers of program graduates, faculty from allied disciplines, or other individuals who are knowledgeable about the objectives of a major and concerned for its quality enhancement. External examiners may involve themselves in any or all of the steps in the student assessment process; they provide both a valuable external benchmark for outcomes evaluation and a means to help assure the external validity of program evaluation results. Currently, all three base institutions rely almost exclusively on program reviews from visiting accreditors and regulating agencies for this purpose.

Another promising assessment method for majors is classroom research (sometimes called learning research or classroom assessment), originated by K. Patricia Cross and Thomas Angelo (1988). This dynamic, course-level, classroom-based approach encompasses many different specific measurement techniques (one-minute papers, concept maps, goal rankings, annotated portfolios, interim student evaluations). These have in common an emphasis on short-term evaluation of the teaching-learning process for immediate instructional improvement, as opposed to individual student outcomes or broad program evaluation. Instructors in any major can use classroom research techniques for ongoing course-level assessment, and the results can help to refine instructional objectives, teaching methods, or evaluation techniques quickly.

One of the most practical, and possibly underutilized, major assessment methods is data analysis using archival records. Institutional research and academic records offices usually have a wealth of information on students: premajor characteristics and educational histories; major courses of study, with concomitant strengths, weaknesses, and sequences; and cocurricular activities. These are all pertinent factors that should not be ignored, especially to validate or help explain results from other methods.

Now we come to what must be one of the most popular assessment methods, surveys. Well over half of the major programs at our three base institutions and the other respondent colleges report surveying either their active students, alumni, or both. Furthermore, many departments also solicit written questionnaires from other sources, such as withdrawing students, faculty, employers, graduate schools, and parents. Like the testing options with which this section began, surveys come in both standardized or locally developed formats, with essentially the same relative advantages and disadvantages as previously cited for each. Surveys may seek respondents' perceptions on major program satisfaction only or may ask for more detailed responses on program strengths and weaknesses. They may be in multiple-choice or rating formats, may allow open-ended replies in the respondents' own words, or may perhaps use a combination.

Veteran assessors sometimes discover that written surveys turn out to be less valuable than initially hoped since they (1) are much more difficult to design, implement, and interpret than they appear; (2) often produce relatively unrepresentative response rates (perhaps 20 to 40 percent for mailed surveys); and (3) at best only represent what respondents are willing to report. This is highly inferential, anecdotal information that should never be confused with hard data on actual program quality. Despite these limitations, the reported impressions of students, alumni, and others on major programs are important and unique sources of evaluative feedback and should be an integral component of any major assessment effort — provided that survey data recipients do not misunderstand or exaggerate their results.

All three base institutions use this method widely, and Winthrop provides several examples of broadly applied but prudently utilized surveys. Seniors and alumni are surveyed (the latter within one year and again three years after graduation) with questionnaires that can be supplemented for use by individual majors. Also, departments can conduct specialized surveys of their majors or third parties for their own purposes. The social work department surveys graduate programs attended by its majors to monitor student preparation strengths and weaknesses and to modify undergraduate courses accordingly; the schools of business and education use employer survey results in the same ways.

The psychology department at Montevallo has added an interesting and useful twist on survey methodology by using Stark, Lowther, Shaw, and Sossen's Student Goals Exploration instrument (1990) to sample both senior and faculty goals for the major. Comparisons of similarities and differences between the two groups has resulted in modifications in the curriculum and in student orientation efforts to strengthen vocational preparation and make program objectives clearer and more salient to its students.

In all these cases, items are carefully written and revised to obtain as much information as possible, with opportunities for respondents to give examples and the rationale for their opinions. Data analysis and reporting are always cautious. Sampling and validation concerns are noted, and conclusions are limited to data trends that are clearly supported by additional evidence. When used in this manner, surveys offer a relatively quick, inexpensive, and rich source of qualitative program information for both internal and external validity applications.

Finally, just as oral exams offer some important internal validity advantages over written tests, so oral interviews can be powerful alternatives or supplements to written surveys. Although clearly more labor intensive, exit interviews for majors can be extremely valuable in providing a quantity and quality of evaluative feedback unmatched by any other data source. Eliciting *how* graduating students feel about their major experience and *why,* in a candid dialogue with faculty at this critical juncture in students' careers, may well prove the quickest and cheapest source of immediately useful data available to a major department, regardless of discipline, objectives, or size.

The psychology department at Winthrop conducts voluntary, one-on-one, audiotaped interviews with 80 to 90 percent of its graduating majors. Resulting reports are used for longitudinal comparisons of student perceptions of program objectives, courses, instruction, facilities, equipment, and overall program value. Interview data also serve as premeasures of postgraduate success. Curriculum changes motivated by interview results have included a required senior capstone course (to increase program integration, fill in content gaps, and provide a final basis for postgraduate careers), a cornerstone course (to make program objectives and options clear to incoming majors and to begin program assessment earlier), strengthened research methods requirements in several courses, and the initiation of advising tracks for majors with different postgraduate goals (graduate school — experimental, graduate school — applied, paraprofessional-related field, and liberal arts).

It should be noted that these interviews have become very popular with the students and have been successfully used as rewards for volunteering to take standardized achievement tests. In fact, at all our base institutions, interviews were among the most positively reported means of assessing majors for both internal and external validity purposes.

The Importance of Implementation

In addition to considering which assessment methods will be employed, another important factor is how they are implemented. To apply only one valid, feasible measure for each major objective is to maximize the amount of effort and minimize the quality of the results — exactly the opposite of what we want to do. The solution, of course, is to use several methods to assess multiple objectives, thus attaining the greatest validity in the least time. Several measures increase data quality; if each covers several objectives, the overall effort required decreases. Multiple methods used at several points throughout the major (as in Winthrop's music education program) are especially effective.

Two other implementation strategies offering more quality for less effort also deserve mention. Montevallo French and art majors have used an assessment matrix to organize and track program objectives, their location in the curriculum, and the ways they are assessed. This approach helps to create maximum effectiveness and efficiency for instructional and assessment purposes. The political science major at Montclair State and the psychology major at Winthrop both use senior capstone courses as primary outcomes assessment vehicles for comprehensive exams, exit interviews, and the like. Capstones also provide settings for performance-based assessments such as papers, projects, and portfolios and drastically reduce student motivation problems. Winthrop has also extended this logic into a newly required cornerstone course for entering psychology majors.

All these implementation strategies help make assessment a natural part of student and faculty program responsibilities while maintaining a high level of quality.

Examples of Effective Assessment Procedures

As the institutional responses that form the basis for this chapter were being collated, an interesting and somewhat unexpected trend emerged. Although valid assessment methodology was certainly a linchpin of any successful effort to evaluate the effectiveness of a major program, the procedures employed in planning, designing, implementing, and evaluating those assessment methods were also very important. In fact, there was at least as much consistency in the assessment procedures that worked as in any specific assessment methods.

Procedural factors in operating a successful program to assess the major include the following:

• There must be a strong, unequivocal, and well-publicized administrative commitment to implement a high-quality, institutionwide assessment program, which is stated and reinforced through meaningful action on a continuing basis. This commitment implies much more than just making an opening speech or paying lip service to a program and then neglecting it when evaluations and budget allocations are determined.

• Assessment planning, design, implementation, and evaluation should be directed by the faculty through a broadening of existing governance structures and committees as well as the creation of new policy-setting bodies as needed at the departmental, school, and institutional levels. The faculty must be involved throughout the assessment process and at all levels of decision making; they should not just serve as laborers during the implementation phase.

• Although both internal and external pressures and incentives should be acknowledged, the primary purpose of assessment should be to enhance program and institutional effectiveness through improved student learning. This priority should be kept foremost throughout the entire assessment process. One of the best ways to sabotage any HEA program is to tell the faculty that it is being undertaken because assessment mandates require it.

• Assessment of the major works best when it is part of a comprehensive assessment effort throughout most or all units of the institution, not just a few departments or programs acting in isolation.

• Explicit assessment program policies and principles should be promulgated jointly by faculty and administration (and students) regarding goals, implementation, reporting of results, and the potential effects on participating students, faculty, and programs. Faculty and students should be encouraged to do their best to provide an honest assessment of a major's strengths and weaknesses and should not be surprised by what happens afterwards. (Assessment policies can always be revised as needed, but likewise in an open, participatory manner.)

• Objectives should be embedded in course and degree requirements, and assessment activities should be an integral part of course and cocurricular activities. Thus, faculty and staff assessment responsibilities become natural parts of their instructional and program responsibilities, not extra work tacked onto their job descriptions. Capstone and cornerstone courses are especially synergistic options for both pedagogical and assessment purposes.

• Program roles and responsibilities should be clearly designated (for example, through the establishment of an assessment coordinator or office at the institutional level and a departmental assessment coordinator or assessment committee chair), not added to some administrator's job description or lost among the charges of several committees. Likewise, credit for assessment activities should be incorporated into the regular reward structure (salary, tenure, and promotion for the faculty; course credit and graduation requirements for students).

• Lastly, majors should publicize assessment efforts and disseminate results as widely as possible — to faculty, students, administrators, trustees, other institutions, media, regulators, and the public at large — in order to maintain and broaden the motivation of evaluators and assure external constituencies of good-faith efforts.

Benefits of Sound Assessment Programs

As this chapter has shown, there is more than one way, or one *combination* of ways, to assess any major effectively. Regardless of the specific techniques utilized, however, a pattern of procedural and methodological benefits can be expected to accrue for any successful assessment program.

An early benefit is increased faculty interest and discourse regarding the strengths and weaknesses of program objectives and possible means of program improvement. These in turn produce efforts to improve programs, which lead to better assessment quality, which increases faculty motivation to use assessment to achieve that improvement, and so on. The resulting "synergy cycle" can affect program quality and morale for years to come.

Faculty involvement in assessment soon leads to changes in the classroom, usually in the form of more relevant and explicit course objectives and better instruction and evaluation. With clearer course objectives, improved student motivation and achievement follow, widening the synergy cycle even further. Increases in student learning and development motivates the faculty to expand assessment processes to program-level issues.

Revisions in curriculum and program requirements (sequences, prerequisites, new courses) often come next, for purposes of increased quality, relevance to student and postgraduate needs, and other effectiveness and efficiency goals. These revisions result in better teaching and learning, utilization of resources, and service to external constituencies.

All this improvement in faculty-student communication and program relevance can also shore up another weakness in many majors: academic and career advising. When everyone has a shared understanding of program requirements, goals, strategies, and expected outcomes, fewer opportunities for confusion, misunderstanding, errors — even failures — exist.

As important as these quality-improvement benefits to the campus are the effects on those mandating assessment — regulators, accreditors, and other significant external parties. Real efforts to implement valid and timely assessment of majors produce evidence appropriate for self-studies and accountability reports as a natural by-product of the quality-improvement process. With the possible exceptions of proscriptive provisions in a few state laws, colleges can experiment with the methods and procedures advocated in this chapter for their own purposes and satisfy assessment mandates at the same time.

References

Banta, T. W. (ed.). *Implementing Outcomes Assessment: Promise and Perils.* New Directions for Institutional Research, no. 59. San Francisco: Jossey-Bass, 1988.

Cross, K. P., and Angelo, T. A. *Classroom Assessment Techniques: A Handbook for Faculty.* Ann Arbor, Mich.: National Center for Research to Improve Postsecondary Teaching and Learning, 1988.

Johnson, R., Prus, J., Andersen, R., and El-Khawas, E. *Assessing Assessment: An In-Depth Status Report on the Higher Education Assessment Movement.* Washington, D.C.: American Council on Education, 1991.

Stark, J. S., Lowther, M. A., Shaw, K. M., and Sossen, P. L. *Student Goals Exploration: User's Manual.* (preliminary ed.) Ann Arbor, Mich.: National Center for Research to Improve Postsecondary Teaching and Learning, 1990.

11

Attitude and Opinion Data

John A. Muffo
Mary Anne Bunda

Individual scholars and research offices in institutions of higher education have been actively producing models of data collection for nearly a half-century. Although the research has often been geared to factors that influence classroom learning, the broader areas of student development, satisfaction, and use of academic support services (as well as characteristics of the university environment) have been investigated as well. Research on student satisfaction and use of academic support services has always been seen as important to facilitating cognitive learning and growth. The challenge is often in finding the material and applying it to a local situation rather than trying to replicate theoretical research. Published research studies usually report broadly established effects. Though valuable for advancing theoretical perspectives, these effects do not offer advice on specific institutional questions. Single-institution studies are rejected by many journal editors and review boards because they are idiosyncratic or too specific.

This chapter reports solely on the use of perception information in single institutions. The data gathering may not follow standard research methodology, and the solution in one institution may not be applicable to another; however, each of the cases reports a change at a university that was based on a need identified through assessment procedures.

Commonly used methods of garnering opinions include written surveys (Astin, 1981; Pace, 1988), telephone surveys (Fisher, 1988), individual interviews, focus groups (Brodigan, 1992; Jacobi, 1991), observations of behavior (Patton, 1990), logs of conversations between students and service providers (Giles-Gee and Kerns, 1988), and the use of suggestions for improvement. These methods may be used with current students, students who have either dropped out or stopped out, alumni of the institution (Pettit, 1991), or faculty. Assessment of service units such as the library must include the faculty as a crucial client group. The process of identifying who the customers are and how to go about soliciting their opinions in itself can be an important and enlightening exercise in identifying values held at the departmental and college level or within academic and student services units. Samples may be drawn using scientific methods of random selection from either a participant list or a list of class sections; convenience samples may also be used. As with cognitive assessment efforts, satisfaction measures can either be internally developed or secured from outside sources.

The same pros and cons of selection of instruments, participants, and techniques exist in the noncognitive arena as in the assessment of achievement. On the one hand, if the instrument is developed externally, some of its items may not be priority concerns of the institution. Terms used on the questionnaire may differ from those commonly used within the institution. On the other hand, locally developed instruments suffer from lack of benchmarks. Suppose that 12 percent of the alumni say that parking is the worst experience they have on campus. Is this an unusual finding? Should a task force be set up to solve the parking problem? Or is it more important to work on another problem indicated by 10 percent of the alumni? Only normative data allow comparisons to be made regarding such issues. Also, alumni surveys present problems that are different from surveys of current students. For instance, finding alumni addresses may be difficult, and biased results may be produced because of sampling problems. Nevertheless, alumni have a perspective on their experiences that current students do not.

Other kinds of problems result from a sampling technique. It may underrepresent small programs or offices designed to help small target groups. Sampling classrooms ensures a high rate of return, but the reactive environment of the classroom may produce data that have less validity than questionnaires mailed to students individually. The timing of a survey may also influence the results (Pennington, Zvonkovic, and Wilson, 1989). Data from alumni may address issues that were important years ago but are not currently pressing.

A variety of commercial instruments, usually with room for local questions, are available for determining opinions and attitudes. Some are designed specifically for alumni, some for entering freshmen, and some for the entire student population. Among the better-known sources are the American College Testing Program Student Opinion Survey (Hunziker, 1991). Cooperative Institution Research Program (Astin, 1981), and the College Student Experiences Questionnaire (CSEQ) (Pace, 1988). Both the Student Opinion Survey and the CSEQ are concerned with use of services as well as satisfaction with them. The participant-service index allows an institution to contrast its services with those of similar institutions. Using this index may be efficient as well. For instance, if only 5 percent of the student population is using a particular service, it would be unwise to survey all those enrolled on their opinion of that service. Other advantages of such instruments include their quality, ease of use, and low actual cost. Their biggest drawback is their generic nature; they are not aimed specifically at a single institution or topic.

Given the variety of procedures available, it is not surprising that the most basic finding to date in the assessment arena is that there is no single model for excellence. Any assessment effort intended to make a difference eventually has to become part of the fabric of the institution, and to do that it must reflect the institutional culture and environment. Assessment procedures can be operated out of a single unit with information disseminated to operating units, or service units may be responsible for collecting their own information. The focus of any study may be institutional or it may be based on individual units. To be credible, information must be gathered from multiple sources using the best method feasible given budget constraints. Multiple sources of information are just as desirable for studies of satisfaction as for studies of student achievement.

Examples of assessment making a difference abound among those familiar with institutionally based programs. At the campus level, opinion surveys sometimes lead to identification of existing and potential problems and point to solutions. In many cases, initial data collection using a commercial or local instrument reveals a problem. The next step is collecting more information, through personal or telephone interviews of individuals or through focus-group interviews, to analyze the problem and generate possible solutions (for more information on qualitative methods in general and focus groups in particular, see Krueger, 1988; Morgan, 1990; and Patton, 1990). Issues identified and investigated often come from student and academic service functions, but the same sort of perception-satisfaction information can contribute to better understanding and improvement of academic programs as well.

Institutions at Which the Data
Have Made a Difference

While recognizing that attitude and opinion data can be useful at the departmental level, the focus of this chapter is primarily on the institution. Several examples follow in which multiple satisfaction measures were administered, analyzed, and shared in such a way as to lead to improvements in institutional environments. The first example is taken from a medium-sized public institution with a historically strong teaching mission, Miami University; the second is from Virginia Tech, a land-grant university among the top fifty nationally in total funded research expenditures. The third example is from Harvard University (Light, 1992), and the fourth is from Western Michigan University, a public, comprehensive institution that is one of five graduate-intensive universities in Michigan. The final example is taken from a number of institutions but concerns the identification of a common area of need—advising. This example is provided to show various ways that institutions have used data to support the necessity for action and those actions that were actually taken. The variety of assessment plans and activities evident in these examples makes clear that assessment plans are individualized to reflect institutions' values and culture.

Miami University

In a brief summary of responses to a mail questionnaire, Karl Schilling, Miami University of Ohio, has used a locally developed alumni survey, Pace's CSEQ, and Astin's Freshman Survey to gather attitude and opinion data from former, current, and new students. The combination of instruments and participant groups has allowed some of the data to be compared to national norms. Using alumni responses for comparison with those of current students, additional data are linked specifically to program goals at the institution. A conclusion that has been reached in examining the evidence from these multiple sources is that current and former students lack confidence in dealing with quantitative data.

In response to such findings, a grant proposal was written and funded to develop quantitative reasoning skills across the curriculum, as other institutions have done with writing skills. Faculty and administrators report that more quantitative material is beginning to appear in existing courses.

Virginia Tech

At the Virginia Polytechnic Institute and State University, distribution of Pace's CSEQ instrument to a random sample of current students revealed that a low percentage, when compared to the norm group, used the library for study purposes. Two graduate students in education attempted to determine the reasons behind the low usage rate by conducting a series of focus-group interviews. Existing undergraduate advisory groups in the colleges were utilized for at least two reasons. First, they already met on a regular basis and were therefore likely to have good attendance. Second, it was deemed that usage patterns of the library were likely to differ by academic discipline. Focus groups from different academic colleges of the university were likely to be more homogeneous than if they had been selected by other methods across colleges. For this purpose, multiple groups with a homogeneous structure were preferable to heterogeneous groups.

The focus groups revealed a high level of satisfaction with the staff of the library among the students interviewed. This finding was fortuitous in that the director had just resigned and morale was at a low point. There was dissatisfaction, however, with the layout of the current physical facilities and with the availability of parking near the library (over half of all undergraduates live off campus). Suggestions were made to provide for more lounge space and more meeting rooms where groups could work together without bothering others. The report, done by the graduate students, was submitted to the acting director of the library and made available to the university architect as well. Funds had been requested from the state for adding more library space, so information from the report was useful in designing that space.

While studies of student satisfaction are often made at the institutional level, they are also helpful at departmental and college levels. Faculty in an agricultural discipline at Virginia Tech, for instance, were surprised to discover that alumni and employers were dissatisfied with graduates' level of computing expertise. A major reason for the surprise was that the university as a whole had an international reputation for computing excellence. Apparently, the faculty in this department had assumed that somehow its students were being exposed to the computing knowledge and skills necessary to succeed in the profession. In fact, however, these students were falling through the cracks in the system. Department faculty members acknowledged the deficiency and suggested a solution to the faculty of the entire college, since they perceived it as a larger problem. Specific computing skills are now required in core courses in the college. Future surveys should reveal improvement in alumni and employer satisfaction in this area.

Harvard University

The *Harvard Assessment Seminars: Second Report* (Light, 1992) references eleven different sources of information about student attitudes and opinions gathered by a number of individuals, mostly undergraduate and graduate students, as part of their academic programs. Both surveys and interviews were used, usually separately rather than as two stages of the same study. In a meta-analysis of the data, the report summarizes the most important findings as follows:

- Interactive relationships organized around academic work are vital.
- Students value strong writing skills. Many benefit enormously from a few specific suggestions.
- Advisers can help students to make a few key decisions that will shape their entire college experiences.
- Undergraduates have strong views about how science faculties can attract and keep more students.
- Foreign languages and literatures are the most widely appreciated courses — an unexpected finding [Light, 1992].

The report summarizes the results of these eleven studies and offers a number of practical suggestions for improving student learning in writing, the physical sciences, and foreign languages. It provides some advice for improving student advising as well. It does not mention, however, any actions taken at Harvard or any measurable change in student satisfaction as a result of the studies.

Western Michigan University

An ACT Student Opinion Survey has been conducted once every three years for the past fifteen years at Western Michigan. The study is sponsored jointly by the vice presidents of student services and academic affairs and conducted by the Office of Institutional Research. The survey is conducted by drawing a stratified sample of course sections. The 1985 data showed very low levels of satisfaction with the registration process compared to that of other public institutions of similar size. A locally developed alumni survey conducted in 1987 and mailed to a random sample of individuals showed that 10 percent of the alumni felt that adding or dropping classes was their worst experience on campus. The registrar organized a task force to develop a new system of registration that was implemented in the 1987–88 academic year. The Student Opinion Survey results of 1990 showed that the level of satisfaction with the registration process was above the national mean for institutions of this size.

The alumni survey of the class of 1987–88, conducted in 1992, attracted no negative remarks about the drop-add process but did show a strong gender difference in the use of campus recreational facilities. The president began a series of informal meetings with student leaders concerning their perceptions of this issue. Although the result was the emergence of a strong case for a new recreational facility on campus, support from the state for this project was unlikely, given its financial condition. Along with the president, the students designed a plan to use their fees to initiate the construction of a facility that students would own. Ground was broken for the new building in 1992.

Advising: A Commonly Faulted Student Service

Although virtually all institutions of higher education have an advising program in place, no two programs are identical. Some institutions have programs in which faculty provide advising in the major only, whereas career advising and freshman-sophomore counseling are centralized. At other colleges and universities, the faculty is responsible for both career and academic advising. At still others, some faculty members are specifically designated as advisers. Some institutions have peer advising in academic as well as personal areas.

The goals and program definition of advising on campus require different methods for collection of data and uses of the information. Giles-Gee and Kerns (1988) conducted a content analysis of topics of discussion between advisers and students to evaluate the meaning of advising on their campus. Survey responses at Kean College of New Jersey provided by assessment coordinator Michael Knight showed that advising can mean different things even on the same campus. He conducted a survey of current students and found that they and the faculty were using different definitions of and therefore had different expectations for the advising process. The data were used to develop a new student handbook, which included the many purposes of counseling, and the topic was introduced in orientation sessions. Informal feedback at the institution indicates that faculty are now providing more advising services. At Austin Peay State University, according to Linda Rudolph, a student survey indicated a lack of satisfaction with advising, particularly that for careers. As a result, special training for faculty began in 1989, with an emphasis on career choices.

Current student surveys are not the only method that focuses on advising. At Winthrop University, a combination of locally developed alumni surveys and telephone interviews led to the conclusion that there is less satisfaction with career advising and related services than with other aspects of the college experience. In this case, the survey data identified a need area, and the subsequent telephone interview study allowed the institution to collect data that addressed the particular nature of the problem from the graduate perspective.

A number of actions occurred at Winthrop without the aid of outside funding. A forum on career advising was held at the annual faculty retreat. The name of the Placement Center was changed to Career Services to better represent its purpose, and its functions were reorganized and expanded at the same time. In addition, an elective psychology course in career exploration was added to the curriculum. Preliminary findings suggest an increase in alumni satisfaction with career advising.

At Virginia Military Institute, according to Stephen RiCharde, an alumni survey showed dissatisfaction with academic advising, leading to changes in that system and to creation of a new-cadet advising program. Recent graduates have improved attitudes toward advising, and current freshmen have increased grade-point averages. Celeste Hunziker (1991) of the

Office of Student Affairs Research and Information conducted a comprehensive survey at the University of California, Davis, using the ACT Student Opinion Survey. The results, available in ERIC, show how data can be compared to previous studies on a campus and to national norms. The document also discusses procedures used to draw a stratified sample and to mail questionnaires to students, with the resulting response rate. The actions taken on the basis of this study are not available, but it is an excellent resource for those interested in how to carry out such a study.

Importance of the Data

Each of the institutions from which assessment examples were drawn for this chapter uses a combination of methods to gather data. In some cases, actions were taken immediately. In others, results led to further investigation of the situation before a possible local solution was generated. In some situations, actions were accomplished by changing current practice with no additional sources of revenue: in others, the cost of the solution was underwritten either by outside funding or new sources of internal funds.

The key point is that attitude and opinion data have proven to be valid indicators of existing problems at many colleges and universities. They can even point to potential solutions if used in a thoughtful and deliberate manner.

References

Astin, A. W. "The Cooperative Institutional Research Program (CIRP): An Ongoing National Study of Higher Education in the United States." *International Journal of Institutional Management in Higher Education,* 1981, *5,* 31–38.

Brodigan, D. L. *Focus Group Interviews: Applications for Institutional Research.* Tallahassee, Fla.: Association for Institutional Research, 1992.

Fisher, M. B. "Surveying Your Alumni." In G. S. Melchiori (ed.), *Alumni Research: Methods and Application.* New Directions for Institutional Research, no. 60. San Francisco: Jossey-Bass, 1988.

Giles-Gee, H., and Kerns, S. *Advising Topics: A Content Analysis.* Annapolis, Md.: Maryland State Board of Education, 1988.

Hunziker, C. M. *A Report of Student Opinions.* Davis: University of California Press, 1991.

Jacobi, M. "Focus Group Research: A Tool for the Student Affairs Professional." *NASPA Journal,* 1991, *28*(3), 195–201.

Krueger, R. A. *Focus Groups: A Practical Guide for Applied Research.* Newbury Park, Calif.: Sage, 1988.

Light, R. J. *The Harvard Assessment Seminars: Second Report.* Cambridge, Mass.: Harvard University, 1992.

Morgan, D. L. *Focus Groups as Qualitative Research.* Newbury Park, Calif.: Sage, 1990.

Pace, R. *Uses of the College Student Experiences Questionnaire.* Paper presented at the annual meeting of the Association for the Study of Higher Education, St. Louis, Mo., Nov. 1988.

Patton, M. *Qualitative Evaluation and Research Methods.* (2nd ed.) Newbury Park, Calif.: Sage, 1990.

Pennington, D. C., Zvonkovic, A. M., and Wilson, S. L. "Changes in College Satisfaction Across an Academic Term." *Journal of College Student Development,* 1989, *30,* 528–535.

Pettit, J. *Listening to Your Alumni: One Way to Assess Academic Outcomes.* Tallahassee, Fla.: Association for Institutional Research, 1991.

12

Cognitive and Affective Measures of Student Development

R. Stephen RiCharde
Cynthia A. Olney
T. Dary Erwin

The challenge to document the impact of college on students goes beyond assessment of the knowledge of classroom subject matter. Often, the lasting outcomes of college center on the cognitive and affective development of students. Much of the knowledge transmitted in the classroom is not retained in memory; yet decision-making styles, critical-thinking strategies, identity formation, human relations abilities, and ethical-reasoning strategies are nurtured by the college experience and guide much of our later adult functioning in the workplace (Howard, 1986) and society (Erwin, 1991).

The importance of these educational outcomes has been noted in the literature (Feldman and Newcomb, 1969; Pascarella and Terenzini, 1991), in early reports giving rise to assessment in the 1980s with the *Involvement in Learning* study (Study Group on the Conditions of Excellence in American Higher Education, 1984), and, most recently, in the national education goals. For instance, national education goal 5.5 reinforces "critical-thinking, problem solving, and communication skills" as necessary abilities for college graduates (Corrallo, 1991).

In spite of the intrinsic importance of students' cognitive and affective development, less attention has been paid to these areas in assessment than to basic academic skills and knowledge in the major and general education. As will be noted in this chapter, this kind of development can occur as a result of major studies and general education, as well as student affairs and academic services. Decision-making strategies and leadership abilities, for example, can grow throughout the entire collegiate experience — that is, in out-of-class experiences as well as in the classroom.

The purpose of this chapter is to present ways in which assessment has had a meaningful impact on student development at two Virginia colleges: the Virginia Military Institute (VMI) and James Madison University (JMU). The approaches at these two institutions are quite different, but each school has had success in using assessment to better execute its institutional mission.

Making a Difference at Virginia Military Institute

To portray accurately the impact of assessment at the Virginia Military Institute, it is necessary to look at all aspects of the way business is done; assessment has had an impact, albeit subtle in some instances, in all areas. This section will focus mainly on how the use of affective measures of student development has made a difference to the institution and its students.

Although VMI has had a well-established tradition, set of values, and perceived mission for over 150 years, there was initially no clear idea of the role assessment would play in substantiating them. Furthermore, there was apprehension about the possibility that assessment would alter facets of the institution that many felt were tried and true and not readily measurable.

During the process of developing an assessment plan, those involved rediscovered that there are four basic assumptions against which all programs at VMI are implicitly evaluated. These became the starting place for planning. The assumptions are (1) justice: all students are treated equally in all endeavors and the educational process begins with a leveling experience in the freshman year; (2) an adversative model of education: students are placed in a rigorous intellectual and social atmosphere and must prove themselves by succeeding in this context; (3) a constructed environment: the VMI experience is isolated from the outside world and conducted in a self-contained environment; and (4) candor and openness: all aspects of the students' daily lives are open to scrutiny, and honor and integrity are reaffirmed almost daily. If the system is functioning properly, a strong leader emerges from this educational mix.

Assessment personnel next identified three developmental assumptions that reflected the basic values of the institution. First, VMI students develop in periods of rapid change punctuated by plateaus (discontinuous development); second, students appear to develop in the same general direction (unitary development); and third, new learning builds on prior learning (cumulative development). The assumptions were tested by cognitive and affective measures used in the assessment program.

Finally, the long-range academic plan was revised around key educational competencies that contribute to the development of leadership as VMI defines it. These are the following: expertise in an academic discipline, critical-thinking skills, communication skills, a highly developed sense of ethics and values, interpersonal abilities, skills in organizational relations, and physical and mental health. In the plan, each of these was defined in terms of measurable outcomes, and educational strategies were attached to each.

Though presenting some initial organizational problems, assessment has finally undergone a synthesis with institutional planning and resource allocation. The assessment program has now become a central part of academic, cocurricular, and administrative life.

Stress-Induced Attrition

The problem of student retention is greatest during the freshman year; VMI has historically lost as many as 13 percent of freshmen during the first five weeks. Because of the stress-inducing environment, students at VMI drop out both for academic and for nonacademic reasons during this period. The questions that assessment needed to address were "What are the early indicators of attrition due to the stressful conditions?" and "What are the early indicators of academic problems caused by the stressful conditions?" It turned out that the most robust indicators of attrition due to stress were affective measures.

The assessment office began to administer a variety of affective as well as cognitive measures to all entering students during matriculation. Many of the subscales of these instruments proved to be strong predictors of attrition. For example, scores on the Myers-Briggs Type Indicator (Briggs-Myers, 1976) showed that students who were "introvert-sensing-thinking" (IST) types were the highest risks for early dropout because of the initial stressful conditions of the program. Although only 47 percent of the student body were of the IST type, this type made up approximately 85 percent of the early dropouts. The literature on this personality type, verified by follow-up interviews, shows that these students have a strong need to know the purposes of the stress-inducing environment. This type is focused inwardly and thrives on practical information, not on taking things on faith (as do those with some alternative Myers-Briggs profiles).

Another instrument that proved a useful indicator for this purpose was the California Personality Inventory (Gough, 1989). This measure identified students with low well-being and sociability scores as having the highest-risk profile. These students doubted their ability to perform under stressful conditions.

Measures of locus of control (LOC) (Lefcourt, 1982) identified other students highly susceptible to stress. These students could not adequately gain control of difficult environmental conditions and continually looked to others to help them solve their personal problems.

Programmatic changes were made in an attempt to reverse these problems. First, an extended freshman orientation period was initiated. Its purpose was to foster clearer expectations of the first-year experience at VMI. Students were shown videotapes of freshman activities, and programs were conducted to describe the purpose of the rigorous freshman-year experience. Second, a program for parents was initiated during the matriculation program to prepare them to provide support. Finally, an expanded summer transition program was also initiated to provide more extensive summer counseling. These efforts have resulted in the reorganization of the enrollment-management program at VMI, initiated during fall 1992 for the purpose of bringing all retention efforts together.

Changes in retention patterns occurred after these efforts were begun. There was an initial increase in attrition, attributed to the fact that entering students had been made more apprehensive. However, modifications in the orientation program were made to build an expectation of success, and a steady decline in attrition has resulted. Students report that they understand the goals of the freshman year and that they receive adequate information to develop realistic expectations. An important by-product of these efforts has been a broader institutional involvement in all aspects of freshman life.

These programs have contributed to the leveling effect that is the primary purpose of the freshman year at VMI. Even when controlling for attrition due to stress, student affective profiles converge significantly across the freshman and sophomore years. This finding confirms that development during this period is unitary and cumulative. All four institutional values described previously are, to the extent measurable, validated by these results.

Attrition Due to Academic Failure

Stress accounted for only half the attrition during the freshman year. Attrition because of academic failure also needed to be addressed by the assessment program. Traditional measures such as SAT scores have proven uneven predictors of academic success at VMI. Measures were needed that would not only provide predictive validity but also serve as diagnostic tools for individual students.

Cognitive and affective measures were used to fill gaps in student profiles left by traditional measures and to increase the predictive ability of these profiles. An analysis of data on the Myers-Briggs Type Indicator showed that (supporting the literature on the subject) students with the "extrovert-sensing" profile were at highest risk academically. These students are concrete, action-oriented thinkers who have difficulty with the abstract, global requirements of many courses in VMI's core curriculum.

Furthermore, an analysis of the Learning-Thinking Styles Inventory showed that students who were easily distracted and who scored low on metacognition (Flavell, 1979) and reading preference and high scores on concrete thinking were at greatest risk. These students have difficulty in internalizing effective problem-solving strategies and in monitoring their own thinking skills.

Students with an external LOC were at a significantly greater risk for academic failure than those with an internal locus of control. The literature shows that these "field dependent" students look outside themselves rather than accept responsibility for their own academic successes or failures. Also, students with low "self-efficacy" scores (Bandura, 1982; Schunk, 1984), measured in conjunction with LOC, were nearly three times as likely to suffer academic failure as those with high self-efficacy. These students lack the self-confidence and therefore the persistence to overcome academic problems.

Students with low facilitating and high debilitating anxiety, as measured by the Academic Anxiety Test (Gottfried, 1982; Sarason and Mandler, 1952), were high risks for academic failure. Finally, students higher in "dualistic" and lower in "commitment-level" thinking, as measured by the Scale of Intellectual Development (Erwin, 1983), were at risk academically.

Costly new programs have been initiated to assist students in overcoming the kinds of problems identified by assessment. First, the Learning Center was established, and positions were created from private funds for specialists. The Learning Center, initiated during the 1991–92 academic year, provides a broad spectrum of academic support services focused on the problems revealed by assessment. One learning-skills specialist was employed after a national search, and a second position for a specialist in minority advising is anticipated. Academic support modules have been designed to respond to the problems identified by the assessment program, and students receive individual counseling based on their learning profiles.

Second, a sophisticated electronic data base containing individual student information has been created to track student progress. The program can readily monitor changes in affective profiles as well as academic performance. The academic advising program has been modified to provide training in the use of student profiles and assessment instruments, and academic advisers have become the primary referral source for the Learning Center.

Finally, the writing program has been thoroughly revised using an intensive portfolio method of instruction. The program was redesigned to promote the internalization by students of the revision process to assist in building metacognitive skills in writing. Writing competence, the interaction of learning style and writing skill, and metacognitive skills for writing are monitored regularly (Miller and RiCharde, 1991).

Measurable changes in student performance and affective responses have occurred since the initiation of these activities. The attrition rate caused by academic failure during the freshman year has been greatly reduced. Mean grade-point averages for the freshman year have increased, and that increase has remained stable. The greatest reduction in academic failure has been among the minority population. Minority student profiles now show a significantly more adaptive motivational pattern than previously. A list of potential at-risk students is provided to each academic adviser during matriculation, and the resulting counseling has produced a significant improvement in overall freshman performance.

The rapid feedback provided by the electronic profile has permitted more timely and expeditious intervention strategies for students. Freshmen are now assigned to academic support services before the beginning of classes, resulting in a lower failure rate during the first grading period. There has been a measurable improvement among freshmen in overall writing ability in portfolio sections. Writing proficiency in the portfolio classes has increased significantly relative to traditional, literature-based classes. The ability to engage in revision and to monitor long-term writing assignments has increased in the portfolio sections.

Assessment data demonstrate that learning over the first two years is unitary and discontinuous. Further work is needed to make it more cumulative throughout the undergraduate experience. Plans include the initiation of required capstone courses in each discipline to promote the integration of knowledge in the major. Implementation of this change demonstrates the utility of a strong assessment program.

The institutional value of justice is served by the new writing program and academic support services since they assure equal treatment for all students and attempt to equalize entering skills. And although a high level of structure provided by an adversative model has contributed to the success of the Learning Center — students are assigned to activities at the Learning Center on a mandatory basis — a more nurturing environment within the learning modules has proven more effective for correcting academic deficiencies. The nurturing aspects of the learning-skills program within the highly structured framework of the adversative model seems to be a formula for providing meaningful intervention strategies.

Assessment data further show that the learning of writing through the portfolio method is unitary and discontinuous to the same degree as the traditional program. However, the learning of writing is significantly more cumulative as a result of the portfolio method.

Minority Student Attrition

There is higher academic failure but lower attrition due to stress for minority students than for majority students. The attrition of minorities for academic reasons has historically been higher than for other students. Though much concern has been expressed about this fact, little systematic analysis of these patterns and their possible causes had occurred until the assessment program was begun.

The expanded profiles of each student gathered through this program provided insight into the problem of retaining minorities. The profiles revealed that though minority students were at a distinct disadvantage in terms of traditional measures such as SAT scores, there was much about which to be optimistic in other spheres. For example, an analysis of the Scale of Intellectual Development revealed that students with higher dualism and lower commitment scores had consistently lower grade-point averages at VMI. Though minority students entered VMI with higher dualism and lower commitment scores, they reversed the trend at a faster rate; by the beginning of the junior year, there was no difference between minority and nonminority scores, even when other variables were held constant. Scores on this scale foreshadowed a correlative change in grade-point average by approximately one semester. Focus on the skills inherent in the movement from dualism to commitment has made possible more appropriate intervention strategies for minority students.

Students with higher self-efficacy scores are more persistent in their academic endeavors regardless of performance measured by grade-point average. Contrary to the "cultural-deficit hypothesis," minority students entering VMI did not differ significantly on mean entering efficacy scores. This finding showed that minority students required the same kind of assistance as nonminority students in matching their academic expectations to their abilities. However, since the entering skills of minorities were, on the average, lower than those of other students they needed more help in matching expectation to reality.

Students with higher metacognition scores perform better academically than those with lower scores. Minority students entered VMI with lower scores in this area but ascended rapidly to a position equal to that of nonminority students during the first two years of the undergraduate experience. In follow-up pilot programs, minority students showed a propensity to learn metacognitive skills and were motivated to do so. Metacognitive training was viewed by assessment personnel as a fertile ground for assisting minority students to attain academic coping skills more rapidly.

Special programs for minority advising and academic support were designed. A state-supported seed grant was obtained to train advisers. Minority advising was integrated into the new academic support programs, and a specialist was employed by the athletic department and given access to resources for academic support. Assessment profiles are now used by all personnel responsible for providing services to minority students. The summer transition program has taken on a new emphasis by providing tutorial sections for those at risk. Minority students now receive more specialized assistance at the beginning of their VMI experience and more opportunities to correct problems along the way.

A positive change in minority retention patterns has taken place, and deficiency rates have declined significantly. The greatest reduction in total academic failure rates has occurred in the minority population; in fact, the rates are beginning to approximate those for the student body as a whole.

The convergence of minority profiles provides additional evidence of the unitary and cumulative nature of learning and also of the institutional value of justice. Assessment has made differences in other ways at VMI, particularly in the area of curricular revision. However, there is no better demonstration of the impact of programs like assessment than their direct benefits to students.

Making a Difference at James Madison University

The developmental objectives of James Madison University are in marked contrast to those of VMI. JMU is committed to providing a broad liberal arts education to all students, with cognitive and affective development included among the general education goals of the institution. The contribution of curricular and cocurricular programs to student development is systematically assessed.

Developmental outcomes are as integral to the institution's comprehensive assessment plan as are outcomes in skills and knowledge. At the most fundamental level, affective and cognitive changes are assessed longitudinally during the first two years of college. Along with assessment of learning and skills levels, freshmen are tested during summer orientation to determine their (1) establishment of life purpose, using the Student Developmental Task and Lifestyle Inventory (SDTLI) (Winston and Miller, 1987); (2) level of relationship management skills, also using the SDTLI; (3) identity development, employing the Erwin Identity Scale (Erwin and Delworth, 1980); (4) intellectual growth, using the Scale of Intellectual Development (SID) (Erwin, 1983); and (5) moral-reasoning development, using the Defining Issues Test (Rest, 1987). Every spring, classes are canceled for one day so that sophomores can be tested on the same tests they took when they were incoming freshmen. This procedure allows an observation of developmental change during the first two years of college.

Although this approach evaluates changes over time, it does not provide much information about the contributions of specific programs to student development. JMU has been building on the affective development component of the assessment program by adding affective outcomes measures to the major, general education, and student affairs.

Making a Difference in Academic Affairs

A number of academic programs at JMU are including developmental outcomes in their learning and skill objectives. JMU students complete their general education coursework by selecting a specified number of courses within several distribution areas. For example, within the area of philosophy and religion, students choose from a variety of anthropology, classics, English, philosophy, and religion courses. The courses share no common components of knowledge because they represent different disciplines, theories, writers, and time periods. The aim of these general education courses is to change students' valuing and ethical reasoning from self-centered approaches through a peer-centered approach to a humanitarian reasoning style (Erwin, 1991; O'Meara, 1990).

Similarly, the general education distribution area of fine arts/aesthetics has evolved into an aesthetic-developmental framework; there is no expectation of a common knowledge content among art, music, dance, and theater courses. Furthermore,

hierarchical stages of aesthetic development have been concep-
tualized as follows: (1) perceptions of subject matter; (2) perception of emotion-interpretation, (3) historical perspective-syn-
thesis, (4) perception of form-analysis, and (5) perception of
worth-evaluation (Reynolds, 1992). Assessment methods were
constructed locally to measure these developmental approaches
in philosophy, religion, and aesthetic development.

Making a Difference in Student Affairs

The greatest effort to assess the contribution of JMU to student affective and cognitive development has been concentrated
in the area of student affairs. Cocurricular activities at JMU
that provide learning experiences that cannot be simulated in
the classroom are considered an important part of students'
educational experience.

The very process of designing assessments in student
affairs has affected program design. At JMU, departments involved in student affairs often present one-time workshops or
program series covering topics that are loosely associated under
a specific theme such as leadership. Explicit articulation of student outcome goals has seldom occurred. The first step in assessment design, however, is the establishment of expected outcomes. Coordinators found that this process created a different
perspective on program development.

An example of the impact of assessment on program development can be observed in the Emerging Leaders Program.
The program was designed primarily for freshmen who were
recommended to the program by faculty or staff because of perceived leadership potential. The program, with different coordinators each year, consisted of a series of six two-hour sessions
covering topics chosen because they represented some association with the broad topic of leadership and because an appropriate staff or faculty member was available to conduct the meeting.

Throughout the process of designing the program, the coordinators engaged in the task of moving the broad, abstract goal
of developing leadership abilities toward something more focused
and measurable. Knowing that a six-week period had limitations

for making changes in student development, the coordinators chose the objective of developing appreciation of cultural and personal diversity—one not addressed in any other program. The coordinators attempted to introduce students to the complexity of organizational environments awaiting them if they accepted student leadership positions. The coordinators also made a special effort to recruit minority students in order to create a diverse demographic mix. The students were tested with the SID before and after the class to see if they became less dualistic and more committed to their own values as well as more empathic toward others, characteristics that Perry (1970) asserts are representative of higher levels of intellectual development.

Although an analysis of the data revealed that no significant changes in intellectual development occurred, it did reveal that freshmen entered the Emerging Leaders Program with higher levels of commitment and empathy than other JMU freshmen. The Emerging Leaders Program apparently was not sufficiently challenging to change these students' previous levels of intellectual development. This finding has had an effect on plans for a new leadership center that will allow a variety of programs. Coordinators of the center are designing methods to recruit students whose leadership ability is less obvious and also to challenge students at higher levels of development.

The Office of Career Services has used formative and summative assessment results in designing a career-planning class offered for academic credit. This six-week workshop focused on a wide range of career-seeking skills, such as setting career goals, researching careers and companies, and writing résumés. The students were assessed before and after the class on career decisiveness using the Career Decision Scale (CDS) (Osipow, 1987). Results showed a significant increase in decisiveness over the course of the program.

Soon after the class ended, information was released from the Office of Registration indicating that the number of undeclared majors was increasing. This information led the Office of Student Assessment to analyze freshman scores on the establishing and defining purpose subtask (PUR) of the SDTLI. This subtask measures the extent to which students have developed a sense of career and life goals. Freshmen who had not declared majors entered college with significantly lower PUR scores than those who had. Career services coordinators believed that their class, with data supporting its success, could meet this increasing developmental need of entering freshmen. They have added a section of the class to serve more students and hope to offer the class in residence halls.

The use of the PUR scores is one example of how formative evaluation can assist programming in student affairs. Another involved a fall 1990 analysis by the Office of Student Affairs of the students who used the recreational facilities, such as weight rooms, aerobics classes, and the basketball courts. Erwin Identity Scale scores for nonusers were compared to those of high users (five or more times a week). Two different studies were conducted. First, students' EIS scores as entering freshmen and as second-semester sophomores were compared longitudinally to see if frequency of fitness facility use was related to identity development. Second, EIS scores of freshmen were compared to see if level of identity development was related to use of facilities during the first semester of college.

Results indicated that most sophomores who used the facilities showed greater levels of sexual identity development during their first two years of college. Analysis of the freshman data revealed that the high users entered college with significantly lower confidence about their physical appearance. The study was not carefully controlled, so it is not known if use of the fitness facility was the only or even primary effect on sophomores' sexual identity development. The research did, however, yield helpful information. The coordinators of a new, popular fitness facility are now offering programs on sexuality and self-esteem. The programs have been well attended because the facility is convenient and because students who are exercising at the time of presentation often are captivated by the topic.

JMU has conducted a transition program for minority students (primarily African-Americans) who do not meet the entrance requirements of the school. Research had indicated that although the transition students' grade-point averages were lower than those of the average African-American JMU student, retention rates among the transition students were higher. Therefore, an assessment program was designed to explore the contribution of affective development to the transition students' ability to persist in college. In fact, the assessment showed that transition students became more in touch with their African-American identity, more concerned about their wellness, more autonomous and confident about their physical well-being, and better money managers. Several other outcomes — specifically, perceived competence in math, writing, and time management — showed no measurable improvement. The positive information helped document the value of the program, and the other findings have guided program changes.

Another use of assessment data emerged from a study evaluating the effect of Greek life on students' identity and moral-reasoning development during the first two years of college. Males in fraternities did not show as much confidence as non-Greeks of both sexes and Greek females; sorority females did not develop moral-reasoning ability as much as non-Greeks and Greek males (Kilgannon and Erwin, 1992). Students were asked to respond to the findings. For the most part, they decided that the findings were tentative, since students were tested midway through their Greek experience, and requested that a similar study be conducted using seniors. This study is planned for senior fraternity and sorority members to explore further the effect of Greek life on student development.

Effecting Change with Affective Measures

This chapter has provided examples of how affective measures used in the assessment programs of two very different Virginia colleges have helped them implement their missions and have transformed institutional approaches to specific development problems. As assessment programs become increasingly institutionalized and as accountability becomes a routine matter, the students entering our colleges will benefit from dramatic new means of conducting the business of higher education. As indicated here, assessment is helping colleges expand their interest from the traditional curricular concerns to the total developmental processes promised in mission statements nationwide. In fact, the greatest legacy of the assessment phenomenon may be that it helps the nation's colleges find new ways to make good on old promises. The emphasis on developmental outcomes offers promise of documenting the benefit of general education, academic support services, and student affairs. In a changing world where knowledge can quickly become obsolete, cognitive and affective development may be regarded as outcomes upon which higher education can have an enduring impact.

References

Bandura, A. "Self-Efficacy Mechanism in Human Agency." *American Psychologist,* 1982, *37,* 122–147.

Briggs-Myers, I. "Myers-Briggs Type Indicator." Palo Alto, Calif.: Consulting Psychologists Press, 1976.

Corrallo, S. "Critical Concerns in Assessing Selected Higher-Order Thinking and Communication Skills of College Graduates." *Assessment Update,* 1991, *5*(6), 5–6.

Erwin, T. D. "The Scale of Intellectual Development: Measuring Perry's Scheme." *Journal of College Student Personnel,* 1983, *24,* 6–12.

Erwin, T. D. *Assessing Student Learning and Development: A Guide to the Principles, Goals, and Methods of Determining College Outcomes.* San Francisco: Jossey-Bass, 1991.

Erwin, T. D., and Delworth, U. "An Instrument to Measure Chickering's Vector of Identity." *NASPA Journal,* 1980, *17,* 19–24.

Feldman, K. A., and Newcomb, T. M. *The Impact of College on Students.* San Francisco: Jossey-Bass, 1969.

Flavell, J. H. "Metacognition and Cognitive Monitoring: A New Area of Cognitive-Developmental Inquiry." *American Psychologist,* 1979, *34,* 906–911.

Gottfried, A. E. "Relationships Between Academic Intrinsic Motivation and Anxiety in Children and Young Adolescents: Children's Academic Anxiety Inventory." *Journal of School Psychology,* 1982, *20*(3), 205–215.

Gough, H. G. *California Psychological Inventory Administrator's Guide.* Palo Alto, Calif.: Consulting Psychologists Press, 1989.

Howard, A. "College Experiences and Managerial Performance." *Journal of Applied Psychology,* 1986, *71,* 530–552.

Kilgannon, S., and Erwin, T. D. "A Longitudinal Study About the Identity and Moral Development of Greek Students." *Journal of College Student Development,* 1992, *33,* 253–259.

Lefcourt, H. M. *Locus of Control: Current Trends in Theory and Research* (2nd ed.) Hillsdale, N.J.: Erlbaum, 1982.

Miller, E. P., and RiCharde, R. S. "The Relationship Between the Portfolio Method of Teaching Writing and Measures of Personality and Motivation." Paper presented to the Conference on College Composition and Communication, Boston, Mar. 1991. (ED 332 184)

O'Meara, W. "Assessment of Liberal Studies Courses in Philosophy/Religion/Values." Presentation at the 4th annual Virginia Assessment Group/State Council for Higher Education in Virginia Conference on Student Assessment, Virginia Beach, Va., 1990.

Osipow, S. H. *Manual for Career Decision Scale.* Odessa, Fla.: Psychological Assessment Resources, 1987.

Pascarella, E. T., and Terenzini, P. T. *How College Affects Students: Insights from Twenty Years of Research.* San Francisco: Jossey-Bass, 1991.

Perry, W. G. *Forms of Intellectual and Ethical Development in the College Years.* Troy, Mo.: Holt, Rinehart & Winston, 1970.

Rest, J. *Guide for the Defining Issues Test.* Minneapolis, Minn.: Center for the Study of Ethical Development, 1987.

Reynolds, G. A. "Assessment Report: Fine Arts, Liberal Studies Component." Unpublished report, Office of Student Assessment, James Madison University, 1992.

Sarason, S. B., and Mandler, G. "Some Correlates of Test Anxiety." *Journal of Abnormal and Social Psychology,* 1952, *47,* 561–565.

Schunk, D. H. "Self-Efficacy Perspective on Achievement Behavior." *Educational Psychologist,* 1984, *19,* 48–58.

Study Group on the Conditions of Excellence in American Higher Education, National Institute of Education. *Involvement in Learning: Realizing the Potential of American Higher Education.* Washington, D.C.: U.S. Government Printing Office, 1984.

Winston, R. B., Jr., and Miller, T. K. *Student Developmental Task and Lifestyle Inventory Manual.* Athens, Ga.: Student Development Associates, 1987.

13

The Community College Student Experiences Questionnaire

Jack Friedlander
Patricia H. Murrell
Peter R. MacDougall

An extensive body of evidence accumulated over the past two decades demonstrates the strong relationship between student involvement and achievement. The studies show that the more time and effort students invest in the academic and social opportunities available in the college environment, the greater will be their academic achievement and personal growth, their satisfaction with college, and their persistence in college (National Institute of Education, 1984; Astin, 1985; Pace, 1989). This chapter describes how community colleges are using the Community College Student Experiences Questionnaire (Friedlander, Pace, and Lehman, 1990) to understand and promote student involvement and achievement. It concludes with a series of recommendations on how to increase the likelihood that the results of assessment programs will affect college practices.

Description of the CCSEQ

The Community College Student Experiences Questionnaire (CCSEQ) is a standardized self-report survey instrument that evaluates students' level of involvement in desired in-class and out-of-class learning activities. It also measures the degree of progress students feel they have made in achieving desired educational outcomes. More specifically, the CCSEQ measures the amount, breadth, and quality of effort students put into taking advantage of the resources and opportunities available in the college setting: in course-related activities; in the library; in contacts with faculty members, counselors, and other students; in activities related to art, athletics, music, sciences, theater, and writing; and in participation in clubs and organizations.

The questionnaire also assesses student satisfaction with various aspects of college, such as the extent to which they find their courses to be challenging, stimulating, and worthwhile and the quality of their interactions with faculty, counselors, and other students. Achievement is measured by asking students how much progress they have made toward twenty-three important educational goals related to effective communication skills; career development; personal and social development; and knowledge in the humanities, sciences, social sciences, and technologies.

The CCSEQ has been shown to be a valid measure of quality of effort and an effective method of describing the experiences of community college students based on student involvement theory (Lehman, 1991). It has been completed by over six thousand students in thirty-three community colleges. Studies show that there are substantial differences in the levels at which students take advantage of the opportunities available for learning in the college setting; they also reveal that the greater the involvement, the greater the progress students feel they have made. For example, the more time and effort students devote to writing, the more improvement they feel they make in learning how to write clearly and effectively (Friedlander, 1990b). These results are similar to those obtained in four-year institutions using a version of the CCSEQ designed for them (Pace, 1989).

An important finding of these studies (both at community colleges and four-year institutions) is that the amount and quality of participation in learning activities are more important determinants of student achievement in college than such factors as age, ethnicity, number of hours employed, high school grade-point average, and marital status (Friedlander, 1980; Pace, 1982, 1984; Friedlander, 1990b). Such findings support Pace's conclusion (1982): "Granted the importance of all the elements that influence who goes where to college, once the student gets there what counts most is not who they are or where they are but what they do" (p. 19). This conclusion, based on studies of students attending the full spectrum of colleges and universities, is very powerful.

Applications of CCSEQ Findings

Structured interviews were conducted by members of the authors' staffs with individuals involved in administering the CCSEQ at twenty-six of the community colleges located across the United States that have used the instrument. The purpose was to identify how the results of the CCSEQ were being utilized.

The primary reasons for using the CCSEQ were to collect data for an institution's self-study for accreditation or to meet state mandates. Of the community colleges contacted, eighteen reported that the CCSEQ findings were used in devising and implementing specific strategies for increasing student participation and achievement. Of the remaining eight institutions, four were in the process of analyzing the data, and four had no plans to use the information due to the lack of staff resources.

At colleges where the CCSEQ was part of the self-study for accreditation, the results were analyzed by a research or planning office and sent to various campus committees or units to review for possible implications in their areas. The expectation was that the findings would stimulate the development of program initiatives in desired areas. Most institutions indicated plans to readminister the CCSEQ within two or three years to determine if progress was being made in those areas of student attainment that the college was trying to affect. One of the colleges was using the CCSEQ to promote continuous improvement within its total quality management program.

A variety of approaches for increasing student involvement have been based on CCSEQ findings. These efforts include

incorporating a module on the importance of student participation and initiative into a college's new-student orientation program, experimenting with new instructional techniques to promote student involvement in desired course-related learning
activities, awarding extra points to students who participate in
out-of-class activities that had some relationship to the course
content, and revising a humanities course to incorporate general
education areas in which many students reported that they had
not made much progress.

An important finding of the interviews was that few colleges had systematically planned how the results of the CCSEQ
would be analyzed, presented to staff, or incorporated into planning processes. In most instances, efforts to use the CCSEQ
findings to effect changes in instructional and student services
programs arose from individual or department initiatives done
on an ad hoc basis. For example, faculty members in the English
department at one community college in California were surprised to find that a relatively high percentage of the students
at the college had not used the resources in the library in preparing course-related papers and projects. The English department
faculty met and devised strategies to ensure that its students used
the library as a research tool and is encouraging faculty in other
departments to do so as well.

Santa Barbara City College (SBCC), in California, is one
of the few colleges that has systematically included the assessment of student involvement, satisfaction, and achievement in
its institutional planning process. The following case study describes how the CCSEQ has been used at the institution.

Using the CCSEQ at Santa Barbara City College

Santa Barbara City College is a comprehensive community college in California that serves over twelve thousand students each
semester in its credit programs and an additional thirty-three
thousand in its noncredit division. The CCSEQ is an integral
component of SBCC's model for planning and assessing institutional effectiveness. The college administered preliminary versions of the CCSEQ to cross sections of its students in 1987 and

1989 and used the instrument for a third time in fall 1992. In addition, specific components of the CCSEQ have helped in the evaluation of the effectiveness of various classroom and student services research projects.

Involvement of College Staff in the Use of the CCSEQ

The CCSEQ was selected with the clear expectation that it would yield information to assist the college faculty and staff in promoting student learning. To increase the likelihood that the results of the CCSEQ would be used, one or more members of the Institutional Research Committee met with the organizational units in a position to affect student involvement. The purpose of these meetings was to discuss this concept and the way it is measured by the CCSEQ and to explore possible applications of the findings by members of the organizational unit, such as the Social Sciences Division, counseling department, and Student Senate. The discussion of this effort with each of the units was guided by the principle that institutional change happens at the program, departmental, and individual level.

Integration of the CCSEQ into the College Planning Process

The college's planning committee reviewed the findings and implications for college practices resulting from the CCSEQ study. This committee recommended that efforts to promote student involvement be included in the institution's two-year plan and that student involvement and achievement be included in SBCC's measures of institutional effectiveness, further integrating these ideas into the way the college does business.

Statement of Institutional Directions

The comprehensive planning process at SBCC is guided by its mission statement and specifically its Statements of Institutional Directions (SIDs), specific strategies for achieving institutional objectives. The SIDs focus on measurable outcomes. To illustrate, the following goal statement related to promoting student involvement was included in the 1991–92 Statement of Institutional Directions: "The College will strive to increase student participation in College activities and to promote student responsibility. To achieve this goal, the College will: (1) increase student participation in department-based clubs, associations, and applied learning opportunities; (2) develop systems through which students may evaluate periodically their progress toward achieving educational goal(s); and (3) increase faculty emphasis on promoting active modes of student learning in their courses" (Santa Barbara City College, 1991, p. 3).

Initiatives for Promoting Student Involvement

The faculty and staff included in their two-year unit plans a variety of excellent strategies for increasing student participation in desired learning activities (Friedlander and MacDougall, 1992). The efforts proposed by the department and units were in response to specific findings and recommendations emanating from the CCSEQ assessment project.

Efforts to Increase Student Participation in Course-Related Activities. In each of the past three years, SBCC has allocated funds to support faculty classroom research projects designed to try an array of instructional strategies for increasing student involvement. Faculty have developed projects to encourage student participation in activities that would enhance their skills in such areas as critical thinking, independent inquiry, writing, class participation, and collaborative learning with students from different cultural and ethnic backgrounds. The evaluation component in many of these projects contained CCSEQ items measuring the student behavior that the instructional strategy was designed to affect.

Efforts to Increase Student Contacts with Faculty. CCSEQ responses revealed that almost half of the students at Santa Barbara City College had not met with a faculty member outside class, and many had had only minimal individual contacts with their instructors. These results were similar to those found at other community colleges (Lehman, 1992) and also at four-year institutions (Pace, 1989). These findings were significant because research studies have consistently shown that the more extensive the interactions students have with their instructors, the greater will be their personal growth, their satisfaction with college, and their persistence there (Astin, 1985).

In response to these findings, a faculty advising program was introduced to increase the frequency and depth of out-of-class contacts between students and faculty in their major field of study. Faculty selected to participate in this program receive training in advising students and in working collaboratively with counselors assigned to their majors. An evaluation of this program (Friedlander, 1990a) showed that it has had a positive impact on student-faculty interaction and student retention.

Efforts to Increase Student Involvement in Out-of-Class Activities. CCSEQ responses revealed that a large percentage of students at SBCC, like students at many commuter campuses, had not taken advantage of the out-of-class learning activities provided by the college. This was particularly the case in the degree of student participation in fine arts activities (art, music, and theater performances), activities sponsored by campus clubs and organizations, and special events designed to enrich campus life (such as the college's noon-hour lecture series). The faculty and staff responded to these findings by developing a number of ingenious programs.

To increase the likelihood that students would attend the theater, faculty members from the English and theater arts departments devised the idea of having English 1 classes (college-level reading and composition) study a play that the theater arts department would be performing that semester. Students in the English 1 class discussed the play with the director and the cast from theater arts, attended a performance of the production in the SBCC theater, and participated in a postplay discussion. This interdepartmental project, which has been in place for three years, has exposed over a thousand students who might otherwise not have seen a play to the theater. Participation in subsequent college-sponsored plays has also increased.

Several faculty and staff members responded to the challenge by linking the out-of-class events for which they were responsible to specific courses. For example, students in philosophy classes were required to write a critique of the presentations made by speakers participating in the noon-hour lecture series. The students were asked to identify the presenter's thesis, to discuss how it was supported, and to describe how much they were persuaded by the arguments presented. Students who could not attend the live lecture were asked to view a videotape of the event. Linking course-related assignments to this extracurricular activity revealed to hundreds of students the enjoyment of attending public lectures; it also taught them how to be active listeners who can critically evaluate information. Such an outcome is particularly important in a media-intensive information society.

Efforts to Increase Student Involvement in Educational Planning Activities. The CCSEQ includes items for assessing student participation in goal-setting and academic-planning activities designed to facilitate achievement of their transfer and career education objectives. By allowing students to seek information on routine matters, the college was unwittingly creating unnecessary dependency. Members of the SBCC counseling department have therefore developed transfer task and career advancement inventories. These checklists provide students with a detailed structured map of the activities they should complete to achieve their transfer or career objectives in the most efficient and educationally sound manner. The responsibility for accomplishing educational objectives is thus shifted from the college staff to the student.

As an additional effort to reduce student dependency, the college has revised its orientation, advising, and counseling programs to encourage students to be active participants in their use of these services rather than passive recipients of information provided by college staff. For example, the college is experimenting with approaches that require students to complete directed preliminary work on the questions to which they are seeking answers before they can meet with an academic or career counselor or other support staff. Subsequent administrations of the CCSEQ may include items to assess the extent to which students use independent learning strategies to acquire needed information.

Changes in College Practices
to Encourage Student Involvement

At Santa Barbara City College, the commitment to promote student involvement has been incorporated into procedures for faculty hiring, department program review, and staff development. To illustrate, candidates for faculty and administrative positions are questioned about their knowledge of strategies in this area. Questions about the efforts taken by faculty and staff to promote student involvement have also been incorporated into program review procedures.

As a result of responses to the CCSEQ, the Campus Center renovation plan was modified to allow for more meeting space for student clubs and organizations and to provide a comfortable environment for students to study together. The changes also accommodate the college's goal of increasing the number of students who participate in campus-based jobs and organizations.

Using the CCSEQ at a Tennessee Consortium

Four west Tennessee community colleges administered the CCSEQ as part of a consortium effort in collaboration with the Center for the Study of Higher Education at Memphis State University. Shelby State Community College, Dyersburg State Community College, Jackson State Community College, and State Technical Institute, Memphis, each wrote its own research questions and selected a population to study. Results of the various efforts have provided the basis for a dialogue among the institutions as they search for ways to improve the involvement of their students. The group has discussed several major questions, including: What does involvement mean in a predominantly part-time, commuter student body? How can involvement be accomplished when the student's major interaction and contact with the institution is the classroom? How can students be encouraged to connect their classroom learning with their out-of-class activities, whether on or off campus?

Institutional uses of the instrument are varied. Dyersburg State Community College reports extensive use of the CCSEQ data in strategic planning that has involved people from the president to alumni representatives. Faculty view the instrument very positively; they report that it finally gets to something they care about and can influence, like writing assignments, library use, and what happens in their classrooms. State Technical Institute at Memphis draws on the CCSEQ findings as baseline data about the quality of operations in various aspects of the institution as it moves into a program of total quality management. Consortium members are consistently positive in their views of the CCSEQ. One individual stated, "It has made us a more learned learning community!"

Use of the CCSEQ to Address Special Concerns

The Tennessee Board of Regents funded the consortial project in an effort to ascertain similarities and differences in the social and academic integration of black and white students at the four campuses. Data from the four institutions were aggregated for 633 students, 176 black and 457 white. Social integration was gauged by work and family responsibilities, time spent on campus, involvement with extracurricular activities, views of the campus environment, and interactions in classrooms and with students, the faculty, and other personnel. Data about academic transfer and vocational aspirations; student status and course-taking patterns; science activities; vocational studies; writing, speaking, and learning skills; library and computer use; gains in dispositions and content relative to general education; and self-reported grades were viewed as representative of academic or programmatic participation.

On the whole, black and white students' experiences were not dramatically different. In fact, the similarities in quality of effort, engagement, and participation, both socially and academically, are remarkably strong. Both groups appear to be involved in social and academic experiences at about the same levels of regularity and intensity, with modest variations. Although the scope of the study and the size of the sample were both quite small, the instrument proved its merit as a valuable tool for making comparisons across many groups (Faith and Murrell, 1992).

Use in Alumni Studies

One of the consortium members, Jackson State Community College, incorporated fifteen items from the CCSEQ into the survey instrument sent to alumni two years after they graduated. A comparison of the alumni responses with those of current students revealed that the two groups felt that they had made inadequate progress in basically the same areas. The results of these surveys are being reviewed by the Strategic Planning Commission at Jackson State. The ability to connect alumni satisfaction more directly to student involvement gives institutions solid evidence on which to base programmatic changes. The findings of this pilot project conducted at Jackson State Community College are consistent with results of alumni surveys of graduates of four-year institutions. These studies have shown that the patterns of the graduates' activities and interests as adults, and the particular benefits that they attribute to their college experience, are generally parallel to the patterns of emphasis in their major field curriculum and the environment of the college they attended (Pace, 1989).

Use of the CCSEQ in Institutional Self-Studies

As previously noted, most of the colleges that used the CCSEQ did so as part of the self-study process for institutional accreditation or to meet a state assessment requirement. This fact attests to the strengths of the CCSEQ in enabling colleges to examine the extent to which students are making progress toward a range of goals, particularly those emphasized by the college.

The CCSEQ brings the added dimension of evaluating the interactive processes between students and the institution. Much of the assessment of the effect of college on students has centered on the links between age, ethnicity, entering test scores, high school grade-point average, or number of hours employed to variables such as persistence, achievement test scores, grade-point average, or other exit criteria. The opportunity to determine exactly where the learner and the environment make contact and to examine the degree of interaction between the two informs educational leaders about ways to influence and balance the delicate social contract that exists between students and their institutions. Such information provides important depth to assessment efforts.

Use of the CCSEQ in Assessing Student Preparation for Transfer

Many of the items on the Community College Student Experiences Questionnaire are also included in the version of this instrument used in four-year colleges and universities (Pace 1984, 1990). The responses of students at Santa Barbara City College who planned to transfer to a four-year college or university were compared to those of freshmen and sophomores attending four-year colleges and universities represented in a national data set (Pace, 1989). The purpose in making these comparisons was to determine the extent to which the lower-division experiences of transfer-oriented students at Santa Barbara City College were similar to those of lower-division students who began their studies at a four-year institution. The results of these comparisons revealed that in many ways the educational experiences of SBCC students were at least comparable, if not richer, than those of students in four-year colleges and universities. Areas in which the college needed to work harder were identified and addressed.

The CCSEQ, used in conjunction with the College Student Experiences Questionnaire administered to students at four-year institutions to which the college's students transfer, can compare the involvement, satisfaction, and gains toward achieving desired educational outcomes among comparable groups of students at the respective institutions. Such information could also serve as a valuable advising tool in showing community college students the level of effort they will need to make to be successful at a particular four-year institution.

Recommendations

Are assessment programs involving the use of the CCSEQ making a difference in student learning and development? At many community colleges, the answer is yes. When coupled with the experience of other institutions, several factors emerge as instrumental in ensuring that the results of the CCSEQ translate into practices that promote student learning:

1. Decisions to use the CCSEQ will have the greatest impact if based on strong commitment from the college president, faculty, and staff leaders to student involvement theory and the research upon which it is based. This high level of visibility and support is a critical factor if student participation is to become embedded in the culture or ethos of the institution.
2. Commitment to student involvement and the means for assessing it should be integrated into the ongoing institutional planning and evaluation process of the college and should be reflected in its measures of institutional effectiveness.
3. The involvement of faculty and staff in the design and implementation of the process, the interpretation of the results, and the development of recommendations for their respective areas is essential. This approach is consistent with the premise that institutional change happens at program, departmental, and individual levels.
4. Departmental strategies for promoting student involvement and a high priority for their funding can result in the development of many creative initiatives for enhancing student participation in desired learning activities.
5. Faculty and staff should be encouraged and given visibility for their efforts in promoting student involvement. Recognition can be provided in public forums, college publications, and memos from the president and deans; it can also take the form of internal funding of projects and assistance in acquiring external funding to support innovative ideas.
6. New initiatives to promote student involvement should contain an evaluation component. Such studies conducted at the

local level can heighten interest in and commitment to student involvement.

7. Decisions to use the CCSEQ should include plans for analyzing and disseminating the results. The amount of data generated can be overwhelming, and care should be taken to translate the data into information useful to both institutional decision makers and practitioners.

The CCSEQ gives community colleges a blueprint for operationalizing the theoretical concepts of student involvement and engagement. Items translate neatly and easily into institutional programs, policies, and classroom practices that make sense to both faculty members and administrators. If attributes such as responsibility and accountability are not developed in students, the danger is a culture of dependency in which students expect more and more of the institution and spend less of their time and effort on their educational endeavors. The result may not only be increased labor and costs for the institution but also the stunted growth and development of students. Creating an environment that teaches the value of effort encourages self-directed learning and habits of responsibility that will carry over into the work setting and into family and civic life.

References

Astin, A. W. *Achieving Educational Excellence: A Critical Assessment of Priorities and Practices in Higher Education.* San Francisco: Jossey-Bass, 1985.

Faith, E. S., and Murrell, P. H. "The Social and Academic Integration of Black and White Students: A Pilot Study of Four Two-Year Institutions in West Tennessee Using the CCSEQ." Memphis, Tenn.: Center for the Study of Higher Education, Memphis State University, 1992.

Friedlander, J. "The Importance of Quality of Effort in Predicting Student Attainment." Unpublished doctoral dissertation, Graduate School of Education, University of California, Los Angeles, 1980.

Friedlander, J. "Evaluation of Santa Barbara City College's Faculty Advising Program." Unpublished paper, Santa Barbara City College, 1990a.

Friedlander, J. "The Quality of Students' Educational Experiences at Santa Barbara City College." Unpublished paper, Santa Barbara City College, 1990b.

Friedlander, J., and MacDougall, P. R. "Achieving Student Success Through Student Involvement." *Community College Review,* 1992, *2*(1), 20–28.

Friedlander, J., Pace, C. R., and Lehman, P. W. *The Community College Student Experiences Questionnaire.* Los Angeles: Center for the Study of Evaluation, University of California, Los Angeles, 1990.

Lehman, P. W. "Assessing the Quality of Community College Student Experiences: A New Measurement Instrument." Unpublished doctoral dissertation, Graduate School of Education, University of California, Los Angeles, 1991.

Lehman, P. W. *CCSEQ: Test Manual and Comparative Data.* Los Angeles: Center for the Study of Evaluation, University of California, Los Angeles, 1992.

National Institute of Education, Study Group on the Conditions of Excellence in American Higher Education. *Involvement in Learning: Realizing the Potential of American Higher Education.* Washington, D.C.: U.S. Government Printing Office, 1984.

Pace, C. R. "Achievement and the Quality of Student Effort." Washington, D.C.: U.S. Department of Education, 1982. (ED 227 101)

Pace, C. R. *Measuring the Quality of College Student Experiences.* Los Angeles: Center for the Study of Evaluation, University of California, Los Angeles, 1984.

Pace, C. R. *The Undergraduates: A Report of Their Activities and Progress in College in the 1990s.* Los Angeles: Center for the Study of Evaluation, University of California, Los Angeles, 1989.

Pace, C. R. *The College Student Experiences Questionnaire.* Los Angeles: Center for the Study of Evaluation, University of California, Los Angeles, 1990.

Santa Barbara City College. *Statement of Institutional Directions, 1991–92 to 1992–93.* Santa Barbara, Calif.: Santa Barbara City College, 1991.

14

Classroom Assessment

Susan Sellman Obler
Julie Slark
Linda Umbdenstock

Most current measures of institutional effectiveness in community colleges focus on the end product: transfer rates, number of degrees earned, grades, job placement, salaries. These measures tend to be taken after the fact and do not contribute easily to program transformation. However, a number of cross-institution assessment projects in California have helped community colleges focus on student learning as it happens, using classroom assessment to improve learning on the spot. Because the long-range purpose of educational assessment is to assist teaching and learning, colleges need models and developmental processes that yield immediate and relevant information about how education occurs. Such information could be used by the person on the front line—the classroom teacher—to shape the teaching and learning process while it is still in progress.

Classroom research, an approach developed by K. Patricia Cross of the University of California, Berkeley, and Thomas A. Angelo of Boston College, involves teachers in ongoing, systematic study of teaching and learning within their own classrooms in order to understand and improve them. Unlike other evaluation initiatives, classroom research begins with the premise that faculty are uniquely empowered to lead the research in teaching effectiveness and, by extension, student learning. Classroom assessment is one method under the larger umbrella of classroom research. Through classroom assessment, instructors learn more about how their students learn and how they respond to particular teaching approaches.

The purpose of classroom assessment is twofold: (1) to improve student learning, especially in higher-order cognitive skills such as synthesis, analysis, and evaluation, and (2) to revitalize faculty members' engagement in their students' learning. Classroom assessment narrows the gap between research and practice in higher education by providing direct, immediate, and continuous feedback on the effect of teaching on student learning, giving teachers the opportunity to immediately modify their strategies.

Cross and Angelo (1988) prescribe thirty such assessment methods in *Classroom Assessment Techniques: A Handbook for Faculty*. A much-revised and expanded second edition is now available (Angelo and Cross, 1993). Most of the techniques are simple to use and yield results that are quick and easy to interpret. One of the simplest, for example, is to ask students to write two or three sentences in a "one-minute" paper in which they summarize recently acquired concepts or skills. Students' responses are not graded; they merely provide the instructor with information on whether students actually learned what was taught. A teacher of history, for example, might want to know what students have learned during three class meetings covering a particular phase of the American Civil War. If the *range* of responses suggests that students will not grasp the next phase without further help, the instructor can provide a handout reviewing the material. Another classroom assessment technique (CAT), described in the second edition (Angelo and Cross, 1993), has to do with the "muddiest point." Here, students would be asked to jot down the most and least clear points made during a class session. Most users of classroom assessment ask for anonymous feedback so that students can respond as honestly as possible. These methods do not replace testing, but they provide quick, routine, and frequent feedback on classroom learning. Some teachers use these techniques six to eight times in a term; many use them for up to five minutes every time the class meets. Invariably, the best results occur when faculty report results directly to their students, thereby increasing the collaborative spirit of a shared learning experience.

Launching Classroom Assessment Through Consortia

In California community colleges, a series of consortia have spread the training and uses of classroom assessment. Cross and Angelo began the Classroom Research Project with support from the Pew Charitable Trusts and the Ford Foundation in 1988. In that same year, they began working with community colleges in the San Francisco Bay area. In 1989, two major consortia began their work with classroom assessment. The Learning Assessment Retention Consortium (LARC Network) received a grant from the Fund for the Improvement of Postsecondary Education to develop training programs for thirty-six community colleges across California over three years (Kelemen-Lohnas, 1992). Rio Hondo College in southern California also received a grant (Title III) for projects in classroom assessment in four colleges over five years (Obler, 1992). In these projects, many faculty participants were trained by Thomas Angelo. Often, six to ten faculty members, from a range of disciplines and programs, worked together for a semester to use and to adapt various Cross-Angelo techniques and to refine their teaching and learning approaches in response to student feedback.

Other consortia have evolved from these projects. One is a two-year, ten-college network known as Beacon Associate Colleges (which is also coordinated at Rio Hondo College). This project is funded by the American Association of Community Colleges to expand the training and piloting model developed in the Title III consortium. The special focus of the Beacon College project is on training faculty to advance and assess "prodiversity" goals with their students (Sigala, 1992). The goals are to increase materials and methods fostering this approach to the curriculum and to reduce the negative images of or attitudes toward groups on the margin of American society (this effort is sometimes known as the antibias curriculum).

Another consortium stems from the LARC-FIPSE project; it came about as a result of a 1992 California Community College Chancellor's grant, which provides funding to twelve colleges for classroom assessment projects in northern California. Coordinated at Napa College, these colleges will continue the training and the classroom assessment work that began with the FIPSE project.

Still another and broader California project integrates classroom assessment into training in adult education principles for the occupational education faculty. Funded in 1992 through the Carl Perkins Act, it includes regional workshops accessible to all of the over one hundred California community colleges (Kelly, 1991). The authors of this chapter directed or were involved in three of these consortia: the LARC-FIPSE project, the Title III consortium, and the Beacon College project. The reports and documentation of these and similar programs are the primary sources for this chapter.

Documenting the Difference

Each consortium project employed numerous and distinct ways of documenting how and when it was making a difference in teaching and learning. The data included in the extensive project reports were gathered through retention statistics, open-ended student surveys, faculty surveys and interviews, faculty and student focus groups, classroom assignments such as learning logs, and numerous complete sets of classroom assessment responses. Some colleges produced training videos; others converted their results into readers' theater dramatizations of how the classroom was affected by the use of classroom assessment. Within this extensive documentation, the projects have realized consistent, promising results, including some consequential effects on the culture of colleges and their classrooms. Across the colleges, concrete changes in teachers and teaching and in students and learning are in evidence. In addition, the impact on curriculum, staff development programs, and overall college climate has been positive and pervasive.

Choosing Promising Program Models

The pattern or model of these California classroom-based programs is common to many classroom assessment programs around the country. They are, however, far more comprehensive and directly applied to classroom learning than typical faculty development efforts, which are often limited to occasional speakers or workshops that focus on teaching tips. The classroom model allows faculty to work together while trying new methods in the classroom over time, and it includes training in setting learning goals, using classroom assessment techniques, and documenting the results for at least a full semester. In each group, eight to ten faculty members meet to solve problems and document teaching changes and learning results (Obler, Arnold, Sigala, and Umbdenstock, 1991). Incentives for faculty participation in these programs include both extrinsic and intrinsic rewards; they range from stipends or reassigned time to the pleasure of sharing classroom war stories. A college may conduct up to four or five of these pilot projects in a year, covering up to forty teachers, each with at least one class of thirty to sixty students. After classroom assessment is established with a critical mass of faculty members, many projects go on to try new teaching methods like collaborative or cooperative learning. They then assess these methods with classroom assessment techniques.

Working from the Outside in:
Generating and Sustaining Change

The networking approach to establishing classroom assessment programs has helped colleges by providing external training, leadership, and support. On many campuses, resistance to changing teaching and learning makes starting a local campus project very difficult. In a recent issue of *Change,* Parker Palmer suggests that movements begun *outside* organizations are likely to support more long-range change than internal programs. Education systems — the guardians of tradition — typically resist change from within and may render new ideas and their champions ineffective (Palmer, 1992). In a consortium, by contrast, project leaders can meet routinely with their counterparts from neighboring campuses and exchange achievements or woes within a relatively safe environment — unencumbered by the political agendas on their own campuses. They return to their campuses, equipped with problem-solving tactics and ideas.

Implications of Classroom
Assessment: Active Learning

The use of classroom assessment in the projects has shown faculty where changes in teaching and learning are needed. The teaching methods that have been the most successful with students, according to their classroom assessment responses, are those that are known as active learning (Obler, 1992). Of these, the most commonly used methods include collaborative or cooperative learning, learning logs, interactive computer-assisted instruction, and classroom assessment itself. These approaches demand that students actively apply, contrast, evaluate, synthesize, and interact with concepts, especially when a *product* demonstrating those skills (a paper or performance, for example) is involved. At most campuses, faculty have discovered the importance of increasing this kind of learning and varying these methods.

Project leaders who do the training of their colleagues have recognized the need for continued support during the initial stages — especially when active learning requires teachers to rethink their role in the classroom. They often find that they become learning coaches, rather than information dispensers. As Bonwell and Eison suggest in their Association for the Study of Higher Education review of active learning, "The instructor shares control with the students" (1991, p. 63).

Learning logs, another active learning approach, require that students keep notes on vertically divided pages. On the left half, students record key points from labs, discussions, texts, field study, or brief lectures. Shortly afterwards, students respond to the notes on the right half of the page: posing questions, relating ideas, and applying concepts or skills. Like cooperative learning, learning logs require students to *practice* learning skills along many dimensions. Through routine assessment, faculty can trace the problems and progress of students using the logs. At Rancho Santiago College, faculty in the psychology department report that persistence in classes using the logs is much higher than in their former courses where logs were not kept (Anthony, 1992).

Campus projects in the Title III consortium are developing computer-assisted instruction (CAI) and assessment techniques to find out how CAI changes student learning. The best faculty-developed and commercial software allows students to learn interactively — individually or in groups — rather than passively reading textbooks on the screen. Immediate feedback from the interactive software exercises provides students with incremental, motivating information with which to practice thinking skills. Faculty in CAI projects are already working with classroom assessment feedback gathered from three-by-five cards stacked near monitors. In some cases, faculty are working on ways to assess the software itself. Routine classroom assessment of all these methods has helped faculty recognize students' need for and appreciation of active learning — especially in the practice of higher-order thinking skills (Kelemen-Lohnas, 1992).

Classroom assessment is the cornerstone of these programs that introduce active learning methods. Cooperative learning teams, for example, are assessed through simple classroom assessment techniques designed to evaluate their work: team members are asked to characterize the productivity of their group in one sentence and to pose one way to improve its performance next time (Whalen, 1992). Students using learning logs can inform the teacher how and when the logs are increasing their application of course concepts; on a three-by-five card, students can specify the most useful or most difficult aspect of using the logs. In each use of the CATs, faculty must report results to students and, where appropriate, make adjustments in pace or emphasis.

The Critical Difference:
What We Are Learning About Learning

Angelo's 1991 volume is cautiously titled *Classroom Research: Early Lessons from Success.* These early lessons gathered from the many consortia projects illustrate the range of changes occurring in the culture of teaching and learning on many campuses.

Changes in Students and Learning

Faculty and students alike report that classrooms are more charged with the energy of learning; students are more involved in their learning than ever before (Slark, Anthony, and Sharpe, 1991). Systematically asking students whether and how they have learned, and providing them feedback, makes students active participants rather than passive learners. The result seems to be higher course retention rates over time (Whalen, 1992). On the various campuses, the focus of the classrooms has shifted from the teacher and the teaching process to the learner and learning outcomes.

Some local campus projects have found that students transferred the skills acquired in the projects to other classrooms and experiences (Anthony, 1991). Students have asked instructors outside the projects for the opportunity to provide feedback through CATs. When students are asked focused questions about what and how they learn, they acquire long-term insights about their own learning styles and skills. A semester-end survey done at Fullerton College after a semester's use of CATs indicated that the anxieties of students about asking questions in class were significantly reduced and their sense of involvement in class was increased (Kelly, 1991).

Perhaps one of the more rewarding results of the use of CATs for the learner and the teacher is the partnership that is created. Classrooms become dynamic environments, charged with learning energy. The following comments from the LARC-FIPSE project demonstrate the pleasure and motivation that students get from this natural classroom alliance. One student reports, "It makes me feel good that I have a teacher that cares about the way she teaches for the student. Keep on doing [CATs] because the student will feel more pleased and willing to work, without feeling lonely and confused." Another says, "I feel it is important that you ask questions of us because then you find out what helps us better. We learn better and in return you become a better teacher." Still another states, "By being asked these questions, I see a teacher who cares; therefore, this will encourage me to work harder" (Kelemen-Lohnas, 1992).

Furthermore, students acquire improved communication skills and class participation abilities (Slark, Anthony, and Sharpe, 1991). By articulating their own ideas routinely on the CATs, students eventually became more self-confident and assertive in their interactions with teachers and other students. In cooperative learning teams, this growing learning confidence was even more apparent (Whalen, 1992). Some projects reported an increase in intercultural student contact, which promoted mutual student understanding and the breaking down of cultural barriers. A faculty member in the Beacon Project, for example, said, "The class seems very cooperative and friendly and willing to express ideas about what they need and what they do not understand" (Sigala, 1992).

Finally, campus leaders have reported that the use of CATs democratizes the classroom; all students have an equal voice. The practice of collecting feedback anonymously ensures that the reactions of less assertive students were not overshadowed. Faculty discovered that speaking up in class is considered rude behavior in some cultures; thus, CATs allowed particular students a voice and a way to practice expression without shame or embarrassment. The CATs also provided teachers with feedback on how prevalent this discomfort was. If they wanted to use cooperative learning groups, they could therefore address the uneasiness ahead of time. Faculty on some campuses found that properly structured learning teams offered a more comfortable learning environment, especially for those who preferred group cooperation to individual competitiveness (Whalen, 1992).

Changes in Teachers and Teaching

Observers in the corridors outside rooms where classroom assessment and active learning are used report seeing students engaged with each other and the course material. Teachers are less likely to be in front, talking straight through the session and reading from dog-eared notes. In fact, many faculty are beginning to use CATs routinely and to see their benefits to themselves and to students. The following comments from the Rancho Santiago College project were typical of those in other colleges: "I've always taught using a traditional lecture-discussion style. I am now getting my students more actively involved in organized small group activities which are really working well! I am constantly aware of how effectively my students are learning and can make adaptations when needed. I still believe that students are responsible for their own learning, but I now feel more responsible for constantly monitoring that learning and not just measuring it for their grades—that's quite a philosophical shift" (Anthony, 1991).

In sum, teachers have begun to focus more on what and how students are learning rather than on what they are teaching. As Marilla Svinicki so aptly said, "The learner is at center stage" (1991, p. 27). As faculty concentrate more on their students, they become aware of the benefits of sharing the stage. The natural link between teaching and learning and the partnership between teachers and learners have created a shared context for more in-depth understanding. As a result of gathering routine student feedback, teachers are trying new techniques to see what will strengthen student learning. They are now deeply involved in assessing not merely the acquisition of facts as tested on multiple-choice forms but also skills in questioning, comparison, and analysis from different perspectives; these advanced cognitive abilities distinguish experienced learners.

Faculty report that they enjoy the contact and the richness of talking with each other on substantive issues in teaching and learning. Regular meetings and time for problem solving are an integral part of the training model in the consortia projects. Local project participants talk about trying out the active learning methods and adapting each other's techniques to fit their own discipline, program, style, or objectives. Participating teachers function as a support team. As one faculty member put it, "Enthusiasm is infectious when peers can meet and discuss success and failures of the techniques of instruction" (Anthony, 1991).

On some campuses, faculty admitted that they were once

reluctant to discuss what was happening in their classrooms; it was too painful for those who cared about students or too demoralizing to admit defeats. Some teachers admitted to coping with underprepared students by lowering standards, others by becoming thick-skinned or detached. In the past, when faculty got together to discuss the classroom, they attributed problems to the students' limitations — a form of blaming the "victim." They saw the students' home life as beyond classroom scope, their lack of preparation as someone else's job, or a lack of materials as an administrative problem. After working within the classroom projects and listening more carefully to students' CAT responses, faculty are beginning to reframe their thinking: they are beginning to see how their teaching affects learning.

What is evident in all the projects is an increased collegewide emphasis on teaching and learning that has generated faculty revitalization. Because the training and introductory process is both individual and shared, the increased energy is truly transforming the classroom. On many campuses, the projects have spawned a growing peer leadership of faculty-directed training and discussion of student learning. Enhanced networking, brainstorming, and communication among faculty has occurred within and among colleges. As faculty collaborate about substantive issues of teaching and learning, long-range change can occur. Palmer (1992, p. 16) points out that "when the language of change becomes available in the common culture, people are better able to name their yearnings for change, to explore them with others, to claim membership in a great movement."

Changes in Staff Development, Curriculum, Climate, and the System

Campuses using classroom assessment have begun to notice the effects of the programs on the culture of the college in other areas beside teaching and learning.

Changes in Staff Development

At some institutions, staff development programs have changed their focus because of these evaluation efforts. On some campuses, the credibility of staff development has been increased through use of classroom assessment techniques (Kelemen-Lohnas, 1992).

At a regional meeting of staff development officers examining how to evaluate and strengthen the programs on their campuses, several officers strongly advocated the move away from one-time workshops, conferences, and individual projects toward more systematic efforts to affect student learning through ongoing training and support sessions encouraging use of CATs and sharing (especially within disciplines).

Changes in the Curriculum

The use of classroom assessment also ultimately focuses faculty — both individually and in departments — on revitalizing the curriculum itself. As the use of CATs progresses and the amount of student feedback increases, teachers recognize the need to review and discuss their instructional goals and curriculum. Working collaboratively and reviewing the curriculum through the eyes of *students* have helped teachers in these consortia identify content gaps, sequencing problems within and between courses, and the exclusion of cultural perspectives. Mathematics faculty members, for example, have asked themselves whether mastery of fewer concepts provides a better grounding than a poorly retained overview of a comprehensive curriculum (Anthony, 1991). Teachers have also begun to retool their testing to concentrate on active learning strategies, rather than on the rote retention of facts and principles. They have found that old testing techniques may not test the skills and knowledge that they expect of students; they have thus changed the curriculum and testing to focus on critical thinking, practical application, and written expression.

Changes in Campus Climate

In California, *campus climate* is an ambiguous term; it can refer to staff morale and attitudes, the way diverse student groups may be perceived on campus and in classrooms, or the ambiance of the initial registration process. The classroom assessment programs of the consortia have had effects on college climate quite beyond the classroom. These projects have contributed to college environments where assessment techniques are well accepted, routine, and even welcomed (Sigala, 1992). For instance, more than one college uses CATs to measure the effectiveness of administrative meetings and ways of making the meetings more productive and pleasant for participants.

Relationships between faculty and research departments and between teachers and administrators, have changed and improved because students are a shared concern. This student focus arises from the visibility of the campus projects and from the credibility won by teachers as a result of this research. The availability of teaching and learning resources — materials, leaders, and project centers — has increased as a result of the financial resources provided by the various grants acquired to fund the activities.

Changes Beyond the Campus

In a recent session of the California Community College Chancellor's Office Commission on Innovation, corporate business leaders were asked how the total quality management process could directly effect improvements in the classroom. A college president in attendance responded that classroom assessment techniques were in line with TQM principles because they represented continuous improvement via students — the "customers" of our colleges. He further noted that this was an innovation most likely to have the greatest impact in transforming education. In another statewide setting of presidents, managers, and faculty innovators, high technology was at the center of discussion about instructional improvement. The faculty at the meeting, however, stated that classroom assessment was more important than technology to the kind of change needed in student learning. These faculty members, who were not participants in the consortia projects, had heard about the strengths of classroom assessment from their colleagues.

Changes in the Culture of Teaching and Learning

In addition to the multiple benefits of classroom assessment in local programs, the consortia colleges have learned the value and power of networks. Networks have provided the colleges with validation, credibility, and accountability that would not have occurred otherwise. The consortia process as a vehicle for change has been crucial to the success of the projects. Moreover, critical, far-reaching changes in teaching and learning philosophies and practice have taken place because the efforts were spearheaded by faculty and students, not by administrators. By contrast, most large-scale outcomes assessment programs are not so readily converted to immediate and noticeable change. In these consortia projects, the participating colleges have noted the following results:

- Increased campus focus on teaching, learning, and assessment
- More student motivation and involvement in learning
- Greater use of active teaching methods
- Increased pleasure in learning, which improves students' communication skills and revitalizes the classroom
- Renewal of teachers and teaching through the discussion of innovative classroom methods and through improved student learning
- Creation of teacher-student partnerships in the teaching and learning process
- Increased use of active learning and critical thinking
- Enhanced metacognitive skills (awareness of learning) in students
- Identification of the need for training, support, and incentives for faculty who want to try alternative teaching, learning, and assessment approaches

The evaluations and project reports have almost unanimously suggested that some organizational hurdles and program limitations remain. Of course, classroom assessment is not a panacea for ills that have been part of higher education for a long period. Practitioners wanting to start similar programs should note that in the early stages the programs should remain small (under twenty teachers). Most program leaders found that some faculty members have difficulty at first in translating student feedback into useful changes in their teaching or learning strategies. Campus leaders and program proposals must include more direct training and preparation for teachers in active learning methods that work with the students that community colleges serve. Many of these students are adults who are the first generation in their families to attend college. Usually, they have a wide range of preparation, are often older than freshmen, and come from diverse cultural backgrounds.

Further, the consortia projects found that they need what all innovation requires: strong leadership support at the top and a keen awareness of the vulnerability of new programs. Premature evaluation is a major pitfall that the programs should avoid. In fact, during a national teleconference on developing centers for teaching and learning, Paul Elsner, chancellor of the Maricopa colleges in Phoenix, and Mardee Jenrette of Miami Dade Community College noted that programs of this type should not be evaluated until the initial work is stabilized. In some cases, three to four years are necessary before evaluation (Elsner, 1991).

Without a doubt, the documentation of learning is just beginning to advance. To date, the field has failed to address these issues adequately, but the programs and studies reviewed in this chapter have made important strides toward the gathering of essential data. Classroom research is ready to use classroom assessment information to define and monitor student progress; indeed, this assessment has already created substantive change in the culture of teaching and learning.

References

Anthony, M. A. *Classroom Research Project: Year 2 Report, 1990–91.* Santa Ana, Calif.: Rancho Santiago College, 1991.

Anthony, M. A. *Classroom Research Project: Year 3 Report, 1991–92.* Santa Ana, Calif.: Rancho Santiago College Press, 1992.

Angelo, T. A. (ed.). *Classroom Research: Early Lessons from Success.* New Directions in Teaching and Learning, no. 46. San Francisco: Jossey-Bass, 1991.

Angelo, T. A., and Cross, K. P. *Classroom Assessment Techniques: A Handbook for College Teachers.* (2nd ed.) San Francisco: Jossey-Bass, 1993.

Bonwell, C. C., and Eison, J. A. (eds.). *Active Learning: Creating Excitement in the Classroom.* ASHE-ERIC Higher Education Report No. 1. Washington, D.C.: Association for the Study of Higher Education, 1991.

Cross, K. P., and Angelo, T. A. *Classroom Assessment Techniques: A Handbook for Faculty.* Ann Arbor: National Center for Research to Improve Postsecondary Teaching, University of Michigan, 1988.

Elsner, P. "Academic Excellence: How Teaching-Learning Centers Respond." North American College and University Video Teleconference, Rio Hondo College, Dec. 5, 1991.

Kelemen-Lohnas, E. *Final Report: The LARC-FIPSE Three-Year Project in Classroom Research and Assessment.* Santa Barbara, Calif.: Santa Barbara City College, 1992.

Kelly, D. K. *The Effects of Classroom Research by Part-Time Faculty upon the Retention of Adult Learners.* Practitioner-Based Research Report. Fullerton, Calif.: Fullerton College Press, 1991. (ED 335 076)

Obler, S. *Title III Consortium: Year 3: 1991–92, Executive Summary.* Whittier, Calif.: Rio Hondo College Press, 1992.

Obler, S., Arnold, V., Sigala, C., and Umbdenstock, L. "Using Cooperative Learning and Classroom Research with Culturally Diverse Students." In T. A. Angelo (ed.), *Classroom Research: Early Lessons from Success.* New Directions for Teaching and Learning, no. 46. San Francisco: Jossey-Bass, 1991.

Palmer, P. "Divided No More." *Change,* Mar.–Apr. 1992, pp. 10–17.

Sigala, C. A. *Beacon College Project, 1991–92 Annual Report.* Whittier, Calif.: Rio Hondo College Press, 1992.

Slark, J., Anthony, M. A., and Sharpe, W. *Classroom Voices.* Santa Ana, Calif.: Rancho Santiago College Press, 1991. Videotape.

Svinicki, M. D. "Practical Implications of Cognitive Theories." In R. J. Menges and M. D. Svinicki (eds.), *College Teaching: From Theory to Practice.* New Directions for Teaching and Learning, no. 45. San Francisco: Jossey-Bass, 1991.

Whalen, M. *The Collaborative Learning Project: Year 3 Report, 1991–92.* Walnut, Calif.: Mount San Antonio College Press, 1992.

Part Four

Approaches with Promise for Improving Programs and Services

As we have seen, Part Three of this volume contains descriptions of assessment methods that are widely used in higher education today to suggest improvements in academic programs and student services. Part Four presents four relatively new approaches that are just beginning to prove their worth in stimulating change. Each holds promise for making a difference in the future.

In Chapter Fifteen, Robert Millward describes the assessment center — the quintessential authentic assessment method that evaluates students' abilities in simulated versions of the settings in which they are expected to apply what they have learned in the classroom. Experience with assessment centers at three institutions in Pennsylvania has led faculty to increase their use of portfolios, simulations, projects, and early field experiences in order to promote students' application skills. Millward's own studies indicate that teacher education majors who are taught via simulations are more likely to use them in their own teaching and that simulations can improve creativity and sensitivity as well as skills in communicating, playing a leadership role, and planning and organizing.

In Chapter Sixteen, Carl Waluconis describes self-evaluation as an assessment technique that employs essays to help students analyze their own learning. Typically, students are asked to respond to such prompts as "What did you learn?" and "How do you plan to use what you learned?" Applied in a given course, self-evaluation is a form of classroom assessment. Waluconis describes a relatively unique application of this technique undertaken at Seattle Central Community College (SCCC): a course in self-evaluation wherein students evaluate all the courses in which they are concurrently enrolled. This author, who also is the developer of the SCCC course in self-evaluation, provides evidence that students become more responsible for their learning, more motivated to engage in lifelong learning, more aware of diverse perspectives, and less likely to drop out of college as a result of the course. Waluconis suggests that quantitative appraisal methods applied to students' self-reflective essays can provide numerical scores for presentation to external decision makers as evidence of student learning.

In Chapter Seventeen, James Ratcliff and Elizabeth Jones furnish a glimpse of the potential of their Coursework Cluster Analysis Model (CCAM) for linking assessments of general learning with the coursework that students take in college. The purpose of this methodology is to identify patterns of coursework (or learning subenvironments) within an institution that are particularly effective in promoting learning for students having specific backgrounds, achievements, aptitudes, and interests. Courses that are consistently shown not to assist learning should be improved or dropped. Application of the CCAM can also help faculty determine which assessment measures explain the most variation in student learning and should thus be included in the assessment program of an institution.

In Chapter Eighteen, Darrell Krueger argues that educational programs cannot be improved by measuring only the resources going into them, their outcomes, or even the two in combination. In addition to assessing resources and outcomes, we must carefully analyze the *process* of education, including student involvement, faculty-student interaction, the setting of high expectations, and provision of frequent and immediate feedback concerning performance. Krueger advocates the application of total quality management principles to the process of improving student learning. Many campus administrators are currently attempting to use TQM to increase the efficiency and effectiveness of administrative functions, but few have applied TQM to teaching and learning. Krueger believes that this application holds enormous promise for improving higher education in the remainder of this decade and into the next century.

15

Assessment Centers

Robert E. Millward

During the early 1980s, several faculty members at Indiana University of Pennsylvania (IUP) questioned the value of using multiple-choice tests to predict future success in teaching. For this reason, we began to explore the assessment center concept to diagnose the beginning teaching skills of college sophomores, juniors, and seniors. With financial assistance from our university and two other state universities, Slippery Rock and Millersville, we were able to contract with one of the nation's largest assessment firms, Development Dimensions International (DDI), to help us design and implement a diagnostic teacher assessment center. Douglas Bray, DDI chairman of the board and former AT&T assessment director, worked with us in developing the guidelines for our teacher simulations. He has written several books on the validity of the assessment center approach and has had over forty years of experience in designing assessment simulations.

With the help of Douglas Bray and the consultants from DDI, we began to identify skills that we considered critical for effective teaching. After agreeing on these, we began to develop

231

a set of simulations to assess an education major's teaching potential. By 1987, we were ready to implement a teacher assessment center at IUP and Slippery Rock University.

Description of Methods

Presently, the Teacher Assessment Center is being used at Slippery Rock, Carlow College in Pittsburgh, and the Alaska State Department of Education, as well as Indiana University of Pennsylvania. During the past five years, we have evaluated over six hundred students. The following paragraphs provide a brief description of each simulation.

• *The School Museum.* This two-hour exercise involves events related to a very boring set of educational exhibits that are almost hidden on the second floor of the town's museum. The superintendent and the board are concerned about the value of supporting a school museum. The simulation contains letters from concerned citizens, letters from school personnel, budget information, maps, charts, and graphs. After studying the problem, the student must make a ten-minute presentation of his or her findings. This simulation is designed to assess planning, problem analysis, oral communication, initiative, sensitivity, and innovativeness.

• *Vignettes.* During this one-hour simulation, students view a series of classroom episodes on a videotape. At selected intervals, the tape stops, and questions such as "If you were the teacher, how would you handle the situation?" or "What would you do now?" appear on the screen. Students respond to these classroom episodes in writing.

• *Education Fair.* This exercise focuses on a variety of problems encountered in organizing a districtwide education fair. Once again, the students must read charts, budgets, letters, graphs, and reports regarding this long-running fair. The students have two hours to complete this simulation.

• *Actual Teaching.* Each student is given a packet of material containing lesson plans, objectives, overheads, handouts, and background information. He or she is given two hours to prepare a fifteen-minute presentation of ways in which the lesson could be presented as well as innovative techniques that could be incorporated into it.

At the end of the assessment process, students receive a written narrative of their overall performance. Here is an average profile of IUP education majors in each of the thirteen dimensions over the past three years, on a scale of one to five (with one being low and five high):

Skill Dimensions	Performance Rating (N = 280)
Problem analysis	(3.1)
Planning and organizing	(3.2)
Leadership	(2.3)
Sensitivity	(2.7)
Strategic decision making	(3.0)
Tactical decision making	(3.4)
Written communication	(3.5)
Oral communication	(3.6)
Oral presentation	(3.2)
Initiative	(2.7)
Innovativeness	(2.0)
Tolerance for stress	(3.7)
Monitoring	(3.1)

The intent of our preteacher assessment is to provide an early diagnosis of teaching skills prior to student teaching. It was not designed to discourage students from teaching but rather to enhance their training. The profile shows that in four dimensions (leadership, sensitivity, initiative, and innovativeness) a majority of the students who have been assessed scored below average. Only 5 percent of the students have scored above average in developing innovative ways for solving problems, and the same figure holds true for leadership behaviors. About 25 percent of the students score above average in initiative and sensitivity.

If the results are valid, we must ask ourselves why students do poorly in these four dimensions. Faculty have speculated that colleges do not promote skills that enhance creative and innovative behavior. Students seldom get a chance to assume leadership positions within the classroom. We defined initiative as going beyond what is expected. Students too often are satisfied with attaining a basic competency, earning a passing grade with minimum effort.

The descriptive data in the profile of IUP's college sophomores provide direction for our methods of teaching courses to help future teachers become more sensitive to children, issues, parents, and the unexciting teaching strategies currently used in many of our classrooms from kindergarten through college. Methods of teaching here at IUP are now emphasizing portfolio development, simulations, projects, and early field experiences to promote the development of both innovative classroom teaching techniques and leadership behavior of future teachers. Meaningful assignments accompanied by an insistence on high standards are being used to encourage the learning of innovative teaching strategies that consistently enhance the learning of others.

Initial Advantages of the Assessment Center Method

The assessment center method developed at IUP is used to develop a profile of an education major's strengths and weaknesses in thirteen skills. This information is being used to redesign current methods of teaching courses. For example, we are finding that when required to develop a series of presentations that are videotaped and then evaluated by the college teacher and by their peers, college students develop much more refined skills in oral presentation and planning. We have learned that students who take part in simulations in a college methods course will use simulations for teaching specific concepts when they begin their own teaching experience. Our goal is to show students how to move from simulations to authentic assessment projects. The first step, however, is to introduce the college students themselves to simulations, to describe how they can be used to evaluate basic skills, and then to show them how to use simulations in turn to promote their students' development.

The assessment center method also helps college education majors improve their abilities in observing, analyzing, and interpreting classroom behavior. In addition, students learn to evaluate student performance using simulations rather than relying on pencil-and-paper examinations. When schools begin to adopt performance assessment techniques, instruction becomes more exciting; teachers promote the development of student portfolios; and instructors begin to expand their concept of assessment beyond traditional exams (O'Neil, 1992; Fiske, 1992).

Typical Assessment Schedule

We have found that the typical two-day assessment schedule used in industry does not fit into a college student's schedule. Students cannot be expected to miss classes just to attend a two-day assessment. We solved this problem by scheduling one assessment simulation at a time at the end of Monday afternoon classes. Thus, over a four-week period, a student can complete all four assessment simulations and then receive a written diagnostic report regarding strengths and weaknesses across the thirteen assessment dimensions.

The overall design of our simulations permits us to assess twenty-four to fifty students at one time; this figure far exceeds the typical industrial models, which evaluate only six to twelve candidates at once. For example, fifty students can be scheduled to complete the education fair and the vignettes simulations without the need for assessors to be present. The completed simulation exercises can then be sent to a trained group that consistently scores either the education fair or the vignettes simulation. Our objective is to help an individual to become an expert at scoring just one of the four simulations and thus increase the reliability of the scoring process. The school museum and the actual teaching simulations require the student to make an oral presentation to a trained evaluator. Prior to the presentation, students have two hours of preparation time to complete the exercise. They work on it for two hours late Monday afternoon, return all materials to the proctor at the end of that time, and then arrange a time slot on Tuesday for making their oral presentation. Presentations are scheduled throughout the day using three different rooms to accommodate simultaneous presentations. We have completed fifty in one day by using both a video camera and actual evaluators. Since many evaluators are public school teachers, they prefer to have the video presentations sent to their school or to their homes rather than to spend a day at the assessment center.

Assessor Reliability

In most industrial assessment centers, six evaluators must reach consensus on a candidate's overall performance. The discussion includes a review of the candidate's behavior for each simulation, as well as how the behavior was scored by the assigned assessor. As a result, modifications are sometimes made on the candidate's original scores simply because of new insight or better interpretations of the data. Once consensus is reached, evaluators are asked to score each dimension on a scale from one (little skill) to five (substantial skill). The assessors must agree within one point of each other on each dimension. Table 15.1 presents a typical scoring pattern for an assessment of a candidate's performance in problem analysis skills.

Table 15.1. Candidate's Scores for Skill in Analyzing Problems.

Assessors:	A	B	C	D	E	F
Example 1	3	3	3	4	4	3
Example 2	3	2	3	4	4	3

Example one presents a set of six assessor scores that are within a one-point range (threes and fours) and are therefore acceptable. Example two shows a range from a low of two to a high of four. Since the range exceeds one point, the evaluators must continue their discussion until they can reach consensus.

Unlike industry evaluation, the preteacher assessment simulations were designed to be scored without a consensus discussion of each candidate's attributes. This decision was made because of the large number of students who must be assessed within an academic year. It would be too costly to organize

twenty or more six-person teams during a typical college semester. Therefore, we developed guides for each of our four
assessment simulations that would guide scoring decisions for
each candidate. The guides focus attention on specific behaviors
and furnish checklists that help to provide more structured information than do the traditional open-ended scoring directions
used in industrial assessment centers. As previously noted,
another way to increase rater reliability is to have assessors
specialize in scoring just one simulation rather than all four.

We recently compared the ratings of over fifty IUP assessors who scored the education fair and vignettes simulations
with the ratings of two experts. Of the eight dimensions that
are assessed in the education fair simulation, six (planning and
organizing, leadership, decision making, problem analysis, written communication, and initiative) attain high percentages of
agreement between evaluators and experts. Only two dimensions, sensitivity and innovativeness, had scores that varied by
two points. A comparison of evaluator and expert ratings on
the classroom vignettes simulation shows that four of the five
dimensions have a consistent scoring pattern (Millward, 1990).

Content Validity

We began the development of our simulations by reviewing the literature on the characteristics of effective teachers as well as by conducting on-site observations. The behaviors that we identified
were then organized into a variety of categories that eventually
became the thirteen skill dimensions. These were reviewed by
three panels across the state whose members included college
faculty, public school teachers, and educational administrators.
The reviewers helped us clarify the definitions for the dimensions.

We addressed basic issues as we designed each simulation. First, each had to be designed for sophomore education
majors who had no experience in actual teaching. Second, it
had to elicit the kinds of behaviors that were identified as essential teaching skills. Finally, the simulation had to be easily
scored. Content validity, according to Virginia Boehm (1982)
in her booklet *Establishing the Validity of Assessment Centers,* is the

relationship between behaviors measured in the simulations and the actual behaviors needed on the job. Thus, the review of the literature on effective teaching and the three separate panel reviews helped to establish the overall content validity of the preteacher simulations.

Predictive Validity

Douglas Bray and Ann Howard coauthored a thirty-year validity study of the AT&T Assessment Center and concluded that this method is probably one of the best predictors of future performance (Howard and Bray, 1988). In education, assessment simulations, portfolios, and work samples all have the potential of more accurately sampling a student's potential than do traditional pencil-and-paper examinations. If Bray and Howard are correct, our preteacher assessment simulations should provide an early indicator of future teaching ability.

To test this assumption, I observed five student teachers over a fourteen-week period to determine whether their teaching performance matched that exhibited at the assessment center. In order to reduce any observer bias, I did not review any assessment results for the five student teachers until after I had rated their behavior at the end of their student teaching experience. Overall, my observer scores and those of the assessment center matched 80 percent of the time on four dimensions (oral communication, leadership, innovativeness, and planning and organizing). I focused on these four rather than on all thirteen since scoring on two of the dimensions, leadership and innovativeness, has been consistently low and skills in oral communications and planning are relatively easy to observe and to rate. The results show a relationship between assessment center scores and actual classroom behavior and provide evidence that the simulations can be used to help diagnose a student's teaching strengths and weaknesses.

Improvements in Teacher Training

At IUP, we have designed a series of follow-up training tapes to help students improve particular skills; these focus on communication, sensitivity, leadership, problem analysis, planning and organizing, and innovativeness. For example, the training tape that demonstrates innovative teaching strategies depicts various teachers using such strategies. After our education majors view the tape, they participate in a series of problem-solving activities with their peers that are designed to promote the application of creative solutions to specific problems. In addition, we provide examples of traditional lessons from various basal texts and then have our students collaborate on innovative approaches that enhance the content of the lesson.

We have also produced training tapes that model leadership skills and sensitivity and a tape that illustrates a set of beliefs about teaching. We are currently introducing a series of activities that can be used to complement the tapes. One activity that has proven to be successful poses a problem that we adapted from James Adams's book *Conceptual Blockbusting* (1986). The students are presented with a four-inch iron pipe that is eight feet tall and securely bolted to the floor. At the bottom of the pipe are three very fragile ping-pong balls that must be extracted within thirty minutes. Sitting next to the pipe is a box full of objects that students are permitted to use to solve the problem. They are also allowed to use anything within the building, within reason, to help them. Students work with five or six of their peers. The students are often videotaped, and the college instructor focuses on leadership, planning, problem solving, innovativeness, sensitivity, and communication skills. Students learn how to observe, analyze, and interpret behaviors.

Of course, colleges can derive the benefits of videotapes without going to the expense of producing their own. A number of commercially produced tapes (including those developed by major publishers and the Association for Supervision and Curriculum Development) can be used to demonstrate effective teaching.

Strengths and Weaknesses of the Assessment Process

The strength of a college assessment center program is its ability to focus on specific skills that education majors need to develop to become successful teachers. For example, the finding that only 5 percent of our education majors score above average in leadership and innovativeness led us to create activities for teaching the methods that force students to solve problems, make decisions, and work cooperatively with their peers.

At the same time, college teachers must act as models for education majors. College lectures must be kept to the minimum. Students should begin applying methods of teaching within the first week of class; more learning often takes place through making mistakes than by getting a good grade on an examination on curriculum theory. The assessment process can have a positive impact on changing the ways methods classes are taught.

Another positive effect of the evaluation process is that students and faculty rediscover the impact of simulations on learning. In simulated situations, students learn that problems can be solved by using a variety of strategies. They learn the value of group problem solving and brainstorming. Students learn that decisions made with a lack of background data often lead to delays and blind alleys.

A major weakness of the assessment center approach is the amount of time required to administer and score the simulations. Evaluators must be given sufficient training; learning how to assess is a developmental process that requires a great deal of practice. Assessors must discriminate between effective and ineffective performance; they are expected to know how to analyze, evaluate, and develop written narratives; and they must have a thorough understanding of the dimensions of the task. Industrial assessments have been successful because industries have their own staff of assessors or contract with a professional firm. Colleges have to rely on volunteers who may work only in one, or at the most, two assessment centers per year.

Another stumbling block lies in the way the current curriculum is structured. Within most schools, classes occur in fifty-minute blocks, and simulations do not fit neatly into this structure. Simulations incorporate skills in all subjects, and this presents a scheduling problem for some teachers and administrators.

The last major weakness in the use of diagnostic assessments is the lack of follow-up strategies designed to improve skills that are below average. If students score below average in leadership and innovativeness, they should have the opportunity to correct the deficiency while in college. Methods of teaching that focus on following a format for designing lessons, not on examining the actual content of the lesson, are merely promoting a "recipe" approach, and the student is not really learning any new skill. A better way would be to ask the student to design a series of lessons that would be innovative and interesting and would encourage leadership, require group cooperation, and include a multicultural theme. Such an assignment would promote skills in the areas of problem analysis, decision making, leadership, initiative, sensitivity, and communication. Furthermore, if students were required to implement this series of experiences during their student teaching experience, the planning would become much more practical. If the assessment process is not directly linked to college methods courses, there is little chance the concept will survive.

Are We Making a Difference?

We are making a difference, but on a small scale. The assessment center, diagnostic assessment, authentic assessment, and performance assessment are concepts that are not being introduced on a large scale in colleges of education. In addition, the follow-up developmental activities are much more useful than a one-time assessment. The methods that we use to measure student performance must be expanded to target what Howard Gardner labels multiple intelligences (1983, 1991). Can tests be exciting, interesting, and challenging? Grant Wiggins says they can and calls upon test makers to be "creative designers . . . not just technicians" (1992, p. 26).

Oral communication skills can be improved among education majors by getting them to videotape classroom presentations that are critiqued both by their college teacher and by their peers. Their ability to plan and organize increases when education majors are required to develop and introduce simulations to be used in actual classrooms. Student teachers begin to concentrate on what their students need to learn by designing simulations to enhance these skills rather than developing a set of boring work-sheet questions that merely emphasize rote recall of facts.

Leadership skills are improved by having education majors work with their peers in designing simulations. They learn how to work in groups, how to use brainstorming techniques, and how to delegate tasks.

Sensitivity toward people and issues grows as students take part in initial assessment simulations and later as they begin to get kids involved in simulated situations. We have introduced a multicultural simulation that provides the student with an opportunity to explore both the cognitive and affective dimensions of multicultural concepts.

Innovation is encouraged as students begin to go beyond the parameters of traditional basal textbooks and explore issues in more depth. Content knowledge takes on new meaning when student teachers concentrate on authentic assessment (Perrone, 1991).

Some of our students have tried using simulations to diagnose such dimensions as leadership, problem solving, judgment, organizational ability, and sensitivity. But they need help in developing methods for observing and recording behavior and in analyzing the data they collect.

We have also developed authentic assessment strategies for elementary students that are designed to increase their understanding of in-depth issues. When education majors see the impact these strategies can have on learning, they begin to incorporate authentic assessment into their lesson plans. The few student teachers who have attempted to use assessment simulations have reacted positively toward the process.

Assessment centers, authentic assessment, and performance evaluation can all have a significant impact on changing the way we train future teachers. The course syllabus for every testing and measurement course should include methods for implementing assessment center techniques. Methods courses must be redesigned. Students need help in understanding what should be evaluated as well as in designing new ways to measure learning. The May 1992 issue of *Educational Leadership* focuses on how performance assessment is being implemented within classrooms across the country. The articles clearly illustrate the need for colleges of education to begin restructuring their methods courses to include performance assessment concepts. It is time to stop measuring teaching effectiveness by the number of credits amassed. Instead, we need to consider specific essential behaviors. We should ask whether education majors can design innovative teaching strategies that enhance student learning. We should inquire what books our students have read recently and what impact their reading has had in improving teaching performance. We need to find out what kind of projects or tasks education majors have designed to promote in-depth learning of concepts. When colleges of education begin to focus on performance rather than course credits, we will see a dramatic improvement in teaching. Authentic assessment has the potential for creating a revolution in teacher training programs.

References

Adams, J. L. *Conceptual Blockbusting*. Reading, Mass.: Addison-Wesley, 1986.

Boehm, V. *Establishing the Validity of Assessment Centers*. Pittsburgh, Pa.: Development Dimensions International, 1982.

Fiske, E. B. *Smart Schools, Smart Kids*. New York: Touchstone, 1992.

Gardner, H. *Frames of Mind*. New York: Basic Books, 1983.

Gardner, H. *The Unschooled Mind: How Children Think and How Schools Should Teach*. New York: Basic Books, 1991.

Howard, A., and Bray, D. *Managerial Lives in Transition: Advancing Age and Changing Times*. New York: Guilford Press, 1988.

Millward, R. "Assessor Reliability of Preteacher Assessment Simulations." Unpublished manuscript, Indiana University of Pennsylvania, 1990.

O'Neil, J. "Putting Performance Assessment to the Test." *Educational Leadership*, 1992, *49*(8), 14–19.

Perrone, V. (ed.). *Expanding Student Assessment*. Washington, D.C.: Association for Supervision and Curriculum Development, 1991.

Wiggins, G. "Creating Tests Worth Taking." *Educational Leadership*, 1992, *49*(8), 26–34.

16

Student Self-Evaluation

Carl J. Waluconis

Assessment of learning is most valuable and pleasing to faculty, administrators, and students when the activities involved enhance the process of higher education. If learning is improved, often the assessment activity or technique itself is also expanded and takes on new life and meaning. This is the case with student self-evaluation.

Student self-evaluation is a technique that asks students to describe their own learning. When students complete this process in an extended essay, the benefits seem to be especially productive. Student self-evaluations can be used to gain a better perception of learning in an institution, thus benefiting the faculty while at the same time providing students with necessary skills that improve their learning.

To be effective, the learner's description needs to be more than a checklist of accomplishments and facts. In self-evaluation essays, students should eventually create a synthesis of thought about their own learning, including plans for its future use. Therefore, for these self-evaluation essays, students are asked some form of the questions "What did you learn?" and "How do you plan to use it?"

We felt that if students responded to these questions, it would add a new voice — that of the student — to the outcomes assessment picture at Seattle Central Community College (SCCC). Since we wanted to look at education in such a way that it would make a difference at our institution, we thought the student perspective would be especially useful in making necessary improvements. We quickly discovered that these two questions caused a high rate of anxiety for students the first time they had to address them because their opinions had seldom been solicited before. We also ultimately found that providing a place in the curriculum for students to reflect on their own learning initiated changes in the institution that made a difference in the quality of undergraduate education.

A Brief History of Student Self-Evaluation

Student self-evaluation was not something we created. It has been used in different forms in a variety of ways. In looking at its past uses, I found four places where this technique had been successfully employed in the learning process: (1) in individual classroom situations, (2) in capstone courses (Eaton, 1992), (3) in schools with an institutional culture of self-reflection (Curtz, 1991), and (4) in interdisciplinary programs (Gabelnick, MacGregor, Matthews, and Smith, 1990) like the Coordinated Studies Programs at Seattle Central Community College. In all of these places the effectiveness of student self-evaluation was sufficiently promising to suggest that a separate course might be tried at SCCC in which students assessed their learning in the other courses in which they were concurrently enrolled.

In individual classes, student self-assessment can include a wide range of activities. As described by Cross and Angelo (1988) in *Classroom Assessment Techniques,* weekly or even daily short descriptions by students of what they learned in class and what they hope to learn next, written on a card and turned in at the end of a class period, have been helpful to many faculty. This kind of self-reporting from students can have an immediate impact on a faculty member's next lesson plan. In some classes, instructors use self-assessment as an assignment. In English composition classes at SCCC, a student's final essay is often a critical comparison of his or her own writing at the beginning of the term with that at the end. Even when used in a single class, the student self-assessment reflects a change in the student's relationship to the material: "I wanted to shout while I was writing; I wanted the words I was speaking to have a voice, to shout as loud as I would if I was speaking. I wanted to say something through the essay; I wanted to make sense instead of counting the words and wondering if they met the amount of words our teacher told us to write. I was conscious of what I was doing; it was like I was speaking. I have learned more about writing this quarter than ever" (SCCC student).* Student self-assessment provides a place to speak explicitly about whether or not the learning was meaningful and important; this benefit of student self-assessment encouraged the development of a class in which that was a focus.

Fairhaven College (FC) at Western Washington University has used a capstone course in which all students write summary and evaluation (S&E) papers. In these papers, students examine their years at the institution, "paying attention both to ways in which the institution helped or hindered their progress and to their own developing knowledge of subject matter and themselves as learners" (Eaton, 1992, p. 56). The papers often reflect attitudes indicating that learning has become an ongoing, lifelong process: "This seminar has provided a wonderful structure within which I have been able to thoughtfully look back over my four years, reviewing, questioning, bringing to articulation a portrait in words of my experience here. . . . Writing my S&E was a chance for me to come to a sense of completion at FC and to also see I take with me much work still to be done" (student quoted in Eaton, 1992, p. 56).

Student self-evaluations are an intrinsic part of the curriculum at Fairhaven College. They are also used extensively at other schools as a process of evaluation and as part of a student's transcripts. In Washington State, their use over a long

---

*Unless otherwise indicated, quotations by SCCC students are taken from papers submitted to the author's classes and have been used with the permission of these students.

period at Evergreen State College and Antioch University has helped to shape the culture and climate of those institutions. At Evergreen, in addition to assessing their own work every quarter in evaluation conferences, students also evaluate the faculty, and students and faculty assess the programs in which they just participated: "Through these experiences of reflection, writing, and discussion, students gradually learn that there are variances in judgment, for which reasons can and should be given" (Curtz, 1991, p. 25).

When the community colleges in Washington began to import interdisciplinary, coordinated studies programs, the programs included student self-evaluation as part of the assessment process. In that setting, student self-evaluations again offered students a place in which they could reflect on their own learning and what was important to them about it: "I have gained a new outlook on science from this class. Before, science always seemed to be some vast institution that allowed only certain people entrance. It was on some imaginary pedestal. I now see that science is just another form of human creativity and that it can be a very fulfilling subject to study. Because of this class I am not intimidated by society's myth that science is only for the geniuses of the world and I plan to study it further" ("Self-Evaluation Project," 1990, p. 123).

The self-evaluation essays from the programs reflected changes on many levels for the students, much more than a standardized evaluation could do. As one student commented, "I think that the most significant learning experience I had this quarter was realizing the depth and repercussions of my own stereotypes and prejudices" ("Self-Evaluation Project," 1990, p. 117). The faculty concluded that writing the essay—putting the thoughts on paper—helped students to see learning in new ways.

Findings and Improvements:
The Self-Evaluation Class

Student self-evaluations always offered a new window on learning for faculty who used them. The new perspective that this method offered led faculty to suggest to the Outcomes and Assessment Task Force at SCCC that a separate course in self-evaluation be developed. The idea was accepted. In this class, a humanities offering called Ways of Knowing, the final essay would be a student self-evaluation of the courses in which they were concurrently enrolled.

One of the reasons this approach was supported by the task force was that it would offer a picture of what was going on in different parts of the school. What was working and what was not could be described by students and later addressed by the faculty. It was thought to be a new way of generating conversations about the school and learning but still relied on the standard method of finding a problem and then later solving it. Possibilities exist for that linear method of problem solving, but the course specifically and student self-evaluations in general created a new sort of problem solving. The course uncovered important missing areas in the curriculum, but as it did so, it also provided a solution.

The changes produced by the course included greater curricular coherence through reinforcement and integration of ideas, expanded student responsibility for learning, the promotion of lifelong learning, more exploration of diverse perspectives, greater student retention, and enhancement of faculty development.

The need for curricular coherence as students move from one subject to another was identified by students as they wrote their self-evaluation essays. Along with this, the essays provided an opportunity to reinforce ideas. This approach helped to solve a special problem that has evolved in higher education. Implicit in lectures and class work is the assumption that the student should take the material seriously. The professors, of course, know why it is serious; they have spent the better part of their lives studying it. However, the reasons are often not made clear to students. As the following quotations from students in the class make clear, self-evaluation can provide a time and place for students to understand these reasons for themselves. One student in the class wrote, "I find that learning Algebra is like learning the most succinct language of all. If within this language I chose the incorrect 'word,' the 'meaning of the sentence' would be totally erroneous." Students also used the class essays to link different courses in which they could use similar ideas: "Another important idea I expanded upon this quarter was my ability to speak out, to use my voice. This idea is probably the most connected idea of this quarter because of the fact that I've used it in every class and area of my life. In English, I was using my voice the second week of class when I read my paper on lesbian and gay youth aloud. In Japanese, I found my voice when I found the courage to talk with my teacher face-to-face about my grade at midterm. And at home, I found my voice when I told my lover that I needed time alone and I told myself that, yes, I was a victim of all forms of childhood abuse" (SCCC student). As students made the reasons for study more explicit to themselves, they also demonstrated a greater ownership of the material.

A constant effort in education is to have students assume greater responsibility for their own learning. The class and essay helped them confront this need on their own: "I realize there is nothing anyone can do that will help me change if I'm not going to try. I must discipline myself and only then will I know what true success feels like" (SCCC student). Along with this responsibility for learning, a new sense of ownership may cause students to repudiate standard grading procedures in education. A participating student wrote, "It is not grades that define me or my learning, a reality that I can easily forget at times."

The important elements of what can be done with learning in the future, often missing from anything except vocational and exit courses, can be discovered by the students themselves: "I don't know what my major will be, but what I have learned about critical thinking, working with other people in groups or as partners, and being able to visualize things as they are being related to me, will be of benefit to me throughout my life. Equally important is the realization that I have a right and a responsibility to question what I don't understand or agree with. I hope that I can instill this in my son" (SCCC student).

Lifelong learning is further reinforced when students obtain a broader view of the subject matter. Whether they are obtaining such a view is hard to discover in many of the traditional testing modes. A new perspective can often be provided by the student's own words.

> I kept thinking this would get easier once I wrote it down. It only got harder. I kept hitting wall after wall, coming to no conclusions with my ideas and my time was running out fast. A classmate called me two days before it was due and said, "I want to read your notes, let's go have dinner." We went out and ended up just talking about things we'd been afraid to say in class because we thought we were wrong. It dawned on me that these "wrong" things were the things we thought to be most important about the readings and they directly related to the questions on the exam. Suddenly, we both began writing furiously. We both had our answers. Before this dinner I had thought two things: (1) my writings aren't good enough to let anyone read, and (2) I do not need anyone else's input on my writings; that will only distract me. I was dead wrong [SCCC student].

In a less complicated manner, students also wrestled with coming to terms with a new field. One student commented, "American Sign Language is a foreign language. I had to forget the use of complete, descriptive sentences in ASL, and instead concentrate on concepts. The key to learning ASL is knowing that a concept has to be created and a formulation of images connected." In this way, the larger understanding of subject matter helped the student develop strategies with which to absorb it. The course offered a way to use the material that is often not a part of other methods of evaluation: "That is what I enjoy most about this class [Anthropology], actually being able to enjoy the terms and concepts. It isn't about memorizing from a book, but about thinking" (SCCC student).

Self-evaluation also reveals values a particular subject matter may have or not have for students: "The book gave me information that enables me to carry on a conversation about topics in psychology, but the teacher has taught me more about life, causing me to take a look at my surroundings, actions, friends, and values and make some changes for the better that open doors" (SCCC student). If the student has opened up to more diverse perspectives, self-evaluation is a means to express it and the way it happened. One student wrote, "In a school like SCCC, which has such a multicultural population, we are learning from everyone's cultural experiences as well."

Often a better understanding of the subject matter and one's self can be obtained, but at the same time a course may not have gone especially well for a student. When he or she recognizes some value in such a situation, it can lead to an overall higher rate retention: "I do believe I have regressed to a certain degree this quarter. I could say that this quarter has helped change my goals, because it has, but now I'm stuck in that huge box called square one. The goals I started the quarter with have been dispersed in a new wave of possibilities" (SCCC student).

These are perspectives on student learning that are often not revealed. These documents can be much more valuable to faculty members in determining whether or not they have been successful in a course than a checklist evaluation would be. A description of what students have learned may not correspond to the faculty member's intentions. At the same time, it can also be surprising and gratifying when new perspectives are offered. A student's self-evaluation can tell faculty if the class and the institution are making a difference. The following quote from an SCCC student is not from the Ways of Knowing class, but from an interdisciplinary, coordinated studies program.

> This particular quarter was more than I expected. I have found out not only does this class, "The Televised Mind," include a multi-cultural environment, but it also showed me how many people from different backgrounds can come together as one and make a difference. . . . This quarter showed me that a person from a different culture was more motivated to attack a touchy issue than I expected. When I say touchy issue, I mean . . . confronting

> issues on the government, and how women are be-
> ing treated in the 90's by men and other women.
> This class sort of reached out and slapped some
> sense into my head. It also popped me back into
> reality. . . . "The Televised Mind" showed me that
> we can all get together on a positive level and work
> together.

When individual courses do not have sufficient time for effective self-reflection on learning, then a separate course in self-
evaluation, or self-assessment practices attached to a required
course, can fulfill that need.

Other Uses of Self-Evaluation

The self-evaluation essays have also been used to measure learning outcomes at Seattle Central Community College. Faculty
trained each other in scoring and then read collections of student self-evaluations written at the end of the quarter. Faculty
scored whether or not students described certain kinds of learning, including gains in developing a sense of self-esteem and
community, acquiring knowledge of ideas and experience, becoming a lifelong learner, using critical thinking, and acquiring fundamentals. In order to compare selections that revealed
an outcome, each faculty reader also highlighted specific pas-
sages in the essays. Each essay was read and scored by three
individuals, who worked without consulting the others. The
scores reflected no large disagreements concerning what outcome was being described by students. If two of the three faculty
members indicated that a student had described growth in an
area, a score was assigned.
    The results showed that while enrolled in Ways of Know-
ing, students described gains in the following areas of learning:
94.1 percent — sense of self-esteem and community, 91.2 percent — knowledge of ideas and experience and associations between them, 92.6 percent — lifelong learning, 82.5 percent —
critical thinking, and 77.9 percent — fundamentals.
    The way in which a student is asked a question will help

determine the answer. The richness conveyed by statements about outcomes from the self-evaluation essays is impossible with a checklist. Beyond that, the essays themselves appear to bring the students to a point of reflecting on their learning and, in so doing, discovering more that they had learned. The class in self-assessment gave students even more opportunity to do that than did the coordinated studies classes. This kind of emphasis understandably produces comparatively less reflection on gains in fundamentals. A question about learning basic skills seemed to elicit more positive responses when it was confined to a checklist.

Turning the content of the essays into numbers still has unexplored possibilities. However, much more valuable to the students and faculty involved were the essays themselves. As previously stated, by making ideas about learning and what was being learned more explicit, they helped fill missing parts of the curriculum even as they exposed them. Also, the essays helped build a relationship to the material, one that sustained learning by insisting that it be the student's own.

Strengths and Weaknesses

Student self-evaluation is a method that makes a difference even as it allows faculty to see if educational approaches are working. It does not need an expensive testing procedure to support it. In addition, time devoted to it is time spent in learning; it is therefore not wasteful — unlike tests.

Past studies in which students were asked in an interview to reflect on their learning (such as those by Perry, 1970, and by Belenky, Clinchy, Goldberger, and Tarule, 1986), reported that students looked forward to having that time to reflect on themselves as a learner: "I didn't know all these things had happened. I mean, I wouldn't have realized . . . put them all together and seen them all so clearly. But there they are" (student quoted in Perry, 1970, p. 26). Perry says that "in subsequent years . . . most students would report having 'looked forward' to the occasion, saying that they had noted this experience or that during the year as important to tell us about" (1970, p. 26). The importance of this time and place for students to reflect on their learning was not Perry's focus, but the student response indicated that the experience was very helpful to students. In a parallel fashion, the interviewers in another study found that their own lens changed as they listened to learners speak of their learning (Belenky, Clinchy, Goldberger, and Tarule, 1986).

This mutual growth in learning and the perception of learning is reflected in the process of students' writing self-evaluations. In creating a separate course, other aspects of the process can be expanded upon. The course itself reviews aspects of knowing through learning styles; stage theories of learning; and the student's learning history, including in family, among friends, at work, and in prior enrollment in school. Also, different cultural definitions of learning are explored, as well as barriers to learning. The coursework includes a journal in which students complete weekly entries involving an aspect of the Ways of Knowing class and also an entry on learning in their other classes that week. The midquarter essay asks the students to write a profile of himself or herself as a learner. This practice allows students to tell their own stories within an institution and receive credit for it. With that story and their place made at least somewhat explicit, they can then go on to match that profile against the school and their current classes.

One of the weaknesses of the self-evaluation essay is its tenuous relationship to grades. Setting criteria for what is to be included in the essays is not any harder or easier than that task for any writing assignment. However, the criteria could dangerously limit the potential response and violate the entire idea of student self-evaluation. If students thoroughly engage in the process, they will in nearly all cases be successful. The result is not an automatic or easy grade, because the same statement about student engagement might be made for any task on which they will be graded. Grading poems and paintings are frequent endeavors in institutions of higher learning, and this process raises some of the same difficulties as grading self-evaluations. The problem seems to be in the grades, not in the activity. Although the concept of grading with a single number or letter is accepted, it need not be used to keep valuable learning processes out of a school.

Another weakness of student self-evaluation is one of its strengths. If the axis of power is shifted and students are given the control to describe their own learning, teachers must be prepared to be surprised, even dismayed. However, if teachers are interested in knowing if they are really making a difference, this is an excellent method of obtaining answers.

References

Belenky, M. F., Clinchy, B. M., Goldberger, N. R., and Tarule, J. M. *Women's Ways of Knowing: The Development of Self, Voice, and Mind.* New York: Basic Books, 1986.

Cross, K. P., and Angelo, T. A. *Classroom Assessment Techniques: A Handbook for Faculty.* Ann Arbor: National Center for Research to Improve Postsecondary Teaching and Learning, University of Michigan, 1988.

Curtz, T. "Teaching Self-Assessment." *Washington Center News,* 1991, *6*(1), 23–25.

Eaton, M. D. "Student Self-Assessment: Thinking About the Way We Know." Proceedings of the 10th annual conference on nontraditional-interdisciplinary programs, George Mason University Center for Professional Development, 1992.

Gabelnick, F., MacGregor, J., Matthews, R., and Smith, B. *Learning Communities: Creating Connections Among Students, Faculty, and Disciplines.* New Directions for Teaching and Learning, no. 41. San Francisco: Jossey-Bass, 1990.

Perry, W. G. *Forms of Intellectual and Ethical Development in the College Years: A Scheme.* Troy, Mo.: Holt, Rinehart & Winston, 1970.

"Self-Evaluation Project: Coordinated Studies Evaluation." Unpublished manuscript prepared for Title III: Evaluation Model for Coordinated Studies. Institutional Outcomes Library, Seattle Central Community College, 1990.

17

Coursework
Cluster Analysis

James L. Ratcliff
Elizabeth A. Jones

During the 1970s and 1980s, great strides were made in the *technology* of assessment. The procedures and practices for using student portfolios, surveys, and focus groups are testimony to the progress that was made. We have reviewed and refined the ways we measure students' writing and critical-thinking abilities and faculty's instructional techniques. Substantial gains have been made in the ways we organize, operate, and articulate assessment programs at the classroom, institutional, and statewide level. Yet there has been no clear improvement in establishing the link between the courses students took in college and the general learning they demonstrated through evaluations. If through our assessments we discern that students' writing abilities are deficient, we have little to direct improvement beyond redoubling the charge of the English department in this regard or implementing a writing requirement across the general education curriculum. If the English department takes up the charge, normally all students must be forced to enroll in a sequence of writing instruction regardless of their prior writing ability. For writing across the curriculum to work, faculty teaching subjects as diverse as oboe and obstetrics must include objectives and activities for assessments of student writing skills.

What is needed is a way to identify which patterns and sequences of courses are chosen by students with limited or unsatisfactory writing abilities and then to set about enhancing that skill in those classes. For a university with three thousand to five thousand courses or a four-year college with eight hundred to eighteen hundred courses in its catalogue, the task of focusing resources toward the improvement of one or more general education or liberal learning objectives is daunting.

During the past two decades, most of us designed assessment programs based on conceptualizations of the effect of college on students derived from the pioneering work of Kenneth Feldman (1969) and Alexander Astin (1970a, 1970b). According to their thinking, assessments needed to account for inputs (students' background, prior achievement, aptitude, and interests) and for college effects (the curriculum and extracurriculum) to determine outcomes (progress, persistence, performance, and learning). The conceptualization led to value-added and talent-development models of student learning (Astin, 1985). Scholars interested in student learning and persistence used multiple regression models. Student learning was regressed on background characteristics and college effects to determine factors that best explained student learning. Regression models look for the "line of the best fit" — that is, the one best set of curricular and extracurricular variables that influences student learning (Pascarella, 1985). Given that most colleges and universities pride themselves on the variety of curricular and extracurricular programs available to students (Toombs, Fairweather, Chen, and Amey, 1989), looking for the line of best fit in assessment data was tantamount to searching in a department store for the one pair of shoes that best fits the feet of most students. There was increasingly disturbing evidence that students had very few formal learning experiences in common in the overwhelming majority of colleges and universities where distributional education requirements were the norm (Boyer and Ahlgren, 1987; Ratcliff, 1987, 1988).

While the undergraduate curriculum was being declared

incoherent and in disarray (American Association of Colleges, 1985) and calls were being issued for the abandonment of distributional requirements in favor of a core curriculum (Cheney, 1989), evidence was mounting that the variation in student learning was greater within colleges than between them (Baird, 1988; Pascarella and Terenzini, 1991). A curricular corollary of this finding was that students who take different patterns of coursework learn different knowledge, skills, and abilities (Adelman, 1988; Benbow and Stanley, 1983; Ratcliff, 1987, 1988). The idea was advanced that the task of assessment ought to be to identify the best fit of student and learning environment rather than to search for a single environment that suits all students. Given this conceptualization, a goal of assessments of general education and liberal learning should be to identify subenvironments or learning communities within an institution that are particularly salient for students of a specific set of background, achievement, aptitude, and interest characteristics (Pascarella, 1985; Pascarella and Terenzini, 1991).

Methods

The 1980s were also a decade in which the state and quality of educational programs were scrutinized. National reports exhorted faculty and academic leaders to improve baccalaureate programs. The Study Group on the Conditions of Excellence in American Higher Education (1984), formed under the U.S. Department of Education, urged colleges to provide students with clear academic direction, standards, and values. It asked postsecondary institutions to use assessment information and to explore the use of transcripts as resources in understanding more about what subjects students study in college and what they learn. The techniques and findings from student assessment described in this chapter are a direct outcome of those recommendations. Beginning in 1985, we developed specific procedures to determine the gains in student learning that were directly attributable to enrollment in different patterns of undergraduate coursework (Ratcliff, 1987, 1988).

No single curricular model and no single analytical process

clearly identified the effect of coursework patterns on the general learned abilities of students. Therefore, over the past eight years, we have developed a model for linking assessments of the general learning of undergraduates with their courses (Ratcliff, 1987, 1988, 1990a, 1990b; Ratcliff and Jones, 1990; Jones and Ratcliff, 1990a, 1990b, 1991). This research has proceeded under the rubric of the Differential Coursework Patterns (DCP) Project, and the model for linking courses to student assessment has been referred to as the Coursework Cluster Analysis Model (CCAM). Its development and testing were supported first by the Office of Educational Research and Improvement of the U.S. Department of Education. Subsequent qualitative validity studies of the model, trend analyses of coursework patterns, and studies of the applicability of the model to curricular reform, assessment program development, and academic advising have been supported by the Exxon Educational Foundation. The DCP Project and the uses of the CCAM continue as part of the research of the National Center on Postsecondary Teaching, Learning, and Assessment at Pennsylvania State University. Beginning in the fall of 1992, the CCAM will be used with a national sample of five thousand entering first-year undergraduates at twenty-two colleges and universities across the country. We will be evaluating the patterns of coursework most closely related to gains in student learning in reading comprehension, written communication, the sciences and mathematics, the social sciences, critical thinking, and the development of student values and attitudes toward learning.

The CCAM was originally developed and tested at six institutions: a community college, a women's liberal arts college, a nontraditional liberal arts college, a comprehensive college with a professionally oriented curriculum, an urban doctorate-granting university, and a selective research university. In addition, CCAM has been applied to student reports of course enrollment patterns and ACT-COMP and College Basic Academic Subjects Exam (CBASE) scores at the University of Tennessee, Knoxville (Pike and Phillippi, 1989).

In the most typical applications, assessment instruments were administered to graduating seniors. Since 1986, we have examined over seventy-two thousand courses appearing on the transcripts of approximately sixteen hundred seniors. Each group of seniors included a cross section of majors. The samples also reflected the full range of academic ability, as indicated by SAT scores, for the general population of students at each institution. The results of posttests were compared to the results of corresponding pretests of the same students. Such well-known standardized instruments as the SAT, GRE, ACT, and ACT-COMP examinations were used, as well as the Kolb Learning Styles Inventory and locally constructed measures of student-perceived course difficulty.

The Coursework Cluster Analysis Model involves several steps. First, student residual scores are derived. This score is the difference between the student's actual score on the outcome assessment measure and the score predicted by the entrance measure used. Next student transcripts are examined. Courses reported on them are clustered into patterns based upon the residual scores of the students who enrolled. The resulting patterns are then grouped according to any of a wide variety of student or institutional factors. Patterns can be classified according to the entering-ability level of the student, the type of courses selected (general education, prerequisites), the campus at which the student enrolled, or the residence facilities housing the students. The coursework of adult versus traditional-college-age students, commuter versus residential students, and part-time versus full-time students can be compared. Within systems of higher education with course comparability, transfer schemes, and articulation agreements, the model can be used to determine if courses taken by students at branch campuses or other institutions are associated with the same types of improvement in learning as for students on the main campus. The quantitative procedures and techniques are described in greater detail in the *Handbook on Linking Assessment and General Education* (Ratcliff, Jones, and Hoffman, 1992).

This analysis is critical given the diversity of undergraduate education today. Most colleges and universities have an expansive curriculum representing the explosion of knowledge, diversity of students, and modes of inquiry that characterize higher education in the twentieth century. For example, we find that up to 50 percent of the courses found on the transcripts of graduating seniors are not found on transcripts of the preceding year's classes. The reason for this is that annual course schedules do not represent all courses found in the college catalogue. Certain courses are given on a one-time experimental basis, and some are canceled due to lack of enrollment. Typically, the undergraduate student chooses thirty-five to forty-five courses to fulfill the baccalaureate degree requirements from a list of twenty-five hundred to five thousand courses at a large research university or from eight hundred to fifteen hundred courses at a liberal arts college. Therefore, what and how much students learn at a given institution varies from year to year.

A great strength of the CCAM, and an asset that seems to enhance its acceptability to faculty, is that it is not dependent on instruments supplied by external vendors. It can use a variety of locally developed instruments, tailored to particular needs and extensively employing local judgment. A college, for instance, might administer its own essay examinations to freshmen and seniors, and its own faculty might grade them holistically; so long as the final evaluation or its subparts can be translated to a numeric scale, this instrument would be entirely adequate for the purpose of the Coursework Cluster Analysis Model.

Findings

Student learning varies greatly in complex institutions of higher education because of their broad array of curricular offerings. Critical to the success of a general education for students in these institutions is some means of recognizing curricular diversity and its effects. Thus, the more complex the curricular offerings, the greater is the challenge to determine the relationship between coursework taken and learning achieved.

Through measures of general learning and the transcripts of graduating seniors, the courses taken by students who show large gains on these measures can be identified. We have found that clusters rather than single courses produce varied types of gains in learning. For example, sequences in a wide range of disciplines such as business, biology, and philosophy were associated with gains in student learning in analytic reasoning. Improvement in mathematics was linked to work in economics, business, music, physical therapy, math, and quantitative methods in management. Student gains in reading comprehension were associated with studying marketing, accounting, management, music, and history.

These results challenge our traditional views that only mathematics courses improve student learning in math and that only literature or English courses help students to gain in reading comprehension. This project identified a wide range of disciplines that help students to increase their learning in certain areas. Once this cluster sorting has occurred for several years, it is possible to answer questions about the efficacy of particular general education structures and the contribution of specific course sequences to the attainment of educational goals. This project provides some preliminary guidance for revising, reforming, and revitalizing general education for improved teaching and learning.

From our research, we also know that students of low entering abilities (relative to the norms of the institution) took different coursework than high-ability students. For example, we find that low-ability students at the institutions we examined did not complete the science sequences intended to be part of the general education sequence. For instance, Chemistry 101, 102, 103 was a curricular package intended to introduce students to the principal concepts, terms, theories, and nature of inquiry into the discipline. It was designed to produce a depth of learning that could theoretically contribute to student achievement of the general education goals of the institution. Similar sequences might be offered in biology, physics, and astronomy. High-ability students usually select and complete one of these sequences to fulfill part of their general education requirements. However, low-ability students may take Chemistry 101 and receive a low or failing grade. Next they enroll in physics, repeat the experience, and then move on to biology. Depth as intended is not achieved for these students, although they do amass the prerequisite number of science credits to meet general education requirements. Instead, breadth takes on a new and sad definition of sequential exposure to negative education experiences. Our research also provides information to identify positive, as well as negative, general education experiences for low-ability students. The example illustrates that we must do more for these learners.

Two other findings arose from this research. First, what students take in college does have a bearing on what they learn, on the type and extent of their cognitive development, and on their values and attitudes toward learning. Second, the structure of the general education program in the institutions we examined did not have a profound effect on the types of learning we examined.

The finding that studying different courses leads to different types of learning is really part of a larger research finding best described in *How College Affects Students* (Pascarella and Terenzini, 1991). The authors describe and analyze twenty years of research indicating that differences in student learning are far greater within institutions than between them (Baird, 1988). Given this finding, it makes sense that students taking different courses and having different extracurricular experiences should show differences in subject matter learned, in the type and extent of their general cognitive development, and in values and attitudes toward learning.

Strengths and Limitations of the Model

This model and the method of analysis help faculty at colleges and universities to accomplish several things. They can determine which assessment measures best describe the kinds of learning that take place among students at their institutions; they can also select multiple measures that reflect the general education goals of their particular college or university. Using the model to link these measures to coursework, they can then determine which measures explain the most variation in student learning. This information helps the academic leader or faculty committee charged with the development and oversight of the assessment program. If a measure of general learning does not explain much of the variation in student learning, then one option is to conclude that it is inappropriate to the students and the educational program. In short, it can assist in the rejection of that form of evaluation as superfluous or unsatisfactory. An alternative conclusion is that the institution is not devoting sufficient attention to the type of learning measured. Here an examination of the assessment instrument in relation to the curriculum is needed.

The model also determines which patterns of coursework are associated with particular kinds of learning and groups of students. It can measure the extent to which a core curriculum or a program based on distributional requirements produces the greatest gain in learning among different groups of undergraduates at the same institution. It can also be used to identify the extent to which transfer students benefit from the same or different general education courses when compared to courses taken by students who began their baccalaureate program at the institution.

The CCAM also has some limitations. It is intended for the assessment of general education and liberal learning, not of learning within the major. It works best for those institutions that have a distribution plan of general education wherein students have a fairly wide range of curricular choices from which to fulfill the requirements of their baccalaureate. This model will have limited value for those institutions with a core curriculum for general education or a small number of course offerings. In addition, the model requires that institutions have the technical capability to merge student transcripts with assessment measures.

The cluster model identifies coursework associated with improvement in student learning in general education and liberal learning. It does not tell us that particular coursework *caused* the learning. Subsequent research and analysis are required to determine the contributing factors. The model and the accompanying analysis need to be conducted for several years at a college or university. With longitudinal data, consistent coursework patterns may emerge that are associated with improvement in student learning; this information will then be more reliable and valid. Finally, the data yielded by the model are not useful for comparisons across institutions, since each college has its own vision of general education and different goals based upon its mission.

The model described in this chapter is also premised on several assumptions. First, courses are the primary unit of learning in college. Second, learning is not merely the sum of all courses students take, but is actually developmental and cumulative; thus, the identification of combinations and sequences of courses is required. Third, transcripts are an accurate listing of the enrollment patterns of students. Fourth, most undergraduate courses are basically stable in content and instruction. Fifth, the assessment instruments used are appropriate and technically sound. Sixth, students are motivated to perform conscientiously in completing these measures.

Improvements Undertaken

The Coursework Cluster Analysis Model identifies groups of courses associated with improvement in student learning, invaluable information to curriculum planners. One institution that has used this model for several years makes the information available to faculty as they assess their general education component of the curriculum. These faculty members now know what courses consistently contribute over time to student learning. Courses outside the general education requirements can become candidates for inclusion in the curriculum. Those in the general education sequence not found to be associated with gains in student learning can be revised, improved, or dropped. The extent to which general education courses affect the learning of both high-ability and low-ability students has relevance in deciding how widely ranging the distributional options should be, given the educational goals of the institution.

The model is also helpful in the academic advising of students. It has identified those specific courses in which students of comparable interests, abilities, and achievement have enrolled. Faculty can therefore recommend courses that are the most appropriate for students.

With the Coursework Cluster Analysis Model, we have a powerful tool for linking the courses students select with the improvement they demonstrate. The model overcomes the tendency to suppress the effect of specific sequences of courses by aggregating data across all students and all curricular choices. It provides a mechanism for updating, expanding, and enhancing the range and type of measures and indicators used in the assessment program. Faculty have always had a good, solid way of evaluating student performance one course at a time; the CCAM allows assessment specialists to examine the effect of sequences and combinations of courses on different groups of students. In the process, assessment can be reconceptualized. Instead of searching for the one best curriculum for everyone—a task appropriate only for small colleges with extremely homogeneous student bodies—we can begin to identify those subenvironments and learning communities that naturally form on our campuses and that may constitute the best success stories we can unearth with our assessment plans and programs.

References

Adelman, C. "Linking Student Outcomes and Curricular Reform: A New Research Model." Forum presentation at the annual meeting of the American Association for Higher Education, Washington, D.C., Mar. 1988.

American Association of Colleges. *Integrity in the College Curriculum: A Report to the Academic Community.* Washington, D.C.: Association of American Colleges, 1985.

Astin, A. W. "The Methodology of Research on College Impact, Part 1." *Sociology of Education,* 1970a, *43,* 223–254.

Astin, A. W. "The Methodology of Research on College Impact, Part 2." *Sociology of Education,* 1970b, *43,* 437–450.

Astin, A. W. *Achieving Educational Excellence: A Critical Assessment of Priorities and Practices in Higher Education.* San Francisco: Jossey-Bass, 1985.

Baird, L. "The College Environment Revisited: A Review of Research and Theory." In J. Smart (ed.), *Handbook of Theory and Research in Higher Education.* Vol. 4. New York: Agathon Press, 1988.

Benbow, C. P., and Stanley, J. C. "Differential Course-Taking Hypothesis Revisited." *American Educational Research Journal,* 1983, *20*(4), 469–573.

Boyer, C. M., and Ahlgren, A. "Assessing Undergraduates' Patterns of Credit Distribution: Amount and Specialization." *Journal of Higher Education,* 1987, *58*, 430–442.

Cheney, L. V. *50 Hours: A Core Curriculum for College Students.* Washington, D.C.: National Endowment for the Humanities, 1989.

Feldman, K. "Studying the Impacts of College on Students." *Sociology of Education,* 1969, *42*, 207–237.

Jones, E. A., and Ratcliff, J. L. "Effective Coursework Patterns and Faculty Perceptions of the Development of General Learned Abilities." Paper presented at the annual meeting of the Association for the Study of Higher Education, Portland, Oreg., 1990a.

Jones, E. A., and Ratcliff, J. L. "Is a Core Curriculum Best for Everybody? The Effect of Different Patterns of Coursework on the General Education of High and Low Ability Students." Paper presented at the annual meeting of the American Educational Research Association, Boston, 1990b.

Jones, E. A., and Ratcliff, J. L. "Which General Education Curriculum Is Better: Core Curriculum or the Distributional Requirement?" *Journal of General Education,* 1991, *40*, 69–101.

Pascarella, E. T. "College Environmental Influences on Learning and Cognitive Development: A Critical Review and Synthesis." In J. Smart (ed.), *Higher Education: Handbook of Theory and Research.* Vol. 1. New York: Agathon Press, 1985.

Pascarella, E. T., and Terenzini, P. T. *How College Affects Students: Findings and Insights from Twenty Years of Research.* San Francisco: Jossey-Bass, 1991.

Pike, G. R., and Phillippi, R. H. "Generalizability of the Differential Coursework Methodology: Relationships Between Self-Reported Coursework and Performance on the ACT-COMP Exam." *Research in Higher Education,* 1989, *30*(3), 245–260.

Ratcliff, J. L. *The Effect of Differential Coursework Patterns on General Learned Abilities of College Students: Application of the Model to an Historical Database of Student Transcripts.* Report to the Office of Educational Research and Improvement, U.S. Department of Education, 1987.

Ratcliff, J. L. "The Development of a Cluster Analytic Model for Determining the Associated Effects of Coursework Patterns on Student Learning." Paper presented at the annual meeting of the American Educational Research Association, New Orleans, La., 1988.

Ratcliff, J. L. *Development and Testing of a Cluster-Analytic Model for Identifying Coursework Patterns Associated with General Learned Abilities of College Students, Final Report, Ithaca College, Samples #1 and #2*. Washington, D.C.: Office of Educational Research and Improvement, U.S. Department of Education, 1990a.

Ratcliff, J. L. *Development and Testing of a Cluster-Analytic Model for Identifying Coursework Patterns Associated with General Learned Abilities of College Students, Final Report, Stanford University, Samples #1 and #2*. Washington, D.C.: Office of Educational Research and Improvement, U.S. Department of Education, 1990b.

Ratcliff, J. L., and Jones, E. A. "General Learning at a Women's College." Paper presented at the annual meeting of the Association for the Study of Higher Education, Portland, Oreg., 1990.

Ratcliff, J. L., Jones, E. A., and Hoffman, S. *Handbook on Linking Assessment and General Education*. University Park, Pa.: National Center on Postsecondary Teaching, Learning, and Assessment, 1992.

Study Group on the Conditions of Excellence in American Higher Education. *Involvement in Learning: Realizing the Potential of American Higher Education*. Washington, D.C.: National Institute of Education, 1984.

Toombs, W., Fairweather, J., Chen, A., and Amey, M. *Open to View: Practice and Purpose in General Education 1988. A Final Report to the Exxon Education Foundation*. University Park, Pa.: Center for the Study of Higher Education, Pennsylvania State University, 1989.

18

Total Quality Management

Darrell W. Krueger

On a daily basis, the mass media remind us that we are residents of a nation at risk. They tell us the United States is falling behind other industrialized societies in productivity, creativity, and innovation. It seems that American international economic competitiveness has eroded dramatically. Indeed, nearly every indicator employed to measure levels of economic effectiveness reinforces this concern. It takes economic resources to produce a more flexible, capable citizenry; such a base is required for our system to produce tomorrow's problem solvers.

The National Educational Challenge

It seems ironic that our educational institutions, once hailed as strong contributors to the American miracle, are now frequently blamed for the country's problems. To argue the point seems to miss its implication. The fact remains: maintaining—perhaps even returning to—the U.S. position of global preeminence is an incredibly complex, demanding challenge, one that we as educators must accept and meet.

A growing body of "missionaries" in educational circles are actively working for significant, positive change within our educational system. However, the reformers are confronted by well-entrenched and frequently counterproductive values, practices, and structural arrangements. As with every social system, change in educational institutions must confront the vested interests of the status quo.

The Issue of Quality

Fundamental to the improvement of education is the refocus of attention on the appropriate values, purposes, and goals of education. Once these are agreed upon, the next step is to arrive at indicators that can demonstrate that they are being achieved. It is not only the results that should be measured but also the processes and practices of good education. Measuring the processes and practices will lead to the improvement of these activities, particularly when quality becomes the focal point of planning and funding mechanisms. History reinforces the point.

Quality: Traditional Style

Traditionally, higher education has responded to the quality question by asserting that excellence can be measured by quantitative means. In other words, excellence was determined by the financial or resource base of an institution, the size and capability of its faculty, and the size and capability of its student body, as well as various factors relating to its physical plant and support systems.

The questions most frequently asked of educators are "How many students are enrolled at the university?" and "Has the student body increased in size?" This value system is something for which we, as educators, are responsible. During the period of rapid growth in this nation, every public education administrator (superintendents of schools, principals, college and university presidents, vice presidents, and deans) took what now has become a very harmful message to their funding sources. "We need more money," we said, "because we are enrolling more and more students." That message was heard and understood. It resulted in funding formulas based solely on numbers of students and credit hours generated. Tools to analyze "efficiency" quickly followed. The "data-element dictionary" was developed to produce statistics for the national and state reports that were required. Focus on the question of "How many?" still dominates today and undermines efforts to improve educational quality.

Quality: The Assessment Mode

Fifteen to twenty years ago, many in higher education began to question the viability of the quantitative input approach to quality. Its limitations were both obvious and potentially devastating. For one thing, the determination of quality of the educational system is made before the student even joins it. The interaction of the student with the educational process is deemed irrelevant for all practical purposes.

As a consequence, thinking about quality began to focus on the output or product of higher education. The assessment movement was born. Institutions of higher education searched for useful indicators that value had been added to their students. They became preoccupied with developing mechanisms for monitoring student development using a variety of approaches. A few states, among them Missouri and Tennessee, recognized the problem earlier than others.

At Northeast Missouri State University, President Charles McClain asked repeatedly, "Are we making a difference? Can we prove it?" It was those questions—and others similar in nature—that propelled the institution into assessing outcomes. Test scores were examined, and numerous student surveys were developed. The efforts were fledgling. Although the goals were well intentioned, they were shortsighted, principally because student achievement at the national average was being sought.

As late as the mid 1980s, only a few institutions had seriously attempted to design and implement viable assessment programs. At the same time, a number that were engaged in assessment were beginning to identify limitations. The programs themselves were not the problem; they were simply not enough.

For example, assessment failed to provide good direction for improving aspects of the educational enterprise that failed to produce good results. Faculty felt that they had a good grasp of the necessary quantitative input variables from the traditional approach and had made progress in measuring overall student achievement. However, they lacked a clear concept of how their precious resources could be effectively and efficiently converted into successful education.

The curriculum was then examined. Was it appropriate? Were the students taking the curriculum? Were they honestly trying? Were they buying the textbooks? Were they studying? Was there coherence in the curriculum? In ways too numerous to mention, actions were sought that would make a material difference, and some successes followed. Students began to improve, scoring higher on the national tests and follow-up attitudinal surveys. But the reasons for this improvement were elusive.

Then, in 1987, the "Seven Principles for Good Practice in Undergraduate Education" appeared. This article was written by Arthur W. Chickering and Zelda F. Gamson under the auspices of the American Association for Higher Education and the Johnson Foundation following a gathering of noted educators at the foundation's Wingspread Retreat Center in Racine, Wisconsin. Earnest study of its components made some things clearer. A direct correlation could be established between the principles and aspects of programs that had shown clear improvement. Outcomes had risen dramatically in programs where student-faculty involvement had increased, there were more collaborative learning experiences, expectations had risen, immediate feedback was given, learning was an active — not passive — experience, students were treated as individuals, and the diversity of talents was understood and respected. Outcomes also improved when learning communities existed outside the classroom and students had increased the amount of time devoted to studying.

Through the years, thoughts on assessment have changed due to better knowledge of the factors that predict learner outcomes and the educational components that truly are important in bringing about positive change. Those components include creating and assessing learning communities, determining whether and then how much students are studying, and asking how many papers they are writing and how much collaborative work and study is going on. Improvement in these areas can bring measurable progress.

Regardless of the assessment tools utilized (portfolios, tests, or any other measure of student products), linking the program to Chickering and Gamson's seven principles and constantly asking the question "How can we improve?" provide the kind of focus needed to effect genuine improvement.

What has become ever more apparent is that what is valued is what is funded, and what is funded is what is measured. When input measures form the sole basis for funding — where the results of educational efforts are overlooked — the quality of education suffers.

The Minnesota State University System has committed itself to breaking out of the input measures model through its "Q-7: Quality on the Line" initiative, one in which Winona State University is heavily engaged. Assisted by a blue ribbon commission, the Minnesota State University Board and the seven campuses it serves are committed to achieving progress on indicators of high-quality education designed for the future. Those indicators are designed to assist in the process of producing graduates who can think critically and solve problems, possess a global vision and a multicultural perspective, are scientifically literate, are ready to work, and are good citizens who behave ethically. Another component is designed to encourage work with Minnesota's public school districts to ensure that students are well prepared for college. The Q-7 program is a significant step, although only a first one that must lead to others if education is to bring renewed progress and prosperity to Minnesota and the nation.

Total Quality Management

Even with the traditional quantitative input approach, assessment model, and the seven principles, the quest to identify quality in institutions of higher education is far from over. In fact, some additional supplementing approaches are already appearing. For example, to expand our grasp of converting resources into products beyond the student-instructor relationship incorporated in the seven principles, the notion of total quality management is emerging. If developed and modified for higher education, TQM can provide an opportunity to improve performance of the entire administrative and academic apparatus of an institution.

Business has led in the development of TQM, not so much because change was desired as because it was dictated by the ferocious increase in global competition, a competition that U.S. firms were not winning. Winona State is privileged to have a strong association with the Rochester, Minnesota, division of IBM, which in 1990 accepted the Malcolm Baldrige Award for its quality enhancement efforts. Like IBM, Winona State is heavily involved in the training and retraining of people. Because of that common thrust and because the university supplies the Rochester Division with many employees, IBM treats Winona State as one of its customers. One significant advantage of that relationship is that Winona State representatives are included in IBM training sessions.

As Winona State now moves to enhance quality in all that it does and as it seeks ways to measure its gains (both to provide accountability to its publics and to secure badly needed resources), the concept of TQM can be extremely useful. This management approach contains insights into problems that are as useful to policy makers in education as they are to those in business. The first of these insights is that inspections do not improve quality. Inspection occurs only at the end of the process. At that point, it is too late. The assessment movement represents a form of inspection for education. The big flaw in outcomes assessment is that it cannot improve quality by itself. The second insight is that the way to improve quality is to review — and improve — the processes that lead to poor quality. If the performance of students does not meet expected standards, it is the fault of the processes that led to that performance. The third useful insight is that 85 to 90 percent of all problems are the fault of the *system,* not the individual. There are no villains in this piece. Most individuals perform their activities in the manner they believe leads to the best results. Finally, TQM has taught us that higher quality need not result in higher costs. In fact, as we review processes, we discover ways of doing them better that may result in sharp cost reductions, as well as major savings in not having to rework defective products. Beyond these insights, TQM contains a number of elements that are directly applicable to higher education.

Reduced Cycle Time. Some corporations have discovered that major cost reductions can be effected in business through process review when it results in eliminating unnecessary steps that tie up resources. The time to graduation for traditional baccalaureate students today is five-and-a-half to six years. Reducing this "cycle time" by only one term would result in savings of millions of dollars.

Benchmarking. The TQM concept of "benchmarking" shows considerable promise for broadening not only the transformation process but also the assessment program. This notion fixes attention on whoever or whatever carries out a process best. Comparisons may be made within the institution, the state, the region, the nation, or the world. Once the model unit is identified, it is thoroughly analyzed with the purpose of discovering the key variables that lead to success and developing criteria for their measurement.

Benchmarking could be very significant to education as the support for national testing gains momentum. Evaluating ourselves against the best of a kind (whether institutions, departments, or programs), could be much more useful than using test scores, which can only provide information without answering the important question of how to improve.

The Quality Challenge: An Institution's Response

In 1989, discussions at Winona State University began to center on the use of the seven principles as the basis for evaluation efforts. These discussions were conducted in an environment of more than a little skepticism. After initial hesitancy, however, the campus community demonstrated that it was willing to learn and anxious to demonstrate the high quality of education that is at the heart of the institution.

The entire community — faculty, staff, students, and administration — has joined together to take the first steps in implementing a system of academic evaluation built upon the seven principles. Particular attention has been given to the creation of learning communities because of the outstanding role they play in promoting student achievement. Other areas of the university have followed by working to establish the benchmarking element of TQM as their preliminary step in planning for progress.

The retiring faculty union president stated recently that the past two years have been the best of his life. It is reasonable to conclude that his reaction is due to the conscious shift the institution has made to thinking about and acting upon those things that make a difference in education rather than focusing on how many credit hours are produced and tying faculty positions to those data.

In the beginning, an "expectations" document was prepared, patterned on one developed at the University of Tennessee, Knoxville. The statement spells out those things to which the Winona State faculty, administration, staff, and students are expected to dedicate themselves. It was linked to a model for analyzing indicators of effectiveness within the context of the learning environment at three levels — institutional, campus, and students — as well as the resources needed at each level and, of course, outcomes. The model is important because it recognizes the context within which the outcomes were developed. Then the process of establishing the indicators was begun.

With the help of Peter T. Ewell of the National Center for Higher Education Management Systems, Boulder, Colorado, measures were developed (most of them unobtrusive) that will help in evaluating how effectively the institution is practicing the seven principles. Ewell emphasizes that his work is intended to serve as a broad guide for the development of quality improvement efforts. The indicators are not intended to be applied judgmentally, narrowly, or comparatively.

Indicators of Institutional Effectiveness

Examples of the indicators include:

1. *Student-faculty contact:* overall student-faculty ratio, average section size (excluding independent study), percentage of sections with fifteen or fewer students, overall frequency of out-of-class undergraduate contact with the faculty, percentage of students involved in faculty research, average number of faculty hours per week spent advising students

2. *Increased cooperation among students:* percentage of faculty members reporting efforts to create group projects or learning communities, percentage of faculty members reporting the use of noncompetitive grading criteria, percentage of students reporting participation in group study

3. *Active learning:* number of internships, practicums, or other practice-oriented courses; number of independent study sections offered; percentage of graduating seniors engaging in at least one internship, practicum, independent study, or similar practice-oriented course; percentage of courses requiring students to engage in independent research papers, projects, presentations, or similar exercises; percentage of courses requiring students to use the library as a research resource

4. *Prompt feedback:* average number of graded assignments or exercises given per course, percentage of courses requiring a graded assignment within the first two weeks of the term, average turnaround time for submission of final course grades, percentage of students reporting that they generally received graded assignments back from instructors within one week, percentage of students reporting that instructors provided frequent and specific oral comments on performance

5. *Time on task:* average student course load taken, percentage of courses with a clear attendance policy, average number of hours per week spent on academic assignments by graduating seniors, percentage of available library spaces occupied by students from 5 to 9 P.M.

6. *High expectations:* average ACT of entering freshmen, average number of pages of written assignments in humanities

and social science courses, percentage of seniors graduating without writing a major research paper during their undergraduate career, percentage of students reporting not being significantly challenged by class material and assignments, percentage of students completing their freshman year without checking a book out of the library

7.   *Respect for diverse talents and ways of learning:* percentage distribution of undergraduate students by race and gender, percentage of courses requiring students to speak in class and requiring them to view visual material as part of assignments, percentage of students reporting that they were encouraged to ask questions in class when they did not understand something, percentage of students reporting that the grading and evaluation process used by the instructor allowed them to demonstrate what they knew

Incorporation of some or all of these, along with other indicators of effectiveness centered on the seven principles, provides meaningful focus to efforts to improve the quality of undergraduate education. It also begins to create the discussion of the world that "ought to be." When communicated to the publics served by education, this focus can be most useful in shifting the discussion away from the issue of "how many." As education changes the discussion, it will certainly alter the behavior of the people with whom it interacts. It is certain that the support will then exist to bring about the change that will allow this country to regain its competitive edge globally, change that will ensure a bright future for the next generation of Americans.

Reference

Chickering, A., and Gamson, Z. "Seven Principles for Good Practice in Undergraduate Education." *The Wingspread Journal,* 1987, *9*(2), 1.

Part Five

State-Level
Approaches
to Assessment

Alverno College and Northeast Missouri State University administrators and faculty undertook their outcomes assessment initiatives in the 1970s for their own purposes. Presidents at both institutions decided that improving the educational experience to enhance student learning was their highest priority, and they kept that goal before their faculties continuously.

Most institutions that implemented outcomes assessment programs in the 1980s did so as a result of outside pressure, either from state governments or from an accrediting agency. By the end of the decade, four out of five states had taken some action designed to encourage public institutions to assess program outcomes, and all six regional accrediting associations had included outcomes assessment in their criteria for accreditation of private as well as public institutions.

The chapters in Part Five include some information about the influence of the accreditation process in stimulating campus assessment activity, but their principal focus is on the impact of state policies. Although it takes more than a decade for the full force of a new accreditation standard to be felt in all institutions within a region, boards and legislatures can implement requirements much more quickly. Moreover, state requirements are often accompanied by immediate and powerful sanctions — such as reductions in funding — for noncompliance.

Tennessee was the first state to adopt a policy on outcomes assessment. Performance funding, as the policy was called, remains the most prescriptive of all state assessment initiatives — requiring among other things that every public postsecondary institution in the state test all graduates using a nationally standardized test of generic skills and administer a common alumni survey. Although the most specific in its requirements of institutions, the Tennessee policy also offers the most substantial reward for compliance: a funding supplement of up to 5.45 percent of each public institution's budget for instruction.

Initiated in 1979, the performance funding program in Tennessee has been in effect long enough to permit analysis of the effects of improvement actions undertaken on the basis of assessment findings. In Chapter Nineteen, Janice Van Dyke, Linda Rudolph, and Karen Bowyer report that increases in student retention, placement rates, and satisfaction of various constituencies have taken place as a result of making changes in curricular and student services suggested by assessment findings.

In Virginia, a much more flexible assessment mandate was implemented in 1985. Within categories (such as general education and major fields) specified by the State Council for Higher Education, institutions could select the instruments and methods to be used in assessing outcomes. According to Barbara Fuhrmann and Karen Gentemann, authors of Chapter Twenty, the wide variety of institutional responses to this general call for assessment has led to a much more diffuse set of outcomes in Virginia than Van Dyke and colleagues have described for Tennessee. Instead of a specific connection between assessment, improvement action, and result (which is the sequence that must be reported annually to the Tennessee Higher Education Commission), in Virginia, evaluation is viewed as just one of several concurrent influences combining to produce change in higher education. Furhmann and Gentemann believe that a principal contribution of assessment to education reform is "a more self-reflective and student-oriented approach to curricular development."

The College Outcomes Evaluation Program (COEP) in New Jersey is the subject of Chapter Twenty-One by Nina Jemmott and Edward Morante. COEP provided the same kind of flexible approach to stimulating institutional assessment initiatives as did Virginia, but it also incorporated a statewide measure of general intellectual skills. After several years of development and two statewide pilot administrations, the skills testing was terminated. However, Jemmott and Morante report three institutional case studies that provide evidence that COEP has had a lasting impact on institutional climate, program and course review, and teacher evaluation.

In Chapter Twenty-Two, Dorothy Bray and Martha Kanter paint a very different picture of assessment from the perspective of educators in California community colleges. California laws define outcomes in terms of transfer (from two-year to four-year institutions), completion of occupational programs, and acquisition of basic skills. Data bearing on each of these outcomes are collected and aggregated centrally for the state's 107 community colleges. Some 60 percent of the colleges have created new basic skills courses designed to meet students' needs, but economic problems in the state have severely limited implementation of further improvements based on assessment findings.

In Chapter Twenty-Three, Peter Ewell provides an overview of state assessment policies and initiatives and of the roles these policies and regional accreditation practices have played in stimulating campus assessment activity. Following his assertion that the indirect nature of external assessment requirements as inducements to institutional action, as well as their sheer variety, automatically limits generalizations about impact, Ewell nevertheless draws some conclusions about the overall impact of nearly a decade of externally induced outcomes assessment activities. The actions responsive to findings range from more remedial coursework for entering students to more capstone seminars for seniors. Despite these accomplishments, Ewell believes that assessment has opened the door for increasing direction from states concerning postsecondary education practice. If institutions are to maintain substantial discretion in the use of state resources, they will have to provide increasingly specific information about their performance.

Following Part Five, I provide a summary and conclusion for the book in Chapter Twenty-Four, analyzing several difficulties we face in answering the question "Are we making a difference?"

A major difficulty is related to time. Improvements take time to bring about, and even more time must elapse before their effects become apparent. For most outcomes assessment programs, which were begun in the late 1980s, the emphasis has appropriately been on the process of collecting evidence.

A second significant problem is related to measurement. Decision makers are interested in simple statistics that are reliable and valid and can be compared across programs and institutions. Faculty, by contrast, need a rich array of data from a variety of sources to direct improvement actions. The measures that might be employed to provide the kinds of data that would satisfy external or internal audiences either have not been developed or are technically inadequate to address the tasks set for them.

Despite these and other problems, I do believe we are making a difference. This volume is filled with examples of changes in educational processes that have been undertaken on campuses across the country in response to assessment findings. These changes — most often made by faculty who had not previously studied the literature on the impact of college on students — are generally actions that research has shown are most likely to enhance student learning and development now and in the future.

19

Performance Funding

Janice Van Dyke
Linda B. Rudolph
Karen A. Bowyer

External initiatives have influenced assessment activities in many states across the nation. In Tennessee, two independent forces working in tandem made strong early impressions. The first was the Tennessee Higher Education Commission Performance Funding Program, initiated in 1979. This program allocated a portion of the budgets of public institutions on the basis of evidence that faculty and administrators were collecting information about student performance and also that they were using the information to improve programs and services. The second force was the Institutional Effectiveness accreditation criterion of the Southern Association of Colleges and Schools (SACS), which was introduced in 1985. Both agencies were making the effort to base evaluation of institutions on the outcomes of their educational practices rather than on campus resources and processes.

Prior to the adoption of performance funding standards in Tennessee, very little had been done at public institutions of higher education with respect to assessing the outcomes of their educational programs. Furthermore, most of what was being done placed the burden of proof on students rather than on institutions: that is, students in fields such as nursing or engineering were tested on state or national licensure and certification examinations to validate their competence to treat patients, build bridges, or otherwise become worthy of public trust. In addition, students took examinations such as the Graduate Record Examination and the Legal Scholastic Aptitude Test to qualify for admission to graduate or professional education. Though institutions may have worked with the testing and certification agencies to obtain their students' scores, little is known about efforts (if any existed) to make systematic use of the scores on these tests to improve the quality of educational programs at institutions.

Other assessment activities being conducted at institutions of higher education in Tennessee prior to the era of performance funding were regional accreditation (SACS) visits every ten years; accreditation visits for allied health, education, engineering, law, and other professional programs; and reviews of programs receiving federal vocational education dollars conducted by the Tennessee State Department for Vocational Education, as prescribed by law.

Most Tennessee colleges and universities were also conducting student evaluations of faculty. Faculty members in career programs at two-year institutions who were preparing students for immediate employment worked closely with advisory committees to assess the effectiveness of their programs and graduates. In addition, employer surveys were used to elicit information about performance of graduates. At Austin Peay State University (APSU), some departments in the College of Arts and Sciences were conducting simple self-studies. No internal or external evaluators were employed to review the self-studies, but the investigations nevertheless provided information about the effectiveness of the program.

The introduction of performance funding in Tennessee has increased the number and intensity of assessment activities across the state. Beginning in 1983, personnel at all higher education institutions in Tennessee started tracking all of the following criteria: the number of accreditable programs that were accredited, students' aggregate performance on a nationally developed measure of general education outcomes, students' performance on tests in their major fields (nationally or locally developed), peer review of master's degree programs, placement of graduates in career programs at two-year institutions, and alumni satisfaction (Tennessee Higher Education Commission, 1983). Many people thought that the most useful and challenging portion of the performance funding standards was that requiring college and university officials to indicate efforts to improve programs and services on their campuses. The institutional effectiveness criterion of the Southern Association of Colleges and Schools has reinforced performance funding efforts. The criterion stipulates that faculty and staff at institutions seeking accreditation from SACS will evaluate the results of education and use the findings to improve campus programs (Southern Association of Colleges and Schools, 1984).

How Assessment Has Made a Difference

Partly because of these external influences, the assessment movement has made a difference in higher education institutions in Tennessee. Faculty and staff regularly review assessment data to determine ways to improve the teaching-learning process and services to students. The very fact that faculty members are discussing the results of assessment and asking how to improve outcomes is a significant change from earlier years.

Some changes in programs or services were immediate. When alumni survey (ACT) responses suggested to Dyersburg State Community College (DSCC) staff that many students had not attended concerts or theater performances while on campus, actions were taken to improve and increase the means of informing alumni and current students of these opportunities. Some faculty now offer extra credit to students who attend these events. Also at Dyersburg, the failure of some graduates to find employment in their major fields inspired the placement counselor to produce a booklet containing the résumé of each graduate. This booklet was distributed to potential employers and advisory committee members. This initiative has resulted in an improved overall placement rate.

Some changes took more thought, consideration, planning, and implementation. For instance, based on disappointing results on the general education test (ACT-COMP), the faculty at APSU established the Heritage Program, an interdisciplinary approach to teaching general education that promotes integration and assimilation of knowledge. Its major strength is that it encourages the cooperation and collaboration of faculty from many fields. The same low communication scores on the ACT-COMP also prompted the faculty at APSU to accelerate ongoing discussions about how to improve the communication skills. Consequently, during the past five years, there has been a significant increase in the number of student papers required in classes, the number of essay tests administered, and the amount of emphasis placed on writing correctly. Students in the Heritage Program are required to write papers for classes in their major. English teachers grade the papers for grammar and writing, and major field instructors grade them for content.

State Technical Institute at Memphis (State Tech) also experienced disappointing scores on the communication section of the general education test (ACT-COMP). The president of State Tech therefore hired a specialist to assist all instructors in incorporating writing assignments in their classes and to reconfigure the college's learning laboratory to ensure that additional tutoring services in communication were available to all students. The writing specialist worked individually with faculty to incorporate writing exercises into their courses. To date, twenty-four faculty members have adopted writing-across-the-curriculum approaches, and forty-eight major field courses contain new writing components. One year after the learning laboratory was restructured, student traffic through it had increased from an average of four hundred contacts per month to that of five thousand.

As a result of major field assessment in one career program at State Tech, it was discovered that the materials taught in early courses were not being retained as expected. To remedy the situation, a spiral technique of instruction was introduced, which periodically gave students reviews of previous materials throughout their coursework, and more visual aids and alternative teaching strategies were adopted.

At Dyersburg State Community College, a self-reported score from graduates that was lower than the statewide mean on the "gains in writing effectively while in college" item of the alumni survey prompted corrective actions that included having students use computers in composition both at the remedial-developmental and at the college levels. More writing was required in all areas of the curriculum, and a technical writing course was implemented.

Dissatisfaction with scores on the problem-solving sub-test of the ACT-COMP and classroom experiences (a finding that suggested to the faculty that students were not thinking critically) prompted the APSU committee to develop a goal for the future to improve this skill. Several workshops on critical thinking have been presented to date, and instructors are seeking resources to assist them with instruction to improve this component of their teaching.

An item analysis of the ACT-COMP showed that graduates at both DSCC and APSU had difficulty in reading charts and interpreting graphs. To improve performance in this area, faculty in economics and other courses at DSCC have added a unit on the topic. At APSU, this information has been given to the faculty with specific suggestions for addressing this kind of interpretation and analysis in their classes.

A follow-up survey to determine why students were dropping out revealed that financial problems were an important reason for leaving western Tennessee institutions. As a result, the goal for scholarship dollars in the annual fund campaign at DSCC was increased in order to provide additional financial support for students in need. As more scholarships were offered, the percentage of survey responses citing financial reasons in the withdrawal survey dropped from 23.9 percent in 1989 to 17.9 percent in 1991. The response of the president of State Tech to this same finding was to institute the Chance for College Program for all high school graduates in Fayette County, a rural farming community within the service area of the college. In 1991, all recent high school graduates in Fayette County were guaranteed tuition, transportation, and books to attend State Tech. During that year, ninety-one students from Fayette County registered at State Tech (as opposed to seven the previous year).

Early in the 1980s, the faculty in the Department of Nursing at APSU became interested in using the ACT-COMP to look more closely at its curriculum. The faculty believed that the skills measured by this test were important to those students entering the nursing programs and decided that it was the responsibility of the discipline (as well as of general education courses) to provide students with these skills. The department members required all students entering the nursing program to take the ACT-COMP and used the results as a part of their admission criteria as well as for advising. In addition, they began to revise and modify their curriculum to enhance students' abilities in several areas, including those measured by the ACT-COMP.

Data on student outcomes in the nursing department were collected from 1982 through 1986. The results showed that substantial increases were achieved in abilities such as clarifying values and communicating. The nursing students also obtained a higher total score on the ACT-COMP and an exceptionally high gain of 22.5 points over the four years. Admittedly, the faculty in a nursing department have more control over their students' curriculum and other activities than a university has over its student body, but the project does indicate that gains can be made with intentional efforts such as these.

Each year at Dyersburg State Community College, an item analysis of the performance of students on the National Council Licensure Examination for Registered Nurses (NCLEX) is used by the nursing faculty to revise its curriculum. This constant vigilance has produced over two hundred graduates in twelve classes in which *everyone* has passed the NCLEX and become a registered nurse.

State Tech graduates gave the faculty at their alma mater a low score on the "availability outside of class" item of the alumni survey. When this response was compared to the demographic characteristics of students, it appeared that evening students (approximately 50 percent of the student body) had greatly influenced the low score. Faculty began posting evening office hours, and responses to this item on subsequent alumni surveys has improved.

An attrition rate of over 30 percent from semester to semester at DSCC has caused faculty and staff to design an early-warning system to notify students at midterm who are in danger of failing a course. The students have been counseled to seek help from their instructor and their academic adviser. A new advising system has also been implemented. Advising loads for faculty have been made more equitable and manageable. By having all administrators assume advising roles, the loads on other faculty members and on the staff have been reduced. Training for advisers has increased, and a new advising handbook has been developed. The persistence rate from fall to spring has improved from 60.3 percent in 1988–89 to 66.8 percent in 1991–92.

Advising has been a source of student dissatisfaction at APSU for many years, as indicated by the student satisfaction survey. There had been an intuitive feeling that advising was not effective, but the data from these surveys encouraged a study of the process. A program for training counselors has now been implemented, new "freshman experience" classes are being offered, and the early-warning system for freshman and sophomore students provides information to advisers about those students in academic trouble. The survey now indicates better satisfaction with advising, except in the area of career choices. Training methods to improve this area have been scheduled during the coming year.

The student satisfaction survey at APSU also indicated unhappiness with the services of two offices providing support services. The personnel in one office have taken the data and made changes to improve delivery of services. A total quality management team has been developed in the other office to study the areas of student dissatisfaction. Using TQM problem-solving procedures and statistical tools, the group has identified the basic causes of the dissatisfaction scores and collected data about types of telephone calls, the nature of information needed by visitors, and the kinds of services rendered and transactions carried out. The group presented these findings to the vice president for student affairs with recommendations for improvements. All recommendations have been accepted and approved.

Nineteen of the twenty-one accreditable programs at APSU are now accredited. The remaining two are making substantial progress toward achieving this goal. Before the emphasis on assessment began in Tennessee, accreditation of a program was not emphasized, and few faculty members chose to pursue this credential for their programs.

A computerized degree-monitoring system has been designed to address the problem of too-few graduates at DSCC. The evaluation system of the faculty was changed to include review of the progress of each faculty member's advisees toward earning an associate degree. The computerized degree-monitoring system allowed the faculty to have up-to-date information on students' academic progress. Since the implementation of these efforts, the number and percentage of graduates have increased. During the last three years, DSCC realized a 21.2 percent increase in number of students enrolled in the fall and a 60.7 percent increase in number of June graduates.

Athletes whose scores on the placement exam (given in the Academic Assessment and Placement Program) indicates a need for substantial remedial and developmental coursework are advised not to participate in intercollegiate athletics during their freshman year at DSCC. This practice has been initiated to improve the retention and graduation rates of student athletes.

Student dissatisfaction with the registration process at DSCC has resulted in the establishment of a review session by staff after each registration to try to improve problem areas. This approach has improved the registration process so markedly that there are now infrequent complaints from students. APSU undertook a similar review process, and scores on student satisfaction improved significantly over a four-year period.

To address discontent with registration at State Tech, a system for registering students from computer terminals in faculty offices has been implemented. Students know when they leave their advisers' offices that the classes in which they wish to enroll are open to them and that their places will be held until they can pay fees. Prior to the implementation of this system, students could leave advisers' offices with approved schedules only to find that one or more of their classes had closed during the walk to the business office. Readvising time has been reduced markedly with this system.

Using student evaluations of courses at DSCC, the faculty found that students preferred more computer laboratory time in the classes on the introduction to data processing, computer spreadsheet applications, and advanced spreadsheet applications. Based on this feedback, the classes were moved into the computer laboratory, an action that eliminated the need to move from the lecture classroom to the computer laboratory once a week. Now the classes have more experiential activities, and the students are more involved; higher achievement is the anticipated result.

Other positive outcomes for higher education institutions in Tennessee that have occurred as a result of the assessment movement are:

- Increased use of portfolios to assess outcomes in the performing arts
- Changed curricula and faculty in some departments, with assessment results used as part of the rationale for these decisions
- More focus-group interviews with employers
- Testing of *all* graduating seniors in their major each year in order to study longitudinal data for improvement
- Testing of entering freshmen, rising juniors, and seniors to study the longitudinal growth of students
- External program review at both the undergraduate and graduate levels
- Linking of assessment to strategic and long-range planning
- Implementation of persistence studies with data used for planning and enrollment management
- Evaluation of all student activities, such as orientation, special speakers' presentations, and workshops
- Beginning efforts to implement continuous quality improvement
- Increased faculty interest in developing better classroom tests

Funding Considerations

Tennesseans have found that assessment can provide the information needed to accomplish a number of educational goals, as well as to give assurances to other publics that higher education is providing the programs required for a changing and complex society. In fact, assessment has been found to be such a valuable tool that faculty and staff have undertaken assessment projects voluntarily. Staff at both State Tech and DSCC administered the Community College Student Experiences Questionnaire (Pace, Friedlander, and Lehman, 1990) last year without any expectation that their efforts would yield additional performance funding remuneration. They simply wanted to know more about their students. Furthermore, faculty have become so accustomed to receiving assessment reports that they inquire about them when processing and distribution of the reports have not been timely.

Nevertheless, the examples cited previously in this chapter clearly show that assessment is a costly undertaking. Tests and surveys cost money to purchase, administer, and score. Intensive program reviews exhaust computer, faculty, and staff resources. Analyzing scores and using the results of evaluation creatively to design increasingly effective programs and services consume time and human talent. In Tennessee, because assessment and instructional effectiveness are attached to supplemental budgetary funding, institutions are able to recover all of the costs of assessment and are able to improve programs and services with the additional dollars they "earn" through performance funding. Most often, those additional dollars revert to an institution's general fund. However, through personal negotiations, the director of the Center for Assessment Research and Development at the University of Tennessee in Knoxville has been able to recoup a percentage of performance funding dollars to establish an assessment fund for individual faculty members. Faculty members then submit proposals to use funds for their personal or departmental assessment projects. In Tennessee — where assessment was initially imposed by external forces — both faculty and students are benefiting directly from the process.

References

Pace, C. R., Friedlander, J., and Lehman, P. *Community College Student Experiences Questionnaire.* Los Angeles: Center for the Study of Evaluation, University of California, Los Angeles, 1990.

Southern Association of Colleges and Schools. *Criteria for Accreditation — Commission on Colleges.* Atlanta, Ga.: Southern Association of Colleges and Schools, 1984.

Tennessee Higher Education Commission. *Instructional Evaluation Variables.* Nashville: Tennessee Higher Education Commission, 1983.

20

A Flexible Approach
to Statewide
Assessment

Barbara S. Fuhrmann
Karen M. Gentemann

The Commonwealth of Virginia has long valued diversity and institutional autonomy in its higher education. Thus, there is no unitary state system; each of the public colleges and universities exists independently, governed by its own board and answerable to the mandates of that board. The State Council for Higher Education in Virginia (SCHEV) is a coordinating body that facilitates the implementation of state policy but does not act as a governing board. The assessment policy of Virginia is consistent with this philosophy of institutional autonomy. Although higher education activities are coordinated statewide, autonomy is likely to increase even further as a result of new legislation that permits institutions to request freedom from administrative control by a number of central state agencies.

As early as 1981, SCHEV staff began addressing the role of outcomes assessment in program evaluation and between then and 1986 worked to refine the notion of accountability as it pertains to higher education programs. By 1986, SCHEV had studied the emerging issues and recommended that the legislature adopt a formal policy concerning outcomes assessment in all state-supported institutions of higher education. Its report, *The Measurement of Student Achievement and the Assurance of Quality in Virginia Higher Education* (State Council for Higher Education in Virginia, 1986), led to the legislation mandating assessment throughout the state.

The policy was clearly designed to stimulate instructional improvement and curriculum reform through outcomes assessment, and it directs individual institutions to develop comprehensive assessment programs consistent with a set of guidelines. However, it avoids standardized assessment practice and the comparison of results across institutions. Statewide testing was rejected by SCHEV as an option for Virginia. The policy was designed to ensure that all state-supported institutions "establish procedures and programs to measure student achievement" and that the programs "derive from institutional initiatives, the tradition of institutional autonomy, and the capacity of faculty and administrators to identify their own problems and solve them creatively" (State Council for Higher Education in Virginia, 1986, p. 16).

SCHEV and the institutions worked through 1986 and 1987 to develop specific guidelines. At the same time, budget initiatives for 1988 to 1990 were developed to include monies to be used exclusively for assessment. The institutions thus received money earmarked for evaluation, and guidelines that emphasized process and the kinds of assessments to develop. At the same time, the uses the state might make of assessment findings were unknown.

Guidelines

Assessment guidelines, developed cooperatively by representatives of the institutions and SCHEV staff, as well as reporting guidelines, were adopted in 1987. These guidelines are still in effect at the present. They emphasize:

• The unique nature of each of Virginia's colleges and universities and the resultant need for individually designed assessment programs

- Recognition that data collected for other purposes might be suitable for assessment purposes as well
- The critical role that faculty must play in designing and implementing assessment plans
- The necessity to be sensitive to student needs and interests
- A focus on assessment of undergraduate learning, both in the major and in general education
- Entry-level standards for verbal and quantitative skills
- Measurement of the success of remediation
- Requirements for reporting the success of transfer students back to their originating community colleges (this information to be used as part of the community colleges' assessment efforts)
- Evaluation of assessment efforts and of the uses made of assessment findings

Institutions were also informed that they would have to report on the results of their assessment efforts (including at least some quantified data) and on changes that had occurred as a result of analysis of findings by 1989. Institutional reports were also expected to address assessment in the majors and evaluation of general education outcomes. Assessment of affective student development was added later. These reports are summarized in a legislatively required biennial report titled *The Virginia Plan for Higher Education,* which includes a review of statewide issues in higher education, statistical profiles of all public institutions, and snapshots of each of Virginia's institutions of higher education.

Means of Implementing Assessment Policy in Virginia

Five separate but related activities assist in the implementation of assessment policy in Virginia: (1) state-level program review, (2) budget initiatives, (3) the Funds for Excellence program, (4) the Institutional Programs Advisory Committee (IPAC), and (5) the Virginia Assessment Group (VAG).

Program Review

Since the inception of the state mandate, all state-level program review activities have included attention to student outcomes assessment. Current initiatives from SCHEV use accountability for assessment as the basis for a change in philosophy and practice to postaudit review rather than regulation. SCHEV is moving toward looking at program outcomes rather than compliance with rules. At the heart of this move is the expectation that institutions will be held responsible for assessment processes that are designed to guarantee quality. SCHEV is encouraging institutions to integrate their assessment efforts into self-studies leading to both internal program evaluation and external accreditation activities. Consistent with the philosophy of institutional autonomy, the emphasis is on processes that are consistent with institutionally derived goals.

Budget Initiatives

Higher education funding in Virginia is driven primarily by full-time-equivalent formulas. However, additional budget initiatives allow for incentive funding based on identified needs. One example of such funding was a call for institutional initiatives that responded to the statewide "University of the Twenty-First Century" challenge. Individual institutions were asked to request funds for plans for the future, with outcomes assessment processes playing a vital role in the evaluation of the requests. Over the last five years, demonstration of assessment processes (whenever they are appropriate) has become a necessary, though not sufficient, condition of funding requests.

Funds for Excellence

In addition to formula funding and special budget initiatives, the Virginia legislature has set aside monies earmarked for campus-based projects designed to meet specific needs. Funds for excellence are awarded biennially in a highly competitive statewide process. In the last twelve years, over $15 million has been distributed. Since 1990, one of the criteria for funding has been a clear tie to assessment findings. Specific findings of student outcomes assessment must demonstrate the need for funding. As with budget initiatives, the tie to these findings is a necessary, although not sufficient, condition for the awards. Unfortunately, because of severe budget reversions in Virginia over the last several years, available monies have been insufficient for all good assessment-related proposals. The danger, of course, is that the cynicism of faculty is increased when they feel that funding is not provided to respond to a clear need based on assessment data. Moreover, the state of the art of assessment is such that institutional needs cannot always be linked to reported student outcomes.

Institutional Programs Advisory Council

IPAC includes the chief academic officers of each of the four-year public institutions, selected representatives from the community college system, and SCHEV staff. This group meets regularly to address issues of mutual concern and to advise SCHEV concerning statewide policy and practice. From the beginning of the assessment movement, IPAC was consulted on every issue.

Virginia Assessment Group

The Virginia Assessment Group, a loosely organized network of assessment practitioners and state officials, was formed in response to the state assessment mandate in 1987. Despite initial skepticism, major conflicts between SCHEV and the institutions have been avoided. The group has been instrumental in helping Virginia meet the challenge of a flexible policy that relies on the good faith efforts of all involved: "Initially VAG was unstructured and somewhat unfocused. It had no officers, no bylaws, no firm membership, and no specific agenda. Gradually it has evolved from a *vague* collection of compatriots united by little more than their apprehension about where the assessment movement might be headed, to a consortium of seasoned veterans who have more than ever to contribute and gain through collaboration" (Hanson, 1992, n.p.).

VAG has also been helpful in another way. SCHEV's strategy had been to encourage ownership by the chief academic officers (CAOs) by channeling all assessment information and decisions through them. However, this strategy often left assessment coordinators out of the loop, even in the dark about some decisions. VAG was instrumental in helping SCHEV to communicate more directly with those responsible for implementing assessment while supporting the goal of CAO involvement by (among other things) scheduling VAG meetings in tandem with IPAC meetings.

VAG, which includes practitioners from the community colleges as well as the four-year colleges and universities, has elected officers who are responsible for organizing a fall assessment conference, open to participation by faculty throughout Virginia, and a spring coordinators' meeting designed to discuss current issues and reporting requirements. Participation in the fall conference has expanded every year. The 1992 VAG directory includes 335 individuals who have attended the meetings. Modest financial support for VAG activities, including a newsletter, is provided by SCHEV, but the bulk of VAG resources comes from profits from the fall conference. To date, VAG has worked with SCHEV to modify implementation guidelines for all aspects of assessment in Virginia, has publicized assessment activities, and has served as a clearinghouse for both its members and state officials for assessment-related questions. In the summer of 1991, at the urging of VAG officials, SCHEV asked the current VAG officers to serve (along with two national experts) as evaluators of the assessment reports that had been submitted in June from all public institutions. Their reviews contributed to a letter from SCHEV to each institution concerning its report and activities.

Outcomes

Assessment in Virginia has been around long enough to ask the question "What works?" and its corollary, "What doesn't work?"

The answers, of course, depend on the contexts in which the questions are asked. On the campuses, few would say that assessment alone has been responsible for major curricular changes. In those cases where major reform has occurred, several themes have converged to motivate the changes. Usually, the national movement for undergraduate reform, a changing institutional mission, external pressures (including regional and specialized accrediting agencies), and evaluation findings have combined to stimulate institutions to reexamine their academic programs.

At Longwood College, for example, there were pressures of reaccreditation; a conscious decision to become a more "self-regarding" institution; the change from a small, teacher-education college to a medium-sized coeducational, comprehensive college; and the state requirement for outcomes assessment. These factors all expedited curricular reform, particularly in general education, which is now structured around ten goals and stresses diversity. A freshman seminar focuses on academic and cultural motifs that are apparent in other campus activities as well.

On larger, more complex university campuses, the same pressures have had an impact, but change is much slower. Nevertheless, the combined pressures of assessment, general education reform, and a renewed emphasis on teaching and learning have resulted in at least modest curricular change. At George Mason University (GMU), the national reform movement in general education provided an impetus for rethinking general education, while the state mandate for assessment helped shape that effort into a student-focused curriculum. Even as the resulting proposal for a core curriculum was rejected by a faculty vote, the planning and preparation involved reemerged in the pairing of interdisciplinary freshman courses with other already existing ones. Although assessment was neither the sole nor the primary motivator for these developments, it kept the discussion of general education reform alive.

Assessment had the same effect at Virginia Commonwealth University (VCU), where general education had been little more than a loose collection of distribution requirements, varying in scope and integrity from one professional program to another. National calls for coherence in undergraduate education, together with the availability of money from the Funds for Excellence program, allowed the provost to focus on strengthening loose connections among academic units and to develop a shared sense of general education. The state mandate for outcomes assessment in general education provided an additional challenge. As at GMU, the culture of the university prevented the development of a core curriculum; however, eight goals for general education, stated as expected student outcomes, were eventually adopted by the university's undergraduate curriculum committee. Each of the ten baccalaureate-granting schools at VCU is now required to identify where in its curricular expectations these goals are addressed and to present a plan for assessment of its students' attainment of them. The major change resulting from these activities is a significantly improved sense of the intended outcomes of general education and a growing acceptance by faculty in the professional schools that general education is indeed a shared responsibility. No longer, for example, is all blame for students' shortcomings in written expression laid at the feet of the English department.

These cases highlight the importance of multiple movements to bring about change on campuses; at the same time, the examples of both GMU and VCU demonstrate how slow and incremental change is on large campuses. Each set of achievements represents more than five years of effort. On older and more traditional campuses, the process of incremental change is particularly apparent. The University of Virginia (UVA), which has embraced assessment more slowly than most institutions, developed a modest plan calling for alumni surveys and an intense qualitative and longitudinal study of the entering class of 1988. Initial student interviews revealed dissatisfaction with the amount of contact students have with professors in their first two years. Even before the larger study was completed, this problem was addressed. UVA began a program of university seminars taught by senior professors for first- and second-year students. Although clearly not a radical transformation of general education, these seminars show that incremental change in a large, conservative university can occur as a result of assessment.

The apparent ability of the assessment *process* to bring about change was one of the unexpected outcomes of the assessment movement in Virginia — as we are learning it has been throughout the country. Even without analyzed data indicating a need for change, the process of evaluation motivates self-reflection and can produce altered curricular programs in the major, in general education, and in out-of-class experiences, even at large research universities. It may be that a broader definition of assessment is needed to account for this phenomenon. At Radford University, for example, the departments of geology and biology developed a new interdepartmental course focused on professional development after discussion following assessment indicated problems. Also at Radford, the communication department created a capstone course after debating student outcomes from the program. Further, the faculty soon realized that if the desired outcomes were to be achieved, the entire curriculum needed revision, all before any assessment data were collected. In the community college system, one institution added an ethics course to its administration of justice program after an external evaluation (part of the assessment plan but not a component that included data) indicated the need for it.

Learning

It is strange for us, as assessment coordinators, to say that assessment data do not "work," and such a statement is actually not entirely accurate. The reality, however, is that at this stage of the assessment movement, curricular change is more a function of the process than of the outcomes of assessment. As assessment programs mature and as they become integrated into the academic culture, a shift will likely occur and the momentum provided by the process will need to be supplemented by good outcomes data. But for now, while data are still being identified and clarified, the process itself seems to be playing the more important role.

Faculty culture is imbued with a sense of commitment to a discipline or profession rather than to an institution. Virginia faculty members are clearly not alone in their allegiance to their disciplines or professions rather than to the educational enterprise as a whole, but the liberal assessment policy in Virginia has served to highlight this fact. The many small success stories generated by assessment in Virginia demonstrate that improvement within a specific program is far easier to achieve than challenging improvement in the liberal aspects of a college education. SCHEV emphasizes that undergraduate education is the bedrock of Virginia's higher education system: "The preparation of a responsible, adaptable, and skilled citizenry continues to be the most important contribution higher education can make to the economic health of Virginia. The rest of higher education's activities [professional preparation, graduate education, research] follow naturally from this emphasis" (*The Virginia Plan for Higher Education,* 1989, p. 8).

Assessment of such outcomes remains elusive, not only because they are difficult to evaluate, but also because faculty have difficulty accepting responsibility for outcomes that appear to incorporate students' personality, early learnings, and attitudes as well as specific disciplinary knowledge and skills.

For assessment to be successful, it must be seen within the context of program improvement. Early in the process of developing strategies, assessment is too often done for the sake of meeting the requirements of a mandate rather than for purposes of self-reflection and improvement. Much institutionwide testing, for example, produces numerical data, but it often is not related to institutional questions and has no direct implications for curricular developments. Only when assessment questions are designed to stimulate open and thoughtful reflection by faculty members concerning improvement do they become meaningful. Thus, a faculty actively involved in setting departmental goals for student learning is likely to produce curricular revision even before assessment data are collected. In Virginia, the requirements in program review and funding initiatives for demonstration of sound assessment process are intended to encourage institutions and faculty to use assessment for self-reflection and improvement rather than compliance.

At both the state and campus levels, there is conflict between needs for improvements identified through assessment and other needs. State budget initiatives are driven by many concerns and include a variety of political agendas, from athletic accountability to date-rape. Vying for small pots of money already, how long can assessment maintain the attention of legislators, particularly when it is so difficult to tell the campus assessment story? Meanwhile, funding priorities on the campuses are also influenced by a variety of concerns. Even in those cases where top administrative support has made assessment more viable and more visible, how is its momentum to be maintained when funds cannot be allocated to address needs that the process identifies? In tight budget times, how are faculty induced to spend time on assessment committees, when promotion and tenure decisions give little weight to program evaluation, especially programs in general education, and when there are few incentives for the hard work involved in making changes?

At the state level, incentives must be strengthened while also allowing greater flexibility in recognizing the effects of the assessment process itself. Simultaneously, at the campus level, some monies must be publicly connected to assessment. Allocations for faculty and curricula that are tied to assessment will surely go further toward integrating assessment into the culture than mere exhortations from committed administrators. Indeed, assessment will be integrated only if faculty develop and implement meaningful programmatic evaluation and improvement and if administrators at both the campus and state levels link important decisions, including resource allocation, to thoughtful assessment processes and findings.

Assessment faces numerous immediate challenges. In addition to the ongoing dilemma about faculty involvement, the disinterest of many administrators, the questionable attention of state legislators, and our continuing financial doldrums, we hear challenges from some proponents of total quality management who relegate to assessment the primary task of identifying weaknesses rather than supporting improvement. We also hear the voices of those who are becoming impatient with assessment's seeming inability to tell a story.

The real challenge is to ensure that we fulfill the promise of assessment and that we counter the cynics who cry, "Just another fad." The public is not interested in fads. More important, it will not tolerate higher education officials trying one new thing after another while perceptions of us as wasteful consumers of resources continue unabated.

We must tell about the changes that are occurring as a result of assessment processes. These are real, substantial, and important despite their localized nature, or maybe because of it. Ultimately, will we be able to demonstrate improvements in student outcomes because of these small changes? We hope so, though we are certain that these improvements will be incremental and difficult to document. Nevertheless, it is incumbent upon those of us who are witness to the changes to make the stories public.

References

Hanson, D. C. "The Virginia Assessment Group: A Brief Retrospective." *VAG News,* Mar. 1992, *5*(1), n.p.

State Council for Higher Education in Virginia. *The Measurement of Student Achievement and the Assurance of Quality in Virginia Higher Education.* Senate Document no. 14. Richmond, Va.: Commonwealth of Virginia, 1986.

The Virginia Plan for Higher Education. Richmond, Va.: State Council for Higher Education in Virginia, 1989.

21

The College Outcomes Evaluation Program

Nina Dorset Jemmott
Edward A. Morante

In the 1980s, processes were designed in many states to assess the quality of public higher education institutions. New Jersey went beyond its well-established and successful Basic Skills Assessment Program to create a comprehensive outcomes assessment program. The College Outcomes Evaluation Program (COEP) was a state-mandated attempt to improve the quality of higher education while also meeting the needs for accountability. The focus of this endeavor was to improve teaching and learning. This chapter will first provide the context for understanding the significance of the impact of outcomes assessment at state institutions. A brief overview of New Jersey public higher education is followed by a description of the political and economic climate in the state that gave impetus to the creation of the policy. Then reactions to the mandate from institutions are characterized.

Data were obtained through case-study research conducted at one institution in each public sector of higher education in the state: one community college, one four-year state college, and the state university. After a brief discussion of the case studies and the institution, the chapter will review what the institutions report as positive changes directly resulting from the outcomes assessment activities of COEP.

College Outcomes Assessment in New Jersey

Though geographically small, New Jersey has the highest population density of any state in the country. Its approximately 7.5 million people enjoy the second-highest per capita income in the nation, and they are employed in a broad diversity of industries, including baking, insurance, pharmaceuticals, high-tech products, and agriculture. Although highly urbanized, New Jersey is also one of the leaders in the production of fruits and vegetables (thus earning it the title of the Garden State).

The public higher education system in New Jersey is relatively new. Prior to the creation of the Board and Department of Higher Education in 1966, a student majoring in a subject like psychology or business would have a choice of going to Rutgers, the State University, a private institution in the state, or an out-of-state institution. Currently, New Jersey has nineteen community colleges, nine comprehensive state colleges (three of which have been created in the past twenty-five years, while the original six were state teachers colleges), and three public universities (one of which is a graduate medical-dental, one a technological research, and the third a comprehensive research university). The desire of many students to go away from home, geographical and financial considerations, and (until recently) the relative lack of choice have produced in New Jersey the highest percentage of out-migration of college students among the states. The need to demonstrate the effectiveness of public higher education as a means of keeping "the best and brightest" in the state was a key factor leading to the establishment of a statewide outcomes assessment program.

The New Jersey Board of Higher Education coordinates all of higher education in the state. Its control ranges from virtually none (in several private institutions, such as Princeton) to considerable (in the four-year public colleges). Nine of its fifteen members are appointed by the governor, with the remaining six representing the various sectors of higher education. The chancellor of higher education is appointed to a five-year term and has historically been perceived as reasonably independent of the political process. The New Jersey Board of Higher Education is considered to be among the most powerful state coordinating boards in the country. This authority has enabled it to establish broad programs.

History of Statewide Assessment

Responding to concerns about the proficiencies of students entering colleges and universities in the state, the Board of Higher Education created the Basic Skills Assessment Program (BSAP) in 1977. The BSAP called for the testing of all students entering state public colleges and universities, as well as the evaluation of remedial-developmental programs at each institution. Under the leadership of the board-appointed Basic Skills Council, composed mostly of faculty and staff from New Jersey colleges, the BSAP became the first statewide effort in the country to assess the basic skills of entering freshmen with a common test and to evaluate systematically the outcomes of remedial and developmental programs with common definitions and standards. After much initial debate and controversy, the BSAP has successfully established itself as a common practice at every public college and at about a dozen private institutions in New Jersey. The success of this program in implementing both the broad goals of access and quality using student assessment and the evaluation of program outcomes created support for the later development of a broad-based statewide endeavor to assess higher education beyond basic skills. In other words, BSAP demonstrated that assessment and accountability measures *could* lead to improvement and achievement of statewide goals.

In 1983, the Statewide Task Force on Pre-College Preparation, a joint effort of the Department of Education and the Department of Higher Education, issued a report that defined basic skills, called for an eleventh-grade high school graduation test at a level of standards comparable to the exam (the New Jersey College Basic Skills Placement Test) used for student placement at entry to college, and recommended that a statewide test be given at the end of the sophomore year of college.

Two other factors played important roles in the development of this outcomes assessment program: autonomy and the economy. Ever since the creation of the New Jersey Board of Education in the mid-nineteenth century, the state's four-year colleges (originally teachers colleges) have been centrally controlled. The establishment of the Board of Higher Education in 1966, the movement to comprehensive institutions, and the creation of three new state colleges did little to diminish this control. In the mid 1980s, the governor and the chancellor proposed a plan to increase significantly the autonomy of the state colleges in return for increased accountability of outcomes. The booming economy during these years provided the opportunity to sweeten the process by providing millions of dollars through various grant programs, the largest of which was called the Governor's Challenge Grant Program. After much controversy, this legislation was passed in 1985. The implementation of the accountability portion was then needed to provide a balance.

In 1985, the Board of Higher Education passed a resolution calling for the creation of a statewide outcomes assessment program for its public colleges and universities. The College Outcomes Evaluation Program was aimed at accountability and improvement. It called for the assessment of outcomes in three broad areas: student learning and development, institutional impact on the community, and faculty research activities. The board resolution included a specific reference to a college sophomore test.

The COEP Advisory Committee appointed by the board spent two years discussing and intensively studying various options and proposals. It sought and received significant input from a wide variety of individuals and groups from across the state as well as beyond the borders of New Jersey. The board ultimately adopted all of the committee's recommendations and established what some have called the most comprehensive statewide program ever developed for higher education (Ewell, 1989, 1992).

Beginning in 1988, COEP defined, collected, and reported data on retention, transfer, and graduation rates; economic impact; minority access and retention; and community service activities (College Outcomes Evaluation Program Council, 1991). Also, every public institution in the state began a review of its curriculum and created a plan for the assessment of student learning in each major program, as well as in general education, student satisfaction, and student personal development. Workshops utilizing some of the leading experts in the country were organized to assist institutions in assessing their efforts. An ongoing COEP Council and several committees were appointed to provide input, leadership, and coordination to this program. The governor's support was sought and strongly given at the largest statewide conference on higher education ever held in New Jersey, where he gave the keynote address and stated: "I strongly support the COEP effort promulgated by the Board of Higher Education." Opposition to COEP was most vocal from a number of college presidents and from the faculty union representing the state colleges.

GIS Assessment

Without a doubt, the most controversial and arguably the most creative and significant aspect of COEP was the development of a sophomore test. The General Intellectual Skills (GIS) Assessment (Morante, 1991) derives its name from the skills it measures: the ability to gather and analyze information, perform quantitative analysis, and present information. More commonly referred to as critical thinking, problem solving, quantitative reasoning, and writing, these are the skills that a representative segment of New Jersey faculty members and the COEP Council agreed should be taught across the curriculum in virtually all courses at all colleges and universities.

The test consisted of a series of extended tasks on various topics. These tasks contained no multiple-choice items; instead, they asked questions of students requiring responses that were short answers, calculations, map drawings, and extended written essays. All of the content material needed to answer the questions was provided as a part of the test. A two-year, $1 million contract with the Educational Testing Service to develop the test, including two extensive statewide pilots, yielded a valid and reliable exam (Educational Testing Service, 1989). Detailed scoring protocols were also developed and used with a six-point scoring rubric (a four was the core criterion expected of college sophomores). Over two hundred faculty members, representing every public college in the state, participated in the process, including writing and evaluating the items and scoring protocols, setting and evaluating the standards, and reading the students' responses. The test was first administered to a representative sample of New Jersey college sophomores in the spring of 1990 and results were published that July (College Outcomes Evaluation Program Council, 1990). A second pilot administration of the exam took place in spring 1991, but these results were not published by the Department of Higher Education.

The Case Study

As previously stated, case studies were conducted at institutions within the public sector of higher education representing the community colleges, comprehensive four-year state colleges, and universities (Jemmott, 1992). The institutions selected for study were Raritan Valley Community College, William Paterson College, and Rutgers University (the New Brunswick campus).

The purpose of conducting case studies was to find out how each campus had reacted to the state mandate and whether COEP had had any impact on the public institutions that were required to implement outcomes assessment programs. Data collection included a self-administered questionnaire, distributed to a random sample of 25 percent of the institution's faculty and administrators; interviews of a diverse group of faculty and administrators; observations of outcomes assessment–related activities; and analysis of campus documents related to outcomes assessment. The study was conducted over a ten-month period, beginning with the fall 1991 semester. Aspects of the results of this study are summarized here, with emphasis on the outcomes of assessment activities at the institutions.

The Institutions

For a better understanding of the significance of the changes made on the campuses, the institutions should be viewed in the context of their missions and their stated positions on outcomes assessment.

Raritan Valley Community College

Raritan Valley Community College (RVCC) is one of nineteen comprehensive two-year colleges supported jointly by county government, student tuition, and state resources. It is located in a semirural portion of the state and is the only community college in the New Jersey system that is supported by two counties. Like most community colleges, it offers associate degrees, certificates, employment training, and transfer programs. Its over fifty-three hundred full-time-equivalent student population is nearly 70 percent part time, and the faculty of eighty-eight is 70 percent tenured. Most of the faculty members hold the rank of associate professor.

According to the college's accreditation self-study, outcomes assessment is "pervasive across the college . . . [and] serves to integrate the elements of the mission" (Raritan Valley Community College, 1991, p. 181). Raritan Valley has made a deliberate and concerted attempt to ensure that its efforts in measuring the effectiveness of the institution are accomplished.

The approach, process, planning, and orientation to outcomes assessment at Raritan Valley are a model of planned organizational change and innovation. The institution has either planned or already put in place all the critical elements necessary for successfully implementing an outcomes assessment program, including:

- Strong commitment and support by the leadership of the college
- An open and participatory process that involves faculty from all areas of the college
- Clear goals and objectives for the program and the process of implementation
- Widespread and accurate methods for dissemination of information
- Open channels of communication that encourage discussion and debate

- Commitment of resources for assessment and related activities
- Clear articulation of the goals for assessment through formal and official channels and written communication of the goals in institutional documents

Raritan Valley has taken its time in developing its program and assessment plans and considers the process an ongoing one. The institution has been consistently thorough and deliberate in first reporting its information to the state, then using the data to further its assessment goals. It has taken full advantage of the state mandate and created an opportunity for improving its educational experience. The faculty of RVCC have described themselves as proassessment.

William Paterson College

William Paterson College (WPC) is one of the nine comprehensive four-year public colleges in the public higher education system in New Jersey. It has a student body of about ten thousand students, most of whom are full-time undergraduates. The college offers both graduate and undergraduate degrees in three schools with over thirty-three majors. WPC has a full-time faculty of just over three hundred, 73 percent of whom have tenure and 38 percent of whom have attained the rank of professor.

Faculty at William Paterson are represented by a powerful collective bargaining unit that negotiates faculty contracts and "plays a watchdog role in matters pertaining to retention, tenure, promotions, sabbaticals, and merit awards, ensuring that the rights of faculty are preserved," according to its 1990 accreditation self-study (William Paterson College, 1990, p. 80). In addition, the Faculty Senate, representative of all faculty constituents on campus, formulates policy recommendations in an advisory plan within the collegiate governance structure. The 1991 middle states accreditation review team noted that the leaders of the union and of the senate are often the same persons and recommended that each body clarify its roles in the governance of the college.

Faculty at WPC described themselves as proassessment but anti-COEP in the survey conducted as part of the case-study research. Individual faculty members, the union, the Faculty Senate, and departmental and institutional leadership have in the past taken vocal and divergent positions on outcomes assessment. COEP, particularly the administration of the statewide General Intellectual Skills Assessment, has created dissension and conflict within the faculty. However, the college administration, members of the departments, and the Assessment Committee have gone forward with well-developed plans and detailed goals for assessment. At this time, it appears that the institution has not yet resolved some critical organizational issues essential to successful outcomes assessment programs. For example, there is little collegewide consensus on goals and the structure of an assessment program. The commitment of the leadership of the college and the involvement of the faculty have been minimal, and the fractious internal politics and "culture of confrontation," as described by the 1991 visiting review team, has inhibited the development of outcomes assessment on campus.

Rutgers University

Rutgers is a multipurpose research university and the only comprehensive public university in New Jersey. It has three campuses. Rutgers College (established in 1766) was the first of several colleges that made up the university and is one of the bastions of American higher education. The university is a member of the prestigious Association of American Universities.

The combined student enrollment at Rutgers is over fifty thousand. Full-time faculty members number nearly two thousand in over one hundred disciplines in fourteen undergraduate and graduate schools and colleges. The faculty governance structure at Rutgers, like most institutions of its kind, is based largely on collegiality and the authority and expertise of the faculty.

In the case-study survey Rutgers University faculty at New Brunswick described themselves as antiassessment and felt that outcomes assessment was not needed on campus. They view traditional methods of evaluation that are accepted, valid, and widely used by peer research universities to be the instruments of choice and plan to continue to use these methods, in addition to others suggested by the state (Rutgers University, 1990).

According to the results of the study, the response of Rutgers faculty members to COEP requirements was one of compliance. Their position was that the appropriate place for the responsibility for assessment was with the faculty and that it would remain so; they based their position on the 1988 recommendations of the University Academic Forum on Assessing Student Learning. That body put forth principles that in essence found COEP not useful in improving education in individual institutions.

Impact of the College Outcomes Evaluation Program

As we have seen, the three diverse institutions examined here have responded to the New Jersey mandate requiring the implementation of college outcomes assessment programs in different ways, depending on their own processes and reflecting their unique characteristics. As in any planned change, but particularly in change that has been externally imposed, the institutions have experienced some internal conflict.

The conflicts arose because faculty viewed the assessment mandate as threatening. They feared unfair comparisons of institutions based on test scores and the misuse of test and student performance results. They believed that COEP was an evaluation of the faculty and that negative results and poor performance might cause faculty members to lose their jobs or their autonomy as teachers.

In addition, the mandate exacerbated already existing tensions on the campuses — between internal constituents such as the administration and the faculty unions and between the institutions and the state. Although this impact was felt very early in the implementation process, those conflicts and disagreements have lessened over time, primarily as a result of decreased pressure due to the elimination of state funding for COEP (as of July 1, 1991).

In spite of obvious differences in institutions and in the success of the COEP efforts, the faculties at all three institutions reported that they believe the state has a right to require certain kinds of information and to demand accountability to the public. They state that their response to the mandate had nothing to do with accountability but rather arose from the top-down imposition of the mandate by the state, the lack of collegiality in the implementation process, and the perceived threat to the faculty because of the mandate. There was little expressed concern that the mandate violated tenets of academic freedom; however, it was felt that it was intrusive and might lead to "teaching to the test." The faculties of these institutions believed that the framework provided by COEP could be a means for improving higher education in the state if the methods had been more collaborative and reported that the institutions would continue to conduct outcomes assessment in spite of the elimination of funding for COEP.

For these institutions, the negative impact of the COEP process on the organization has been outweighed as a whole by the positive benefits. The mandate made faculty look at aspects of their institutions in the context of the whole organization and at the connections between the parts. It also forced them to examine routinely the effects of what they do. According to the participants in the study, the issue of institutional accountability stimulated discussion and renewed interest in the teaching and learning process. The results of those discussions have created positive changes at the institutions in the areas of institutional climate, program and course review, and teacher evaluation.

Institutional Climate

Faculty at all three institutions believed that COEP had had an impact on the teaching climate. COEP was responsible for creating discussions about teaching and a climate of informational and personal sharing. Before COEP began, faculty report that they had talked mainly about teaching-related issues, such as scheduling, promotion and tenure procedures, and administrative details. They had also talked to colleagues within their disciplines about their disciplines, but not about instruction. For the first time, there was campuswide talk about teaching, learning, and the means to measure both.

Within those discussions, faculty tried to define what constituted the core values of teaching and what made for effective teaching. In having to decide on the outcomes of student learning, faculty had to look at the outcomes of their own teaching and found the discussions of value to them personally and helpful in their classrooms.

The COEP discussions also created new alliances on campus. Assessment committees required interdisciplinary discussions, which allowed for cross-fertilization of concepts, methods, and strategies of teaching. In addition, faculty enthusiastically looked for the common ground in teaching. As a result of COEP, faculty increased their expertise in the areas of assessment and traditional methods of evaluation. In order to be informed and to inform their processes, faculty had to learn about their institutions and about assessment. The research conducted in this process stimulated papers, workshops, conferences, and activities that faculty found to be a valuable source of professional development.

For faculty at Raritan Valley, the COEP process was a significant collegial activity. They reported a heightened sense of their own importance and value to the college as a result. They also felt that the administration of the college valued their input and gained respect for their teaching and expertise in their disciplines. The real importance for them was that this sense was communicated to them during the assessment process.

Finally, as a result of the increased focus on student learning, faculty at Rutgers reported the establishment of instructional improvement centers, designed as centers for academic support of students.

Program and Course Review

COEP required the colleges and universities to report on the access and retention of their students, with increased attention to minority students, and on the development of goals and objectives for general education and study in the major. The General Intellectual Skills Assessment focused on critical thinking and the analysis, synthesis, and presentation of information. Faculty at the three institutions said these requirements forced them to think differently about the courses they offered. The assessment made them question whether the courses and their teaching were effective and whether the former assisted students in developing skills as well as acquiring knowledge of content. Eventually, they began to consider ways of finding out. The faculty conducted surveys of graduates to find out how they felt about their coursework and the level of preparation they had received for graduate school and work. Employers were surveyed to obtain a sense of the kinds of critical-thinking and decision-making skills that graduates brought with them.

A careful examination of courses and programs was initiated. In some instances, the faculty reported looking at courses for the first time, to see whether they were still viable and appropriate — courses that had been approved twenty years ago and were still in the catalogue.

That specific courses and entire programs were to be subject to external review and assessment motivated faculty to conduct reviews that were more thorough and critical. In some cases, the program review process had been "in progress" for years, but the task of defining both academic programs and general education had not taken place. Although some faculty committees had continued meeting, the lack of urgency in completing the task had all but stopped the review process.

Teacher Evaluation

The impact of COEP on teacher evaluation was more significant at Rutgers University than at the other two institutions. Although there had been discussions about teacher evaluation prior to COEP, it was generally felt that COEP provided the impetus for the development of a universitywide faculty evaluation instrument, administered for the first time in the fall of 1992 (the results are to be published regularly). Previously, the student evaluation of faculty had been a function of individual departments, but even within departments it had not been a uniform process. There had also been questions about the validity and use of student evaluations that were so varied in their mode of construction, administration, and use.

Teacher evaluation discussions at Raritan Valley and William Paterson are just now beginning. They tend to emphasize and question the lack of assessment of those faculty members who are tenured full professors and who have been considered above evaluation by both students and peers.

Long-Term Ramifications

Despite concerns about a state-mandated program and a perceived lack of collegiality, the evidence — at least from the three institutions studied — leads to the conclusion that assessment in general and COEP in particular had some positive effects on colleges and universities in New Jersey. The three institutions studied have experienced positive changes in the areas of institutional climate, program and course review, and teacher evaluation. There was a significant increase in attention given to the teaching-learning process with a direct focus on the outcomes of faculty and institutional efforts rather than more tangential working conditions.

In addition, increased focus was placed on studying the institution as a whole. Communication extended beyond departments and disciplines to cross sections of the faculty and to students and the administration of each institution. Program review and accreditation became more meaningful and enduring, and faculty development centers were created.

Would these events have transpired without COEP? Perhaps (Morante, 1991), but there is much evidence to indicate that even as COEP stirred the waters and raised anxieties and some hostility, it also led to beneficial change considerably faster than would otherwise have occurred. All planned change initiatives take time, and improvement of public higher education in New Jersey will prove to be no exception. Morover, the momentum to conduct outcomes assessment created by the College Outcomes Evaluation Program has been diminished by the dramatic ending of funding for the program. Effective July 1, 1991, the Department of Higher Education closed down the College Outcomes Evaluation Program. This followed a series of actions that commenced after the swearing in of a new governor in 1990, including the sudden removal of funds for COEP from the state budget three days before the end of the fiscal year. Although data were sent to each institution describing the spring 1991 GIS Assessment results, no report was made public by the department. Similarly a report on retention, transfer, and graduation rates was distributed to institutions but not presented to the Board of Higher Education. The department continues to collect data from the state's colleges and universities although no reports have been issued in almost two years. Despite all of these events, the colleges continue to conduct outcomes assessment activities.

The New Jersey experience has broad implications for policy in other states. Although it has demonstrated that a well-conceived and carefully structured program can fit into academic institutions that are highly diverse and still have positive results, costs to the institutions (related to internal structures and constituent groups) must be less than the benefits that eventually accrue.

Institutions need to understand organizational issues that are affected by a mandated change and carefully negotiate the complexities of campus policies and culture. States need to consider the implications of planned change that is external to the campuses, avoid the top-down approach in decision making, and develop truly collaborative strategies prior to implementation in order to produce the intended results. Other states can learn much from the COEP experience in New Jersey, including definitions of outcomes, testing methods, and uses of comparative data. Yet they will still need to struggle with time-honored concerns regarding processes of change, institutional autonomy, and arrogance.

References

College Outcomes Evaluation Program Council. *Report to the Board of Higher Education on the First Administration of the General*

Intellectual Skills (GIS) Assessment. Trenton: New Jersey Department of Higher Education, 1990.

College Outcomes Evaluation Program Council. *Report to the Board of Higher Education on Retention, Transfer, and Graduation Rates.* Trenton: New Jersey Department of Higher Education, 1991.

Educational Testing Service. *A Report on the Development of the General Intellectual Skills Assessment.* Princeton, N.J.: Educational Testing Service, 1989.

Ewell, P. "From the States." *Assessment Update,* 1989, *1*(2), 6–7.

Ewell, P. "Assessment in Hard Times: A Tale of Two States." *Assessment Update,* Jan.–Feb. 1992, *4*(1), 11–12.

Jemmott, N. *The Implementation of State Mandated College Evaluation Programs at Selected Public Higher Education Institutions in New Jersey.* Unpublished doctoral dissertation, 1992.

Morante, E. "Assessing Collegiate Outcomes." In L. R. Marcus and B. D. Stickney (eds.), *Politics and Policy in the Age of Education.* Springfield, Ill.: Thomas, 1988.

Morante, E. *General Intellectual Skills (GIS) Assessment in New Jersey.* Washington, D.C.: National Center for Education Statistics, 1991.

Raritan Valley Community College. "Raritan Valley Community College Self-Study Report." Unpublished report prepared for the Middle States Accrediting Association, 1991.

Rutgers University. "Rutgers University 1990 Self-Study Report." Unpublished report prepared for the Middle States Accrediting Association, 1990.

William Paterson College. "William Paterson College 1990 Self-Study Report." Unpublished report prepared for the Middle States Accrediting Association, 1990.

22

Accountability
Through Assessment
in Community Colleges

Dorothy Bray
Martha J. Kanter

During the 1980s, California grew by six million people; the growth rate is two thousand persons every twenty-four hours; roughly one-half of these are newborns and one-half immigrants. The size, rate of population growth, ethnic diversity, changing social fabric, and economic stagnation in California are accelerating change and resulting in a chronic budget crisis as the state struggles to accommodate the health, welfare, and education needs of its citizenry. In this environment, assessment and accountability systems will play a critical role in decisions about student access and success in higher education. This chapter will describe the key factors that have characterized outcomes assessment in the community colleges of California.

From Assessment to Accountability

During the 1970s and 1980s, assessment in California's community colleges was a tool for describing student demographics and basic skills proficiencies at the time of enrollment. Colleges gathered such information largely to create and justify special programs and services designed to help them succeed in serving an increasingly large and diverse student population. Assessment activities centered on basic skills testing for placement into college courses, giving rise to the premise that "assessment at entrance is what mattered the most, not post-testing" (D. Knoell, personal interview, 1992). In the 1990s, community colleges shifted to an accountability or outcomes model based on evaluating institutional effectiveness, measured in large part by student achievement and satisfaction outcomes. Whether community colleges in California can link student access and success into a unified and manageable accountability system, given the growth and diversity of the state, remains to be seen.

Outcomes assessment efforts in California were achieved largely through grass-roots networks during the early 1980s. Prior to the legislature's adoption of community college reforms and in response to the calls of critics who claimed community colleges were "a revolving door" for students, an eighty-college consortium known as LARC (Learning Assessment Retention Consortium) emerged in 1981.

LARC used local talent, research expertise, and resources to conduct studies of the impact of assessment and placement practices on student learning and achievement. Free from the effects of compliance mandates and state bureaucracy, during the ensuing five years, LARC completed numerous studies in the areas of reading, writing, and mathematics, from basic skills through transfer-level courses (Learning Assessment Retention Consortium, 1986, 1987, 1988a, 1988b; Learning Assessment Retention Consortium, English Council of California Two-Year Colleges, and Academic Senate for California Community Colleges, 1988). The study results delineated the impact of college assessment practices on statewide policy and on the success of colleges in remediating large numbers of underprepared students. These studies in particular linked evaluation results to curriculum issues and documented promising practices of assessment, placement, and follow-up. The LARC studies provided the colleges and the state with information that for the most part had not been documented previously.

From a public-policy standpoint, by the middle of the

decade, LARC research had validated remediation as viable in California higher education with the result that it was adopted as one of the three key components of the community college mission in the master plan (Commission for the Review of the Master Plan for Higher Education, 1986; Assembly Bill no. 1725, 1988). LARC studies defined (1) the relationship between student access and success, (2) the link between concepts of student equity and academic quality, and (3) remediation as an essential component of the mission of the community colleges.

Legislated Reforms Based on Student Access and Success Outcomes

Concern about student access and success during the 1980s led to the legislature's passage of Assembly Bill no. 3, known as the Matriculation Act. The six components of the matriculation process are admissions, orientation, skills assessment and student evaluation, advising and counseling, student follow-up, and institutional research. The process thus tries to ensure two student outcomes: access to appropriate programs and courses and success in attaining educational goals. In addition, outcomes assessment in the form of a student-tracking system is required. Under this model, the college is accountable for student success (Assembly Bill no. 3, 1986).

In the mid 1980s, California higher education underwent a major review of its mission and goals. *The Challenge of Change* (Commission for the Review of the Master Plan for Higher Education, 1986) laid the groundwork for the 1988 Community College Reform Act, Assembly Bill no. 1725. That landmark reform legislation designated the community colleges as a postsecondary education system, separate from the university and state university systems. AB 1725 affirmed transfer and occupational education as the primary mission of the system and basic skills and English as a second language (ESL) as secondary tenets, thereby establishing a broad-based mandate for outcomes assessment and accountability. AB 1725 was designed to ensure that state monies would be applied to campus reforms related to mission, access, and quality. These reforms underscore the proposition, growing in importance, that state government can and should expect higher education institutions to be accountable for fulfilling their missions effectively and efficiently, maintaining institutional assets as well as using them well, and contributing to the achievement of clearly articulated state priorities (Jones, 1992). AB 1725 also required implementation of a statewide accountability system for community colleges, signaling a shift in the emphasis in state policy from student assessment to institutional accountability.

State Accountability: From Assessment to Outcomes

Campus energy and attention has thus been redirected from student learning in the classroom to data-based systems. Local models and practices have given way to statewide systems and accountability models, producing several contradictions. (1) There are models, instruments, and forums for assessment, but no statewide operational accountability system yet exists in California; (2) some common statewide data are demonstrated and produced, but in the local rather than the state context; (3) a statewide community college accountability model must be implemented by colleges, a majority of which do not have the requisite data systems and research capabilities; and (4) no statewide budgeting policies are yet linked to performance outcomes in California higher education.

This situation creates several critical new assessment questions requiring review and response. How can the state encourage institutional effectiveness and accountability when community colleges are in an input-oriented, decision-making environment? How can colleges and the state employ data on growth and diversity for outcomes assessment models?

Some practitioners ask, "How can we stop and restart the dialogue, since we don't have consensus on where we are going?" Others question how they can convert multidimensional diverse data into usable information. Still others ask, "How can colleges implement an accountability model if they haven't yet implemented a comprehensive student assessment, placement, and follow-up model?" All agree that the future debate will be shaped differently by the use of data at both state and local levels.

In this environment, community college educators need clarity and direction in understanding the distinction between assessment and accountability. Local campus experiences have been based on assessment models that were people-centered; multiple sources of data and information were used in concert to talk about a person — the student. In contrast, the documentation called for in the California Community Colleges Model Accountability System (discussed in some detail later) is part of a broader information-gathering system. This huge undertaking at the state level spans student demographics, courses, services, and fiscal and employee data across the colleges.

Ingredients of potential outcomes assessment models are reflected in the following elements currently being tested as California experiments with assessment and accountability: demographics of students, success for underrepresented racial and ethnic groups as a measure of educational equity, and institutional effectiveness, as well as individual student success.

Outcomes Assessment: Making a Difference by Measuring the Mission

After AB 1725 clearly affirmed the essential components of the community college mission, state legislators and educational policy makers increasingly demanded concrete data from the community colleges substantiating their success in this regard.

Transfer Outcomes

Since 1989, the Center for the Study of Community Colleges (CSCC) at UCLA has reported transfer data annually on forty-nine California community colleges in a national sample of 240 two-year colleges (Cohen, 1992). Through its Transfer Assembly, CSCC defined the transfer rate as "all students entering the two-year college in a given year who have no prior college experience and who complete at least 12 college credit units within four years, divided into the number of that group who take one or more classes at a university within four years" (Cohen, 1992, p. 7). In contrast, at the state level, defining the transfer rate itself has been studied for nearly a decade to no avail. Competing formulas with high price tags have been developed, and the dialogue continues to focus on the proper measure to adopt (Banks, 1992).

The University of California (UC) and the California State University (CSU) report annually to the state and to individual community colleges the number of students from the two-year institutions who subsequently enroll in and complete baccalaureate courses and degrees. Local community colleges aggregate these data and report progress to their local governing boards.

Additionally, some community colleges are able to share student information with their university counterparts directly. For example, at San Jose City College and at Evergreen Valley College, approximately 70 percent of all students who transfer attend San Jose State University (SJSU). Mechanisms have been established so that administrators and faculty can share data and improve institutional processes that encourage transfer based on outcomes information. A study that tracked the longitudinal performance of ESL students from San Jose City College and Evergreen Valley College through university transfer to SJSU was completed in spring 1992 (Kangas, 1992). Results from this study led to an in-depth examination of assessment and curricular patterns affecting the success of transfer students.

Similarly, in the San Mateo Community College District (SMCCD), which comprises three community colleges (San Mateo, Skyline, and Cañada), the chancellor reports transfer outcomes regularly to the governing board with attention to relationships with college-going rates in San Mateo County, numbers of graduating high school students, and the ethnic composition of their transfers to UC and CSU (Callahan, 1991). The district also analyzes the academic performance of students at the university after they transfer. "These reports indicate that the District's transfer students show high rates of continuation or persistence at universities most frequently attended. Furthermore, they point out that SMCCD students are achieving success in their academic programs as indicated by the competitive grade point averages earned at the universities. This information represents important evidence that District transfer students are well-prepared for the academic challenges of university-level coursework" (Callahan, 1991).

The California Postsecondary Education Commission (CPEC), an independent organization that sets and monitors policy initiatives for the three segments of California higher education, regularly reports on the number of students transferring from community colleges to public four-year universities. Critics generally acknowledge that these data are misleading in that transfers to private institutions within California and to public and private institutions outside the state are not included. Also, the last college attended by a student regardless of the number of units taken is credited as the "sending" institution. Sometimes simplistic analyses are published from these data, unfortunately eroding the credibility of the community colleges (Simpson, 1992). Although problems of definition, rate, and instruments abound, CPEC has done an admirable job in aggregating data that are available systemwide.

Occupational Outcomes

Occupationally related outcomes of students are equally important as indicators of how well community colleges are addressing their mission. During the past decade, the state Chancellor's Office supported the development of a vocational data collection system known as VEDS (Vocational Education Data System) but again has had difficulty compiling results from the colleges to demonstrate systemwide accountability. Despite this, some occupational outcomes information is transmitted every year from the colleges to the state to the federal government.

Most community colleges have implemented the VEDS system and collect and report these data routinely at the local, state, and federal levels. At the state level, the Community Colleges Chancellor's Office contracted for the development of an Occupational Education Program Evaluation System and a Vocational Program Follow-Up System. Local community colleges survey vocational students, instructors, administrators, and program advisory committee members on a regular basis for program review purposes; however, again, these data are not collected for statewide reporting purposes. The Follow-Up System is a survey instrument that enables colleges to gather outcomes information on students who left their institutions. In addition to indicating their employment status, the individuals are asked the following questions: (1) Did the classes you took at our college help you meet your educational goal? (2) Did you complete a degree or certificate at our college? (3) Did you take a license-certification or credential examination? (4) Were the occupational skills and abilities learned through the classes you took at our college adequate for helping you in your employment? (5) What is your hourly wage range?

Basic Skills and English as a Second Language Outcomes

Though transfer and occupational education are the primary elements of the community college mission, the teaching of basic skills and English as a second language is important to the mission as well. Promoting student success is the major goal of California community colleges.

Recognizing the lack of statewide information on student performance in basic skills courses, in 1986 LARC identified the measurement of selected student outcomes as its major research priority. The consortium then developed a generic student outcomes assessment model and tested the model in remedial writing programs through college-level English composition in twenty-nine community colleges, using a representative sample of the system as a whole. After completing that project in 1987–88, twenty-eight community colleges applied the model to their reading courses. In 1988–89, twenty-three community colleges completed the outcomes study in mathematics.

Acknowledging the multifaceted mission of community colleges, LARC defined outcomes assessment using multiple measures, including student educational and course goals satisfaction, persistence in courses and in colleges, and skills acquisition in specific courses. The LARC Outcomes Assessment Model was also designed to be used in evaluating outcomes across the curriculum (in any community college course, program, or set of programs) and across colleges.

Salient findings from the LARC studies included the following:

- Students frequently reassessed and changed their educational goals while they attended a community college. Most indicated their intention to obtain a baccalaureate degree, but the specific means or pathway to that goal changed frequently (for example, they often changed their major).
- Students reported that their reading, writing, and mathematics skills improved as a result of completing the basic skills classes.
- Students acquired competence through remedial courses, and substantial skill gains were demonstrated in all the LARC studies (based on testing before and after the classes).
- Students showed substantial gains within their precollege basic skills courses but usually not enough to achieve the average entrance skills at the next higher level of academic work in the discipline.
- Regarding skills outcomes from examining the proportion of students successfully completing their courses (note: successfully completing was a grade of A, B, C, or credit and not successfully completing was a grade of D, F, or no credit):

> In the mathematics study of approximately ten thousand students who reported taking the pretest, 50 percent were successful, 19 percent were not successful, 31 percent withdrew from their course or received a grade of incomplete.
>
> In the writing studies, 67 percent of the sample of approximately 5,200 students were successful, 18 percent were unsuccessful, and 15 percent did not complete their course of study.
>
> In the reading study, 70 percent of the sample of 3,800 were successful, 15 percent were not, and 15 percent did not finish the course.

- Examining persistence in college, 82 percent of the mathematics student sample enrolled in courses the following spring semester. Corresponding persistence data from the writing and reading studies were 82 percent and 78 percent respectively.

The LARC studies increased community college awareness and use of student assessment, research, and follow-up information. This series of studies underscored the relationship of student retention, persistence, transfer, and follow-up data to ongoing program evaluation and institutional improvement and effectiveness efforts. The studies produced a large data base on more than twenty-two thousand community college students. The findings influenced assessment, curricula, and state, as well as local policy, decisions. Major recommendations include:

- The evaluation of students' skills gains should focus upon college-level preparedness. Accordingly, community colleges should work toward consistent exit criteria related to preparedness in basic skills for each level of remediation; these criteria are more important than a standardized curriculum.
- Students who complete each level of basic skills are not necessarily prepared for the next level; therefore, more time on tasks may be required, especially given the degree of underpreparation in some cases.
- California community colleges can undertake remediation of large numbers of underprepared students. The investment of the state in remediation is appropriate and productive given that students in these courses demonstrate satisfactory progress in basic skills and persist at higher rates than their fellow students in the regular program. Since a large number of underprepared students make significant progress toward college-level skills, an academic floor is not appropriate or necessary.

Beyond these policy recommendations, the LARC studies found that 61 percent of the community colleges created new basic skills courses designed to meet students' educational needs (Learning Assessment Retention Consortium, 1986, 1987, 1988a, 1988b; Learning Assessment Retention Consortium, English

Council of California Two-Year Colleges, and Academic Senate for California Community Colleges, 1988).

California Community Colleges
Model Accountability System of the 1990s

The context for defining accountability in California community colleges is one of shrinking and more centralized funding from the state. During the 1980s, the state sought clarification of "an optimal mix of state funds among the various providers of post-secondary education" (Strategic Planning Associates, 1991, p. 25). Instability of school finances and declining resources caused dual state response from the legislature and the California Community Colleges Board of Governors: tighter and more vigorous oversight of funds allocated to community colleges, and a requirement to pool the diverse data of 107 community colleges within a state data base organized as the Model Accountability System (Holsclaw and Wiseley, 1992).

The AB 1725 legislation specified eleven measures for community colleges, nine of which are related to student access, success, and satisfaction. In 1989, a statewide Accountability Task Force was convened with consultant support from national assessment expert Peter Ewell and local institutional researchers and educators from the community colleges. Incorporating the accountability measures, the task force recommended that outcomes data be gathered in mandated areas of student access, success, and satisfaction; staff composition; and fiscal condition. The task force specified the purpose for evaluating the community, educational, and fiscal effectiveness of the institutions as the improvement of educational quality (Far West Laboratory, 1991).

The Model Accountability System is designed to assess outcomes for the purpose of justifying and distributing increasingly scarce state resources to institutions that demonstrate educational quality, efficiency, and effectiveness. There is, however, a great gap between the capabilities of colleges to implement this system and the management information structure required to pool diverse data from 107 community colleges into a single statewide data base. In addition to infrastructure problems, there is continuing debate about who should pay the cost of implementing and maintaining the Model Accountability System as well as mistrust about whether it will be used for institutional improvement or punishment. As Ewell (1992) suggests, "Linking high stakes and measured performance can have negative consequences. If the stakes are high, campuses will start 'managing to the numbers.' But if the consequences of not participating are few, measured performance will simply be ignored" (p. 14).

In spite of its current implementation problems, the Model Accountability System is seen by many as a promising tool in influencing decisions made at the state level. Grosz (1992) argues that accountability and related outcomes assessment activities have already provided the California community colleges a more comfortable position within the state as the legislature contemplates budget shortfalls and enrollment surges. Nevertheless, a new terminology has emerged: "data burden," "research burden," and "local versus state accountability" are heard frequently in discussions about the Model Accountability System.

When the complexities of design and implementation of the proposed dual system of local and state level accountability are added to the extensive variations among colleges, it is clear that implementing the system may prove difficult. Strategic Planning Associates (1991) concludes that "to assume any single accountability system will adequately fulfill the expectations of all of the actors, local decision makers, the Chancellor's Office, the Legislature, and the Governor is to assume a system that hasn't been invented yet" (p. 27).

Fiscal implications of outcomes assessment create another implementation problem. Historically, assignment of state funds in California has not been based on merit. There have been occasional proposals to reward institutions for increased levels of performance (such as the funds initially provided to colleges to increase the number of students transferring to the university). In the end, however, state budget policies have directed state dollars to campuses that need to improve the most, especially those with large numbers of underrepresented and underprepared students. Without rewards or incentives for doing so, colleges have not been motivated to make changes necessary to improve performance.

New Types of Learning Outcomes: Assessing Educational Equity

Many California community colleges now regularly conduct outcomes studies, measuring student access and success. At the same time, the social, political, and educational interests of state and local policy makers are increasingly focused on the dramatically changing nature of the student body. Outcomes assessment efforts have turned to examinations of the quality of learning for students from historically underrepresented groups. Recent efforts in evaluating these groups make clear that this will be a long-term, intensive institutional and faculty reform endeavor.

One example of this current focus is the study conducted at College of the Desert in 1991–92. Designed and implemented by Sigala and Umbdenstock (1992), the study explored the pertinent variables and outcomes of certain pedagogical practices in improving the college curriculum and classroom climate to ensure educational access and success. Outcomes of this research indicate that when curricula and pedagogy significantly incorporate a "pro-diverse" student perspective, student learning increases, and the classroom climate changes to one that is interactive, alive, and positive.

Integrating recent developmental and adult learning information, findings from women's studies, and multiculturalism in teaching and pedagogy, Sigala and Umbdenstock have identified ways in which faculty can transform the classroom environment to one that is inclusive, supportive, and welcoming, regardless of circumstance, background, ethnicity, race, or any other characteristic that tends to keep students separate from one another and apart from learning. Rationale for this study includes the following:

1. Active learning strategies, when appropriately designed and assessed, extend the cognitive strategies that students use to learn new information.

2. Active learning shifts the focus and the classroom modus operandi from traditional teaching behaviors to learning behaviors.

3. The presentation of diverse teaching methods in the classroom strengthens subject mastery through faculty-student and student-student interactions.

4. Course transformation involves the reorganization of curriculum materials to infuse multicultural information as appropriate core or content topics.

5. The presence of many and pluralistic perspectives in the content of a course provides students with the opportunity to examine critically the essential issues from a variety of viewpoints and exercises students' critical-thinking skills and abilities.

Outcomes of this study may serve as a catalyst for future research addressing faculty, student, and institutional transformation. The data show that conscious and skilled involvement of students in classroom activities leads to greater student investment in their own learning and responsibility for acquiring knowledge. Many faculty members reported genuine progress in their work with underrepresented students as a result of using classroom-based assessment techniques. The faculty also saw an increase in expression in classes. Students changed their preferences in how they learned, and ethnic differences were apparent in their preferences. Students related their learning to experiences outside, as well as inside, the classroom. They became aware of their individual and collective cultural contributions; they also encountered and evaluated alternative ways of learning about diversity, and the range of ideas and interests increased as a result of shared multicultural perspectives within and beyond the classroom.

The faculty at College of the Desert is optimistic that the short- and intermediate-term academic, cognitive, and social gains in learning outcomes and the concomitant significant impact on classroom climate can be translated into standard, quantifiable, and positive long-term student outcomes. The findings of this study represent a new aspect of the challenge facing the state of California: will student outcomes reflect educational equity for all students, including those from ethnic and language groups historically underrepresented in higher education?

The California Postsecondary Education Commission completed a feasibility study on measuring campus climate in 1992 (1990, 1992). It found that it is not only possible but essential to assess campus climate, given the changing demography of the postsecondary student population. Students of color often perceive campuses as inhospitable, isolating them from the mainstream of college life and mitigating against academic achievement. The commission has published a campus climate survey that individual campuses can use to measure the extent to which their environment supports learning, particularly for students of color.

In the 1990s, accountability is the focus for outcomes assessment in California. Student assessment models and institutional accountability models can be linked by the premise that academic quality promotes student achievement and institutional effectiveness. "While neither the process nor the results of assessment creates quality, assessment is essential to the recognition of quality and to providing the kind of information in the light of which quality improvement can occur" (Millard, 1991, p. 170).

References

Assembly Bill no. 3 (1985–86 regular session). *Community Colleges Matriculation* (Seymour-Campbell). Sacramento: California State Assembly, Sept. 30, 1986.

Assembly Bill no. 1725 (1987–88 regular session). *California Community Colleges* (Vasconcellos). Sacramento: California State Assembly, Sept. 19, 1988.

Banks, D. *California Community College Student-Transfer Indicators: How Relevant Are They?* Draft Report. Berkeley, Calif.: BW Associates, 1992.

California Postsecondary Education Commission. *Toward an Understanding of Campus Climate: A Report to the Legislature in Response to Assembly Bill 4071.* Report no. 90-19. Sacramento: State of California.

California Postsecondary Education Commission. *Assessing Campus Climate: Feasibility of Developing an Educational Equity Assessment System.* Sacramento: State of California, 1992.

Callahan, L. *Report on Student Retention.* Board Report no. 91-7-3C. San Mateo, Calif.: San Mateo Community College District, 1991.

Cohen, A. *Calculating the Rate of Transfer from Community Colleges to Public Universities in California: A Report to the California Policy Seminar.* Draft Report. Los Angeles: Department of Education, University of California, Los Angeles, 1992.

Commission for the Review of the Master Plan for Higher Education. *The Challenge of Change: A Reassessment of the California Community Colleges.* Sacramento: State of California, 1986.

Evaluation and Training Institute. *The Statewide Evaluation of Matriculation.* Final Report. Los Angeles: California Community Colleges, 1991.

Ewell, P. T. "Developing Performance Indicators for Community Colleges: Evidence from Two States." *Assessment Update,* 1992, *4*(4), 10, 14.

Far West Laboratory. *Improving It, Accountability by Design.* Sacramento: California Community Colleges Chancellor's Office, 1991.

Grosz, K. Correspondence on Accountability and Outcomes Assessment Affecting the California Community Colleges. Los Angeles: Grosz, 1992.

Holsclaw, M., and Wiseley, C. *Management Information System: Status Report.* Sacramento: California Community Colleges Board of Governors, 1992.

Jones, D. *NCHEMS News.* Boulder, Colo.: National Center for Higher Education Management Systems, 1992.

Kangas, J. *Passing Rates of San Jose City College and Evergreen Valley College Native and Non–Native Speaking Students Taking the San Jose State University Junior Writing Skills Test for Fall 1990.* Research report no. 138. San Jose, Calif.: San Jose–Evergreen Community College District, 1992.

Learning Assessment Retention Consortium. *LARC Student Outcomes Study — Executive Summary.* Sacramento: California Association of Community Colleges, 1986.

Learning Assessment Retention Consortium. *LARC Student Out-comes Study.* Sacramento: California Association of Community Colleges, 1987.

Learning Assessment Retention Consortium. "Beyond Testing, Legal Issues and Promising Practices." In J. Kangas and M. Kanter (eds.), *Proceedings of the Beyond Testing Conference.* Sacramento: California Association of Community Colleges, 1988a.

Learning Assessment Retention Consortium. *LARC Student Out-comes Study: Policy Implications and Recommendations.* Sacramento: California Association of Community Colleges, 1988b.

Learning Assessment Retention Consortium, English Council of California Two-Year Colleges, and Academic Senate for California Community Colleges. *Curriculum Practices in Writing Courses: A Joint Study of LARC, the Academic Senate for California Community Colleges, and the English Council of California Two-Year Colleges.* Sacramento: California Association of Community Colleges, 1988.

Millard, R. M. *Today's Myths and Tomorrow's Realities: Overcoming Obstacles to Academic Leadership in the Twenty-First Century.* San Francisco: Jossey-Bass, 1991.

Sigala, C., and Umbdenstock, L. "Consultants' Report, Project TABS, College of the Desert, 1991–92." In *Project TABS, Desert Community College District.* Final Report. Palm Desert, Calif.: Desert Community College District, 1992.

Simpson, V. "Few Community Colleges Matriculate Core of Transfers to UC System, Report Shows." *Community College Week,* 1992, *4*(22), 3.

Strategic Planning Associates. *California Community College Accountability: State and Local Implementation Costs.* Sacramento: California Community Colleges Chancellor's Office, 1991.

23

The Role of States
and Accreditors
in Shaping
Assessment Practice

Peter T. Ewell

For better or worse, assessment over the past decade at most of the nation's colleges and universities has been decisively shaped by external forces. State government, of course, has been the most visible and direct of these: currently, all but nine states have in place a policy on assessment of some kind, affecting all but a handful of public campuses (Ewell, Finney, and Lenth, 1990). More recently, both public and private institutions have been affected by similar decisions to require assessment on the part of all six regional accrediting bodies. The most recent *Campus Trends Survey* reports the astonishing fact that 92 percent of the nation's colleges and universities now engage in assessment, and strongly supports the conclusion that their decision to begin was made in response to one or more of these requirements (El-Khawas, 1992). It also suggests, however, that many campus leaders remain unconvinced about the real benefits of externally mandated assessment and fear misuse of its results.

What, in fact, has been the impact of these policies? The answer seems simple. There is clearly more activity called assessment at more institutions than there would have been had states and accreditors remained silent. But answering the deeper question of impact is more complicated. By requiring assessment in the first place, by providing (or constraining) the resources needed for its development, and by shaping the public rhetoric surrounding accountability, external actors have decisively influenced local assessment technologies and organizational structures. Yet establishing clear causal connections is difficult for at least three reasons.

One problem is time. Though the first state assessment programs were established by 1982, the vast majority of state mandates and accreditation requirements have been in place less than four years. In an enterprise as slow moving as the academy, expecting the state initiatives to show a real impact in this short period is hoping for a great deal indeed. To date, therefore, most real campus effects of external requirements have been in the area of planning for assessment — in particular in developing the requisite policies and organizational structures to make it happen and in choosing initial instruments and approaches.

A second problem is sheer variety. Though they share many features, no two state mandates are alike. Some were established directly by statute, the majority by the action of a statewide governing or coordinating board, and a few by executive order (Paulson, 1990). Only a few specify common measures. Although most allow substantial campus discretion, they differ considerably in what must be reported, how frequently, and with what consequences. Equally important variations among states in governance, fiscal condition, and political culture will also strongly affect the implementation of assessment as a mandate. The pattern for accreditors is similar (Wolff, 1992). Some focus explicitly on student learning, whereas others incorporate learning outcomes into a more general consideration of institutional effectiveness. Some require reporting of assessment results as a distinct portion of a self-study document; others encourage institutions to report on assessment more pervasively. In short, there is no simple link between what states and accreditors require and what institutions do because the differences in the former are so substantial.

Finally, the impact of any external policy on campus practice is by its very nature indirect. Variations in local leadership, institutional mission and priorities, student clienteles, and faculty cultures and governance arrangements will result in quite different local effects for the same basic requirement — particularly, as has generally been the case in assessment, when the requirement itself encourages local variation. Only very rarely have policies on assessment been blunt instruments. As a result, their impact has more often been manifested in the ways that they have helped or hindered institutional assessment programs themselves to make a difference.

Given these limitations, any attempt to sketch the impact of ten years of assessment policy must be modest. The purposes of this chapter are to provide a brief overview of the evolution of external assessment requirements over the past decade, to present some conclusions about how these policies affected campus action in assessment, to offer some parallel conclusions about how experiences with assessment in turn affected state higher education policy development more generally, and to propose a short set of implications for the future.

Evolution of Assessment Policy

It is easy to forget that external assessment mandates are an extremely recent phenomenon. Approximately a third of the states required that institutions conduct regular program reviews before 1982, but almost none included explicit reporting on outcomes (Barak, 1982). The only external bodies to conduct what we now call assessment were a small number of multicampus public university systems that required common assessment of writing as a condition of graduation (for example, the Georgia and California boards of regents) and a few statewide programs that evaluated entering students' basic skills (for instance, the New Jersey Basic Skills Program). Among regional accrediting bodies, the situation was similar. Some had standards that suggested outcomes (for instance, the criterion of the North Central Association that "the institution is achieving its purposes"), but not one explicitly required institutions to investigate and report on academic achievement (Thrash, 1988).

Early state efforts in the realm of assessment, moreover, varied in both purpose and intent. Those of the two pioneers, Florida and Tennessee, could not have been more different. Arguably, in fact, they were not about assessment at all. Florida established its rising-junior College Level Academic Skills Test (CLAST) in 1982, not as an outcomes assessment but rather as a kind of entrance examination to the upper division. The state policy objective of CLAST was less to evaluate instructional effectiveness than to articulate transfer between two- and four-year institutions in the context of a state system that especially emphasized the role of community colleges as primary providers of lower-division instruction. Scores on CLAST are and always were intended to assist in making decisions about individuals, and it was only in 1988 in a special statewide study that they were for the first time deliberately used in the aggregate to investigate questions of instructional effect (Postsecondary Education Planning Commission, 1988). Because of these unique conditions, the CLAST program remains the only statewide rising-junior examination in the nation.

Tennessee's so-called performance funding program, initiated in 1978 and fully implemented by 1982, remains similarly unique (Banta, 1986). Its origins can be traced to a creative attempt on the part of the Tennessee Higher Education Commission to leverage new money from a reluctant legislature in a period of anticipated enrollment decline (Bogue and Brown, 1982). "Reward for performance" proved a powerful political concept because it was both easy to understand and it clearly signaled quality. Information about performance — embodied in examinations such as the ACT-COMP and a range of major field exams, as well as student satisfaction data and the results of professional program accreditation — was necessary to make the system work but was not in itself the point. Certainly, many campuses in Tennessee (most prominently, the University of Tennessee, Knoxville) did effectively harness this information to make local improvements, and this action was clearly welcomed by state authorities (Banta, 1985, 1988). But the outcome measures themselves and their resulting funding leverage were what state authorities were really interested in.

The main thrust of state-mandated assessment began in 1986–1987, coincident with the appearance of two influential reports: *Transforming the State Role in Improving Undergraduate Education: Time for a Different View* (Education Commission of the States, 1986) and *Time for Results* (National Governors' Association, 1986). Essentially, these reports argued for a more proactive role for state authorities in higher education based on a new conception of public accountability as "return on investment" (Boyer, 1985; Ewell, 1990). Assessment was a key element of this new role, but the reports themselves left its actual structure largely undefined. At that time, many observers expected a parallel evolution to what had occurred earlier in K-12 evaluation — an approach based largely upon large-scale standardized testing. And in many cases, this was what state authorities initially proposed (Boyer, Ewell, Finney, and Mingle, 1987). In South Dakota, for instance, the state Board of Regents mandated end-of-sophomore year testing using the ACT-COMP exam and major-field assessment using nationally normed instruments such as licensure examinations and the GRE in a program based heavily on the model of Northeast Missouri State University (Ewell and Boyer, 1988). In Washington, by contrast, an initial proposal for sophomore testing was turned into a study resolution. After a year of trying out four available standardized general education examinations, it was concluded that not one of these was adequate for informing local improvement (Council of Presidents and State Board for Community College Education, 1989). In the three years that followed, most states came to the same conclusion, though few went to the same trouble to test alternatives. Through a combination of pure political opposition on the part of higher education leaders and sound reasoning about what might really cause campus-level change, most states adopted a different approach.

The elements of this new approach were most clearly exemplified in Virginia, whose assessment program became in many ways a model. In 1986, the State Council on Higher Education in Virginia required all public institutions to prepare a local assessment plan embracing basic skills, general education, major-field outcomes, and alumni follow-up. Subsequent to plan approval, each institution was required to report results of its assessment program on a biennial basis, consistent with the state's higher education budgeting cycle. The Virginia approach allowed each institution a great deal of choice in defining learning goals and in selecting assessment approaches that best fit local missions, curricula, and student clienteles. But while it allowed substantial discretion, it also included a number of positive and negative incentives for compliance. On the positive side, funds were allocated to campuses to support the development of local assessment. On the negative side, institutions that failed to submit an acceptable plan were barred from participating in some lucrative funding enhancement programs — a measure designed particularly to get the attention of the three major research universities in the state.

With a few key exceptions — the complex and controversial College Outcomes Evaluation Program in New Jersey being the most prominent — most states followed the lead of Virginia in developing a decentralized approach to assessment (Boyer, Ewell, Finney, and Mingle, 1987). By 1989, some two-thirds of the states had developed policies roughly along these lines (Ewell, Finney, and Lenth, 1990). Their basic features, though details varied, included the following:

- A requirement that each institution develop an explicit plan for assessment including statements of intended instructional outcomes, proposed methods for gathering evidence, and a proposed organizational structure
- Substantial institutional latitude in developing goal statements and in selecting or designing appropriate methods for gathering evidence
- Mandatory reporting of results to state authorities on a regular schedule, generally coincident with the state's budget cycle
- An expectation that institutions themselves would pay the costs of assessment (Virginia and Washington were prominent exceptions)
- Few real or immediate consequences for institutional com-

pliance or the lack of it (exceptions here were Virginia, as noted, and Colorado, where accountability legislation allowed institutions to be penalized by up to 2 percent of their budgets if they were not in compliance)

- The general expectation that information resulting from local assessment programs would simultaneously induce campus-level change and fulfill growing state-level demands for accountability
- The expectation that results would eventually be helpful in developing state-level academic policies and in determining key areas of need for selective investment

For at least three years in most states, these were the terms under which the majority of public institutions undertook assessment. Meanwhile, though lagging somewhat behind, all six regional accrediting agencies had also developed requirements for assessment (Wolff, 1992). The pioneer here was the Southern Association of Colleges and Schools (SACS), which in 1986 introduced a new institutional effectiveness standard to its procedure for reaffirmation. Unlike most states, SACS did not identify undergraduate student learning as the only domain for reporting assessment results — though it was a clear center of gravity. In essence, however, the requirements that SACS placed upon institutions were the same as those later adopted by other accreditors: develop and articulate clear goals stated in terms of outcomes, select or build appropriate local measures to gather evidence of goal achievement, and provide evidence of the ways that the resulting evidence was used to inform improvement. Though again the details varied (only the Western Association, for instance, followed the lead of SACS in producing a new and separate effectiveness standard), all institutions (both public and private) were thus required by accreditors to engage in some form of assessment by 1990.

Impacts on Institutions

As noted, the indirect nature of external assessment requirements as inducements to institutional action, as well as their sheer variety, automatically limits generalizations about impact. Nevertheless, at least five years of experience suggests a few conclusions—both positive and negative—about what has been accomplished.

On the positive side, clearly the most salient impact of external influences on campus practice has simply been that they provided the motivation to get started. National survey results consistently indicate that steadily increasing proportions of colleges and universities engaged in assessment from 1987 to 1992 and that most of the institutions ascribe their activities to one or more of these influences (El-Khawas, 1988, 1989, 1990, 1991, 1992). Going deeper, the presence of state mandates has helped to sustain an assessment effort once started, provided, of course, that the requirements of the mandate themselves are stable. Institutions in states such as Virginia have now experienced three complete biennial reporting cycles, and institutional and state authorities agree that both the quality and utility of the resulting information have increased markedly (Ewell, 1992; Miller, 1991). A majority of campuses now appear willing to continue assessment locally regardless of what the state requires. Even so, when budgetary downturns occurred in Virginia in 1990, several campuses appeared ready to cut local assessment budgets until explicitly prohibited from doing so by state authorities (Ewell, 1991).

Where the signals coming from the state have been mixed, a year or two of induced response has generally not been sustained. In New Jersey, for example, there is now little local activity at the four-year level despite significant state-level investments in the years 1986 to 1989 (Ewell, 1992). In New York, moreover, an initial state presence quickly became overwhelmed by escalating budget problems, and there appears now to be only scattered commitment among institutions. Overall, the expected mechanism built into state assessment policy does occur: initial, generally reluctant, compliance on the part of public campuses is followed in many cases by the local discovery that the results of assessment are useful and that the process is worth sustaining. But the period of state "pump priming" may be substantial before institutions are ready to see local benefits.

Campus Trends results again are revealing: though almost all respondents report that their institutions are engaged in the assessment process, more than half also agree that to date "all that assessment has resulted in is additional reporting requirements" (El-Khawas, 1992).

Institutional benefits that can at least partially be ascribed to the action of external forces are therefore primarily those associated with the early stages of implementation. Most prominent among them is goal development. Most state guidelines for assessment have explicitly required institutions to develop and report instructional goals in terms of outcomes as a prerequisite for assessment; in several cases (Colorado and New Jersey, for example), separate reporting about goals actually preceded the reporting of outcomes. All six regional accrediting bodies similarly require the development of explicit instructional goals. The required goal development process has admittedly been perfunctory in many cases, but in many others it has occasioned substantial and productive faculty dialogue (especially at the department level) about curriculum structure and pedagogy that would otherwise not have taken place (Banta and Schneider, 1988).

A few additional explicit instructional effects can also be credited with some confidence to the presence of external requirements — interestingly at either end of the curriculum. Substantially greater numbers of institutions, particularly two-year institutions, now conduct mandatory assessments of basic skills such as reading, writing, and computation at the time students enter and require directed placement into remediation for students found deficient. In Florida, Texas, New Jersey, and Tennessee, these processes are a direct result of state action and have been shown to be effective in later retention and course performance in statewide follow-up studies. In more typical states like Virginia and Washington, the need for institutions to report on local basic skills assessment practices appears to be having similar effects. The frequent inclusion in state mandates of a requirement to assess outcomes in each major field has led directly to a reintroduction of some once-common features of the undergraduate curriculum — senior seminars and disciplinary comprehensive examinations. To some extent, these were curricular mechanisms that many faculty already favored, and the mandate to develop a departmental assessment procedure provided the needed impetus to implement them.

Direct impacts of external requirements on campus assessment practice are more easily documented on the negative side, though this does not mean that they outweigh the positive. First, the very existence of an external requirement — especially if it is imposed by state authorities — makes the job of selling assessment internally more difficult. In fact, in several cases at major research universities, the direct involvement of the state converted lukewarm acceptance of an internal initiative into vocal opposition to any kind of evaluation as a violation of institutional autonomy or academic freedom (Ewell and Boyer, 1988; Zguta, 1989).

More subtly, requirements of this kind first enter the institution through administrative channels and are consequently seen by most academics as an administrative responsibility (Ewell, 1988). This perception is reinforced where assessment activities are specifically funded or are primarily located in an office or center created especially for the purpose. Yet the creation of such an office (regardless of what it does) is perhaps the single most visible action that an institution can take to demonstrate immediately to external authorities that it takes assessment seriously. The result in many cases, however, is for assessment to be divorced from existing school and departmental decision-making channels and for the faculty to see its object solely as one of generating reports for external audiences.

Finally, although the vast majority of external requirements are nonprescriptive with respect to the choice of instruments and methods, there is a strong tendency for institutions to second-guess what will be considered acceptable by external authorities regardless of local appropriateness and need. Activities or methods that are noted in external guidelines as examples of what might be done are thus often adopted with little question by institutions because they are viewed as "safe" alternatives for compliance. Similarly, any institutional report or practice that is favorably cited by states or accreditors is likely to be widely imitated regardless of its local applicability. A powerful unintended consequence of external attempts to be helpful may thus be an incentive for institutions to adopt approaches that are not useful to them.

On balance, it is safe to conclude that external requirements have proven a necessary condition for the majority of institutions to act on assessment in the first place. As a consequence, though their presence may have induced some unproductive local practices, they may also claim a legitimate share of any of the campus-level benefits that assessment can more generally demonstrate.

Impacts on State Policy

When state policies mandating assessment first emerged in large numbers in the late 1980s, they signaled a new role for higher education governing authorities. Before about 1985, consistent with a notion of accountability that emphasized access and efficiency, state authorities were concerned primarily with fiscal and administrative matters. Relevant academic policy issues were limited and typically included areas like admissions policy, student financial assistance, and program duplication. With the evolution of a new accountability for higher education based on statewide return on investment, assessment policies pioneered the notion that state government had a legitimate interest in what was taught and how (Ewell, 1990). In the nineties, state policy actions in the academic arena are becoming more comprehensive, proactive, and frequent; and in many ways, the actions are being shaped by the previous experience with assessment.

As for institutions, the impacts of state-level assessment experience on later state policy development have been both positive and negative. One of the most prominent positive effects has been exposure to academic issues. In implementing assessment policies, state-level academic staff typically became engaged in considerable and unprecedented dialogue about substantive issues of curriculum and pedagogy with institutional academic leadership and with faculty generally. Though the primary object of these conversations was to negotiate compliance, they

had the additional effects of better informing state-level authorities about real academic issues and conditions at the institutional level and about the existence of substantial bodies of
campus opinion that were sincerely interested in curricular and
instructional change. Both areas of new knowledge are now proving important as the states evolve new approaches to academic
policy.

Like their campus-level counterparts, state authorities also
quickly appreciated the uncanny ability of assessment to provide gateways into wider, often unattended, instructional issues.
Texas and Hawaii, for instance, repeated the Florida experience of using evaluation results to help reenergize discussions
about statewide articulation and transfer, and to examine more
comprehensively lower-division instruction in such areas as writing and mathematics. In other states, including Virginia and
New Jersey, discussions that began with assessment also provided a way into far more complex deliberations about the structure and content of institutional general education requirements
and campus advising practices. And in Oregon, Washington,
and Colorado, attempts to follow occupational-technical program graduates into the workplace through available statewide
employment records helped inform larger conversations about
work force need and deployment in key areas and about employer satisfaction with graduate skills.

Third, assessment helped state authorities to gain experience about the potential and limitations of some now-common
policy levers for inducing local change and about how these
might better work in concert (Ewell, 1985). In New Jersey,
assessment interacted with the lucrative Governor's Challenge
Grant incentive program in several important ways — most prominently in the development of a nationally recognized assessment program at Kean College (Boyer, 1989). At the same time,
broad inspection of patterns in institutional assessment results
occasionally allowed state authorities to direct additional funds
toward identified statewide problems, such as minority achievement (Ewell, 1990). In Minnesota, small grants to initiate assessment allowed some experimentation with addition-to-base incentive funding mechanisms in the first place. Through the

process of implementing assessment, state policy makers also became more sensitive to the fact that myriad unrelated policies can create contradictory incentives for campuses in addressing problems of undergraduate instruction. Foremost among these are funding mechanisms that tend to discourage investment in the lower division and in initiatives that cut across established disciplines (Jones and Ewell, 1991).

Finally, though examples remain few, some states have used assessment results directly to inform specific policy decisions. In Florida, Texas, and New Jersey, early results of statewide basic skills examinations helped build a case for resource reallocation to better support developmental programs at two-year colleges (Ewell, 1990). And even where few comparable statewide results are available, state authorities are beginning to detect patterns in local results that can be used in their planning and setting of priorities — for instance, in Virginia with regard to general education or in New Jersey and Tennessee with regard to minority student achievement.

But states have also had some negative experiences with assessment. As was the case in institutions, the foremost of these has been policy isolation: assessment implementation and reporting can become a "train on its own track," unconnected to other state-level policies or procedures that also affect undergraduate education (Ewell and Boyer, 1988). To some extent, this phenomenon is a clear consequence of implementing assessment as a distinct reporting requirement and of providing specific funding to support it. The suspension of the New Jersey COEP program in 1991 due to funding shortfalls and lack of political support illustrates one consequence of isolation (Ewell, 1992). Missouri and South Carolina incorporated institutional assessment reporting visibly into a wider rubric of strategic planning to attempt to deal actively with the problem of policy isolation.

A second prominent problem is the growing inability of most states to integrate the results of disparate campus assessment programs into a sufficiently simple and coherent statewide picture to satisfy external accountability demands (Ewell, 1991). Coupled with frustration at not gaining universal institutional compliance, this situation is again putting pressure on state leaders to propose common procedures for gathering evidence. Additional legitimacy for these efforts is provided by the National Education Goals Panel, which in 1991 recommended eventual development of a sample-based national assessment of collegiate proficiency in the areas of critical thinking, communication, and problem solving (National Education Goals Panel, 1991). In 1990–1991, one result was a significant increase in state-level proposals for common outcomes testing and strong reemergence of interest in performance funding alternatives for higher education (Ewell, 1991).

On balance, then, the primary impact of assessment on state policy development has been to open new avenues for systematically considering academic issues traditionally considered off-limits to outside authorities. Though the information collected from institutions has proved occasionally valuable in making specific decisions, the real value of assessment has been in the proactive academic leadership that it has provided.

Some Lessons for the Future

As emphasized, the states have learned a number of lessons through assessment that are growing in importance as they develop more proactive approaches to higher education policy. Through assessment, state authorities have become more comfortable with academic issues in general and less willing to defer automatically to campuses on matters of content and pedagogy. At the same time, they have witnessed the benefits and limits of approaches to change that are decentralized, campus centered, and incentive-based. The ramifications of these experiences are visible in current discussions in many states about restructuring higher education governance and resource allocation mechanisms for the 1990s.

In conclusion, it is therefore useful to note a few of the specific lessons learned by states through assessment and their implications for the future. Among the most prominent are the following:

1. *Requiring assessment to stand alone results in little real impact on campus behavior.* In the future, states will be increasingly

conscious of the need to systematically integrate assessment requirements with other state-level incentives and policies that affect the improvement of undergraduate education. At the same time, they will be unlikely to continue approaches where lack of campus compliance has no consequences.

2. *Decentralized approaches, though they continue to show promise for inducing local improvement, are increasingly unsatisfactory in achieving credible accountability.* In tight budget times and in the context of a national discussion about creating comparative standards of achievement, state governments will be under increasing pressure to evaluate college outcomes directly. Most likely, this task will emerge as part of a more comprehensive one of developing common performance indicators covering inputs, processes, and outcomes such as are currently in place in Texas, Tennessee, and South Carolina (Ewell and Jones, 1992).

3. *Decentralized approaches that preserve considerable campus initiative do work eventually to change local practice, but the process takes time and requires consistent messages and incentives.* States in the future will likely emphasize creating a local "market" for assessment results by building them into requests for addition-to-base incentive funding or performance funding mechanisms. At the same time, they will stress assessment practice as only one component of a more comprehensive agenda of curricular and instructional reform.

4. *Policies that act indirectly to increase the decisional discretion of institutional leaders remain the key to meaningful, long-term campus action.* Despite a more visible accountability context, state authorities will likely continue to stress policies that give local leadership the tools it needs to overcome campus inertia—particularly in such cross-cutting areas as general education. The result will probably be a tighter version of the predominant policy "bargain" of the late 1980s that yielded state-level assessment in the first place: increased management discretion to institutions in the use of resources in return for specific performance as measured by a defined set of statewide indicators.

Consistent with the experience of the 1980s, these anticipated lessons for the 1990s will probably apply unevenly; their impact will be dependent upon local political and fiscal conditions. In this respect, the shape of the future remains uncertain. But a new generation of higher education policy appears to be in the making that, when in place, will trace much of its ancestry to the experiences that states gained in implementing assessment in the late eighties. And regardless of their many impacts on campuses — both direct and indirect — this may well prove to be the most lasting legacy of the external assessment mandates of the last decade.

References

Banta, T. W. "Use of Outcomes Information at the University of Tennessee, Knoxville." In P. Ewell (ed.), *Assessing Educational Outcomes*. New Directions for Institutional Research, no. 47. San Francisco: Jossey-Bass, 1985.

Banta, T. W. (ed.). *Performance Funding in Higher Education: A Critical Analysis of Tennessee's Experience*. Boulder, Colo.: National Center for Higher Education Management Systems, 1986.

Banta, T. W. "Assessment as an Instrument of State Funding Policy." In T. W. Banta (ed.), *Implementing Outcomes Assessment: Promise and Perils*. New Directions for Institutional Research, no. 59. San Francisco: Jossey-Bass, 1988.

Banta, T. W., and Schneider, J. A. "Using Faculty-Developed Exit Examinations to Evaluate Academic Programs." *Journal of Higher Education*, 1988, *59*, 69–83.

Barak, R. J. *Program Review Within and Without*. Boulder, Colo.: National Center for Higher Education Management Systems, 1982.

Bogue, E. G., and Brown, W. "Performance Incentives for State Colleges." *Harvard Business Review*, 1982, *60* (6), 123–128.

Boyer, C. M. *Five Reports: Summary of the Recommendations of Recent Commission Reports on Improving Undergraduate Education*. Denver, Colo.: Education Commission of the States, 1985.

Boyer, C. M. *Improving Student Learning: The Outcomes Assessment Program at Kean College of New Jersey*. Union, N.J.: Kean College of New Jersey, 1989.

Boyer, C. M., Ewell, P. T., Finney, J. E., and Mingle, J. R. "Assessment and Outcomes Measurement: A View from the States." *AAHE Bulletin*, 1987, *39*(7), 3–7.

Council of Presidents and State Board for Community College Education. *The Validity and Usefulness of Three Nationally Standardized Tests for Washington College Sophomores: General Report.* Bellingham, Wash.: Western Washington University Office of Publications, 1989.

Education Commission of the States. *Transforming the State Role in Undergraduate Education: Time for a Different View.* Denver, Colo.: Education Commission of the States, 1986.

El-Khawas, E. *1988 Campus Trends Survey.* Washington, D.C.: American Council on Education, 1988.

El-Khawas, E. *1989 Campus Trends Survey.* Washington, D.C.: American Council on Education, 1989.

El-Khawas, E. *1990 Campus Trends Survey.* Washington, D.C.: American Council on Education, 1990.

El-Khawas, E. *1991 Campus Trends Survey.* Washington, D.C.: American Council on Education, 1991.

El-Khawas, E. *1992 Campus Trends Survey.* Washington, D.C.: American Council on Education, 1992.

Ewell, P. T. *Levers for Change: The Role of State Government in Improving the Quality of Postsecondary Education.* Denver, Colo.: Education Commission of the States, 1985.

Ewell, P. T. "Implementing Assessment: Some Organizational Issues." In T. W. Banta (ed.), *Implementing Outcomes Assessment: Promise and Perils.* New Directions for Institutional Research, no. 59. San Francisco: Jossey-Bass, 1988.

Ewell, P. T. *Assessment and the "New Accountability": A Challenge for Higher Education's Leadership.* Denver, Colo.: Education Commission of the States, 1990.

Ewell, P. T. "Assessment and Public Accountability: Back to the Future." *Change Magazine,* 1991, *23*(6), 12–17.

Ewell, P. T. "Assessment in Hard Times: A Tale of Two States." *Assessment Update,* 1992, *4*(1), 11–12.

Ewell, P. T., and Boyer, C. M. "Acting Out State-Mandated Assessment: Evidence from Five States." *Change Magazine,* 1988, *20*(4), 40–47.

Ewell, P. T., Finney, J., and Lenth, C. "Filling in the Mosaic: The Emerging Pattern of State-Based Assessment." *AAHE Bulletin,* 1990, *1,* 3–5.

Ewell, P. T., and Jones, D. P. *Pointing the Way: Indicators as Policy*

Tools in Higher Education. Denver, Colo.: Education Commission of the States, 1992.

Jones, D. P., and Ewell, P. T. *The Effect of State Policy on Undergraduate Education.* Denver, Colo.: Education Commission of the States, 1991.

Miller, M. A. "Assessment in Trying Times." *Assessment Update,* 1991, *3*(6), 1–5.

National Education Goals Panel. *Building a Nation of Learners: National Education Goals Report.* Washington, D.C.: National Education Goals Panel, 1991.

National Governors' Association. *Time for Results: The Governors' 1991 Report on Education.* Washington, D.C.: National Governors' Association, 1986.

Paulson, C. P. *State Initiatives in Assessment and Outcomes Measurement: Tools for Teaching and Learning in the 1990's: Individual State Profiles.* Denver, Colo.: Education Commission of the States, 1990.

Postsecondary Education Planning Commission. *College-Level Academic Skills Test Review: Prepared in Response to Specific Appropriation 537A of the 1987 General Appropriations Act.* Tallahassee, Fla.: Postsecondary Education Planning Commission, State of Florida, 1988.

Thrash, P. A. "Educational 'Outcomes' in the Accrediting Process." *Academe,* 1988, *74,* 16–18.

Wolff, R. A. *Incorporating Assessment into the Practice of Accreditation: A Preliminary Report.* Washington, D.C.: Council on Postsecondary Accreditation, 1992.

Zguta, R. "Faculty Response to Assessment at a Major Research University." *Assessment Update,* 1989, *1*(3), 7–9.

24

Summary and Conclusion:
Are We Making a Difference?

Trudy W. Banta

The short answer to the question posed in the title of this chapter, a question that has guided the development of this volume, is *yes*. The foregoing chapters provide many illustrations of improvements in programs and services that have been undertaken as a result of faculty and staff involvement in assessment activities. But this affirmative response must be qualified. My task here is to explain the qualifications and justify my positive conclusion. The qualifications may be explained in terms of time, campus leadership for assessment, and the tension between assessment for accountability and that intended to create improvement.

Time

Although we can point to improvements in programs and services that are traceable to campus assessment efforts, the external constituencies of higher education may be disappointed that concrete, objective evidence of better student learning is sparse. Of the many institutional examples chronicled herein, only the pioneers, Alverno College, Northeast Missouri State University,

357

Ohio University, and a few institutions in Tennessee, have longitudinal data on student achievement that clearly show improvement. I would argue that insufficient time has elapsed for us
to be in a position to attribute substantial changes in learning
to the effects of assessment.

Although Alverno and Northeast Missouri have two decades of experience and Ohio University and public institutions
in Tennessee have more than ten, most campus assessment programs are little more than five years old. Thus, barely a single
class of students has benefited from the entire experience of a
comprehensive assessment program at these institutions.

A second and associated problem is that very few controlled longitudinal studies have been undertaken for the purpose of demonstrating whether students are learning more now
than they were prior to this era of assessment. Some systematic
work has taken place at Alverno, Northeast Missouri, and the
University of Tennessee, Knoxville, but most outcomes assessment projects have been undertaken rather quickly (to satisfy
state or accreditation requirements) with insufficient planning
time and resources to set the projects within the context of longitudinal evaluative studies.

Campus Leadership for Assessment

Although periodic assessment of the learning of individual students has been a well-accepted responsibility of faculty since the
beginning of higher education, the concept of aggregating the
results of individual assessments for the purpose of evaluating
educational programs and student services has not met with immediate approbation by most academics. As campus administrators—the first to feel the effects of external pressures from
governments and accrediting agencies—have sought ways to encourage faculty to undertake comprehensive assessment programs, they have turned most often for leadership to good com-
municators within the ranks of the faculty and administrative
staff. Those who have been recruited for the job of campus assessment coordinator are generally respected faculty or staff members who have proven their ability to bring people together to

solve problems. The most successful coordinators are bright, articulate, persuasive, adaptable individuals who can organize a complex set of activities, mobilize numbers of people to carry them out, and follow through to ensure that the results of evaluative activities are used to inform decision making.

By and large, those selected to serve as assessment coordinators are not measurement specialists or scholars in the fields of educational research or developmental psychology. They have therefore been guided more by intuition and a desire to improve the student experience than by theoretical perspectives. Observers who are schooled in the older, better-established research traditions often express frustration that outcomes assessment as it came to be conceived in the 1980s is not more firmly anchored in the theories of student learning and development and of program evaluation, of which it is such an obvious application. They are with some justification critical of the technically crude methods that individuals who lack training in measurement principles have invented to assess student outcomes. This lack of expertise on the part of most assessment practitioners also helps to explain why so few campus programs incorporate a controlled longitudinal design that in time could enable faculty to determine if their assessment efforts are making a difference.

Accountability and Improvement

Permeating the narratives of my colleagues in this project is a palpable tension between the two principal purposes of assessment: demonstrating accountability and improving curricula, instruction, and student services. External constituencies impel us to undertake assessment for the former purpose; but to the members of the academy, only the latter purpose can provide sufficient intellectual justification for the investment of their time and energy in new methods of measuring student learning and satisfaction.

Despite this tension, I believe that both the external audiences and internal participants of higher education are interested in answers to the same fundamental questions: Is college helping students? Is it increasing what they know and can do? The difference between the external and internal constituents may be found in the nature of the evidence that each is seeking.

External audiences (governors, legislators, higher education policy makers, taxpayers) would like to be able to evaluate college outcomes by reviewing performance on a small number of key indicators. Ideally, scores on these indicators would be obtained from substantial numbers of college students at a modest cost. The data would be reliable and valid, easy to interpret, and comparable across individuals and groups. The indicators would permit scores of individual students to be compared over time in order to assess their progress as a result of their educational experiences. The public would also like to see progressive improvement in the aggregate scores on the key indicators. Thus, external and internal higher education constituencies share not only an interest in what students are learning but also a desire to see improvement in the measures thereof.

But there the similarity between the constituent groups ends. Faculty decry the public appetite for simple scores and brief reports because they know that direction for real improvement must come from many sources rather than a few. They desire a broader, richer, more complex body of information that will give a detailed picture of student learning and suggest specific actions that can be taken to improve it for individual students. Data on a few key indicators aggregated across colleges, systems, states, regions, and nations are not sufficiently specific to be helpful in this connection. Improvement must begin with a single student in a single class if it is to be meaningful and long lasting.

Six of the chapter authors for this volume have been selected by the leadership of the National Center for Education Statistics (NCES) to engage in extended discussion of one of the current national goals for education, goals developed in 1989 by the National Governors' Association and subsequently adopted as the "America 2000 Goals" by former president George Bush and former secretary of education Lamar Alexander. America 2000 goal five, objective five — the only objective that focuses directly upon higher education — states that by the year 2000, "the proportion of college graduates who demonstrate an advanced ability to think critically, communicate effectively, and solve problems will increase substantially" (*America 2000,* 1991, p. 40). The NCES initiative in which the six of us are involved has given us an opportunity to write papers summarizing our reactions to this objective and to come together in Washington on several occasions for discussions based on our papers. In my own position paper (Banta, 1993), I have cited evidence that the measurement instruments and techniques currently available to us do not meet the specifications of either those interested in assessment for accountability purposes or those who need assessment to furnish suggestions for improving the student experience.

The character of the experience for students provided on a given campus is a product of the varied talents and backgrounds of the faculty and administrators employed there, and the enormous diversity among institutions resulting from this fact has always been a valued dimension of higher education in the United States. Nevertheless, the range of approaches to the acquisition of knowledge and skills makes it nearly impossible to develop measures of learning or satisfaction that apply equally well at institutions even in a single community, much less in a given state or across the nation. Study after study on campuses reveals that nationally standardized tests contain questions that cover only a fraction of the content that faculty consider important in a given domain of knowledge (Banta and Pike, 1989).

Despite the desire of external constituents for data on key indicators that will spur educators to improve what they are doing, combined scores composed of several elements or subscores provide little direction for specific improvements. If, for instance, a group of students attains a low score on a test of mathematics, is the low score attributable to their failure to do the numerical calculations accurately, to their inability to comprehend the underlying mathematical processes involved, to reading deficiencies that keep them from understanding the nature of the problem to be solved, or to some combination of these factors? To undertake needed improvements in their work, educators require from a test not just a simple composite score but also subscores that help them pinpoint the precise nature of deficits in student learning. Yet the subscores on many of the commercially available measures of knowledge are not sufficiently reliable to permit their use for this purpose (Pike, 1989).

Today's measuring instruments and methods are also inadequate to the task of showing student progress over time. Hanson (1988) has pointed out that test developers know best how to measure static traits, such as verbal ability, as opposed to developmental changes. Measurement of static traits is based on the assumption that the underlying structure of the construct being measured does not change over time. This assumption is not very helpful when faculty are interested in comparing a student's comprehension of prose or poetry or nuclear physics as a freshman with that as a senior.

The issues of comparability, relevance, reliability, and sensitivity to change are but a few of the measurement problems that educators face in attempting to provide the evidence of learning and satisfaction that will serve the purposes of accountability and of improvement. There is little wonder, then, that the preceding chapters in this volume fail to furnish for external audiences a substantial amount of the kind of hard, objective, direct, easy-to-understand data that would help them see in unequivocal terms that assessment is improving student learning. The state of the art of measurement at this point in our history is inadequate to support such a conclusion. Indeed, student outcomes are so complex and multifaceted that we may never be able to derive simple linear cause-effect relationships between what the faculty and staff put into the college experience and what students take away.

Indirect Measures

If the objectives of accountability and improvement require different levels of specificity in the data collected from students and if current measurement theory and practice are inadequate to do a precise job of furnishing data at either level, how can my affirmative response to the question "Are we making a differ-ence?" be justified?

In their position paper on national goal five, objective five, Peter Ewell and Dennis Jones (1991) acknowledge the problems with direct measures of student learning and propose as a tempo-rary alternative the strategy of looking at indirect measures. In other words, while we wait for theory and practice to mature to a point where they can give us the direct measures we require, we might gather instead objective evidence of good practice that re-search has demonstrated to be effective in promoting student learning. Interaction with faculty outside class, active involvement in learning, and collaboration with peers are a few of the campus experiences that the literature identifies as powerful influences on the acquisition of knowledge and skills. Ewell and Jones suggest that we focus our campus assessment efforts on these readily mea-surable experiences. If we can show that more of them are occur-ring over time, we can deduce that learning is being enhanced.

Further support for directing our attention to indirect measures in exploring the impact of assessment comes from the philosophy and practice of total quality management. The fore-father of the TQM phenomenon, W. Edwards Deming, argues persuasively that inspection alone will not improve an outcome (1982). Instead, we must strive continuously to improve the process that produces the outcome. This proposition suggests that in addition to asking if students are learning more, our assessment of assessment should also address several process-related questions such as: Have campus programs been im-proved? Is the student experience fuller and richer? Are faculty members teaching more effectively?

In the sections that follow, I hope to make the case that the attention paid to outcomes assessment in recent years has in fact produced positive changes in the process of educating students on college and university campuses in this country. Moreover, I will demonstrate that many of these improvements are the very processes that traditional research methods have suggested will have an important positive impact on student de-velopment in college.

Several Research Paradigms

I have organized this discussion of the impact of outcomes assessment on the college experience according to an outline based on several important studies of the impact of college on students. In the late sixties, Chickering (1969) identified several conditions for impact on students such as clear and consistently articulated educational and institutional objectives; an institutional size that gives students opportunities to take part in a variety of activities that promote their development; varied curriculum, teaching, and evaluation practices that encourage active student involvement; residence hall arrangements that provide for intellectual diversity and meaningful interchange with other students; student and faculty interaction in a variety of settings; and a student culture that reinforces institutional programs and purposes.

Two decades later, Chickering and Gamson (1987) developed the Wingspread Seven Principles for Good Practice in Undergraduate Education, following a gathering of noted educators at the Johnson Foundation retreat center in Racine, Wisconsin. These principles include encouraging student-faculty contact, cooperation among students, active learning, prompt feedback on student work, time on task, high expectations, and respect for diverse talents and ways of learning.

More recently, Kuh, Schuh, Whitt, and Associates (1991) have characterized "involving" institutions as having clear institutional missions, valuing and expecting student initiative and responsibility, recognizing and responding to the total student experience, providing multiple small subcommunities for students, valuing students and taking them and their learning seriously, and generating feelings of loyalty and a sense of specialness among faculty and students. In their 1991 book, *How College Affects Students,* Pascarella and Terenzini examine an enormous amount of evidence from the research literature on the impact of college and state the major implication of their review for faculty and administrators: "to shape the educational and interpersonal experiences and settings of their campus in ways that will promote learning and achievement of the institution's educational goals and to induce students to become involved in those activities" (p. 648).

Based on this combined body of work, I have developed an outline of ways to make a difference. This synthesis of recommendations for good practice in higher education will provide a framework for considering how the authors of this book and other practitioners reporting in the Jossey-Bass bimonthly publication *Assessment Update* and elsewhere believe assessment is improving the student experience in colleges and universities.

Ways to Make a Difference

The blueprint for improvement that follows organized in three broad areas. Within each, distinguishing characteristics of successful implementation are listed.

1. Build a sense of shared purpose among students, faculty, and administrators based on clearly articulated and communicated statements of mission and educational goals.
    *   Communication begins in student recruitment and orientation and continues throughout the college experience.
    *   Student-institution fit improves.
2. Establish and maintain an institutional culture that is carefully designed to implement the campus mission and goals.
    *   Learning-centered administrators and faculty set the tone for the campus.
    *   Faculty engage in professional development activities and are rewarded for interaction with students.
    *   High expectations are set for student and faculty behavior.
    *   Faculty-student interaction is encouraged.
    *   Student-student collaboration is supported.
    *   Student involvement in learning is emphasized.
3. Create a program of instruction and evaluation that includes methods respecting diverse talents and ways of learning.
    *   Faculty receive assistance in improving their methods of instruction and evaluation.

- Students are encouraged to spend the time to become actively engaged in their learning.
- Students receive prompt feedback about their progress.
- Faculty receive feedback about their effectiveness.

In the sections that follow, I will provide illustrations of improvement actions that faculty and administrators have made in each of these areas in response to the outcomes of their work in assessment.

Building a Sense of Shared Purpose

Alverno College, Northeast Missouri State University, Kean College, King's College, and other institutions that have used assessment to create a new climate emphasizing student learning provide the best examples of the impact that a sense of shared purpose among faculty, students, and administrators can have on a campus. Peter Ewell (1984) has called these institutions "self-regarding" because they exhibit a self-consciousness about the work of the faculty and students that is unique. When students consider entering one of these institutions, they do so with the full knowledge that their progress and achievements will be tracked and that they will take part in assessment activities. At Alverno College, one of the chief goals of the institution is to develop in individuals the ability to assess their own strengths and weaknesses and to take appropriate action guided by this knowledge.

Virginia Military Institute provides another example of the use of assessment to increase the fit between students and institution. The goals for student development at VMI have been carefully studied, and an array of cognitive and noncognitive instruments has been assembled to provide a profile of each student. This profile can subsequently be linked with success or failure in the environment that faculty have developed to implement the unique student development goals of the institution. The profiles of students most at risk were examined, and changes in orientation and encouragement of first-year students were designed to improve progress for those students with the best chance of succeeding and to counsel some students to select other sites for their college education. These actions have dramatically improved persistence of first-year students at VMI.

At Lehman College of the City University of New York, the Community College of Denver, and Western Michigan University, just to provide a few examples, engagement in assessment activities has prompted the faculty to look more carefully at courses and curricula, investigate students' choices of courses, and undertake improvements. At Lehman College, faculty have developed explicit statements of student outcomes and criteria for their accomplishment for the writing program. At the Community College of Denver, much more specific course descriptions have been created, as well as information about entry to each course of study, in order to help students make more informed choices. At Western Michigan, assessment activities uncovered the fact that far too many students were failing courses to which they were admitted without the appropriate prerequisites. This finding led to a study of prerequisites and to strict enforcement of those that were found to be essential. Similarly, at Mount Hood Community College, high failure rates in chemistry and math courses led to an evaluation of placement test cut scores and ultimately to the establishment of higher cut scores.

Establishing a Supportive Institutional Culture

Few institutions can match the remarkable story of change effected at Northeast Missouri State University following the institution by then-president Charles McClain and his chief academic officer, Darrell Krueger, of a learner-centered campus climate. When McClain assumed the presidency at Northeast in 1970, he found what he perceived to be a substantial problem with student motivation. By instilling a sense of pride in institutionwide achievement at or above the national average on appropriate standardized tests, student achievement began to increase markedly. Not only did the scores of graduates go up, but the institution began to attract a significantly more capable group of entering students.

Faculty at the Community College of Denver made the decision that the school's student attrition rate was too high to support its goal of producing graduates at the associate-degree level. A tracking program showed that students who were not associated with a degree-granting program were most at risk. Further inquiry suggested that entry procedures for college curricula were not sufficiently clear to encourage student enrollment. Thus, faculty for every degree program were encouraged to develop new materials designed to help students find their ways into that program.

Most academics consider advising to be an important component in implementing developmental goals for students. At several institutions, however, assessment activities have revealed substantial incongruence between student expectations for career advising and faculty perceptions of that service. This was the case at Kean College, for example. Consequently, the student handbook was revised to include a broader definition of advising, and orientation sessions on advising have been instituted for students and for faculty. Subsequent surveys have shown that both students and faculty are now more satisfied with the advising process. At the University of Tennessee, Knoxville, a low rating for career advising led student affairs administrators to conduct a series of focus groups to learn how career advising was seen by first-year students. Whereas faculty believed that they should handle academic advising and leave career counseling to people specializing in this field, students wanted a combined effort. As a result, the Career Services staff has begun to take part in in-service training for academic advisers in order to help them provide some career advising on their own and make smooth referrals to Career Services for students with specific needs. Similar findings at Austin Peay State University and Winthrop University have also resulted in bringing career counselors and academic advisers together for orientation sessions. At Winthrop, an elective course in career exploration has been added to the curriculum.

Student-faculty and student-student collaboration in assessing instructional effectiveness in classrooms have been increased through the adoption of a total quality management perspective at Samford University. After training in group processes and TQM tools, students become partners with their professors in the evaluation of instruction. Their team activity generates suggestions for improving instruction, and the reporting process brings them into close working relationships with the faculty. This collaborative assessment strategy helps students improve their communication skills, self-confidence, interaction skills, and understanding of others' perspectives and enhances their involvement in learning. The classroom assessment techniques described in Chapter Fourteen by representatives of the California Community College System convey similar benefits in student-student and faculty-student interaction. Student self-evaluation, as described by Carl Waluconis in Chapter Sixteen, constitutes a third example of the value of collaborative efforts in evaluation.

Assessment activities have provided direction for faculty development experiences that increase faculty members' capacity to contribute to a mission-centered campus climate. At the University of Tennessee, Knoxville, a research-oriented campus, the Center for Assessment Research and Development instituted a small grant program that permitted the faculty to develop proposals designed to improve assessment tools and methods. Through this program, faculty were given time and other resources to produce publishable research while also contributing to the improvement of the assessment process. Several faculty-related tests in the major were linked with alumni outcomes in an effort to establish their predictive validity. This scrutiny of the testing instruments led to modifications in the instruments themselves, and, more important, to changes in curricula and methods of instruction. For example, results on the public relations exam were found to be unrelated to grade-point average in core courses. This finding caused the faculty to investigate again the relationship between test content and course content. The conclusion was that the courses were not sufficiently guided by explicit student outcome objectives that were developed and agreed to by the faculty. The faculty then took steps to write such objectives and to align test content and course content to a greater extent than had been the case previously.

At the State Technical Institute at Memphis, student survey responses revealed dissatisfaction with the availability of faculty outside class. Since many students there attend classes at night, the problem was alleviated by assigning evening office hours to faculty. In addition, learning labs previously staffed by nonfaculty personnel now involve faculty members as well.

The faculty assessment coordinating committee at Peace College has developed a particularly effective strategy for ensuring that the results of assessment are used to improve the alignment of the institutional culture with campus mission and goals. The broadly representative Program Review Committee meets twice a year to review campuswide assessment findings. Committee members collectively prioritize suggestions for improving programs and services and list these on forms that are then directed to the office or faculty group they consider most responsible for the activity in question. A date is set for a response by the unit, which should indicate either a date for implementation or a reason for not acting on the recommendation. Because of this process action is taken on more than 90 percent of the committee's recommendations.

Creating Individualized Instruction and Evaluation

Faculty who are deeply involved in assessment of student learning have developed a much fuller appreciation of individual differences in the ability of students to profit from various kinds of instruction and evaluation approaches. For instance, the faculty at Virginia Military Institute has been persuaded to use portfolios to assess student writing because this is an approach that accommodates a variety of learning styles.

Faculty who have struggled to determine the best ways to assess student learning in the major have been so disappointed by the narrowness of available standardized paper-and-pencil tests that they have developed their own creative strategies for assessing student application skills. The assessment centers developed at Indiana University of Pennsylvania to gauge the effectiveness of students' classroom skills provide one example. At the University of Tennessee, Knoxville, faculty have constructed an in-basket exercise to evaluate potential hospital dieticians' ability to make decisions under pressure. Seniors in advertising are asked to design an advertising campaign for the sponsor of a new product; subsequently, they receive an evaluation of their work by that sponsor as well as by their course instructor. Seniors in broadcasting are asked to solve a practical problem that might confront the manager of a radio station, and theater majors view a videotape of an excerpt from a play and then criticize the acting, directing, or set design (depending on their particular focus within the theater major).

Involvement in assessment has alerted faculty to the need to develop assessment strategies that test higher-order intellectual skills. Members of the animal science faculty at the University of Tennessee, Knoxville, who thought the department should be at the forefront of teaching critical-thinking and problem-solving skills, asked that a random sample of classroom tests be evaluated for the inclusion of items that asked students to apply, analyze, synthesize, and evaluate. To their chagrin, the analysis revealed that 80 percent of the questions were at the knowledge or comprehension level of cognitive complexity. This finding led the faculty to request assistance in learning how to write outcome objectives and related test items that would promote and assess higher-order intellectual skills. At Johnson County Community College, student evaluations of instruction suggested a need for the faculty to learn more about writing of test items and test construction. Faculty workshops on these topics were instituted, and now student evaluations of classroom assessment instruments have improved.

Faculty at Alverno College have long provided an example for the higher education community of giving students immediate and continuous feedback about their progress toward clearly identified learning goals. A number of community colleges, Dyersburg State in Tennessee, for instance, are refining student-tracking systems that make it possible for faculty at institutions much larger than Alverno to give necessary periodic feedback. At Dyersburg, administrators believe that a computerized degree-monitoring system and intensified faculty guidance of students have helped to increase the number of graduates by 60 percent in recent years. At Virginia Western Community College, a similar computerized academic advising system has been paired with efforts to strengthen articulation agreements with four-year institutions as a means of increasing progress toward the campus goal of successful transfer.

Internships and field experiences give students opportunities to apply their classroom learning in real-life settings. Evaluations of internship experiences constitute effective performance assessment mechanisms, and use of the suggestions for improvement derived from these has had a substantial impact on the improvement of classroom teaching. To prepare students for their internships, instructors are including more class assignments that engage students in group activities, use of oral communication skills, and creative projects.

The Harvard Assessment Seminars (Light, 1992) have given new emphasis to the importance of active, especially collaborative, learning. Harvard studies demonstrate that students who work in small groups—that is, four to six members—learn how to move a group forward, how to disagree without stifling others' ideas, and how to include all members in a discussion. These are skills that certainly enhance students' employability. At the University of Tennessee, Knoxville, a study of seniors' open-ended responses to the question "What college experiences have contributed most to your learning?" revealed that almost 80 percent believed their learning had been enhanced by opportunities for fieldwork and by discussions and group projects in classes—all examples of active learning. These group experiences helped the seniors gain understanding of others and of themselves as well as increase their understanding of coursework.

At Dyersburg State Community College, employer focus groups revealed a dissatisfaction with the interaction skills developed in college by Dyersburg students and graduates. The college undertook a series of initiatives designed to increase interaction capabilities, and the latest employer surveys reveal increased employer satisfaction in this area.

Final Thoughts

Looking collectively at the chapters in this volume, we sense a renewed enthusiasm for teaching on the part of many faculty who have taken assessment seriously. We also have evidence that these individuals are better prepared for their work as teachers by virtue of the professional development experiences offered in connection with assessment initiatives (Banta, forthcoming). In addition, faculty and staff trained in other disciplines have become more familiar with the literature on student growth in college as a result of their involvement in assessment, and they have begun to apply some of the recommendations from this research in their own work. Actions aimed at improving academic programs and student services have been taken, and there are many indications that the student experience has been enriched by suggestions emanating from the assessment process. At some institutions, increased attention to the individual and collective needs of students has produced measurable increases in student satisfaction levels and in the likelihood that students will persist in their studies until graduation.

The relative youth of most assessment programs and the inadequacy of available measurement methods make it more difficult to give a strong affirmative response to the question "Are students learning more?" Nevertheless, there are so many examples of assessment-based changes in the environment for learning — changes that research has shown to be effective in promoting cognitive growth and student satisfaction — that it seems quite appropriate to assume that student learning is increasing or will increase as the changes have time to achieve their intended purposes.

The authors of chapters in Part Five make it clear that policies developed and implemented by state governments and accrediting bodies have been powerful influences in stimulating colleges and universities to undertake outcomes assessment. But the most successful of these external initiatives have been nonprescriptive, that is, encouraging institutions to define their own goals and related evaluation strategies. Those of us who have presented our experiences in this book are united in our hope that the federal government, the governors, and others who are advocating national assessment for postsecondary students will take note of our positive accomplishments in improving the all-important processes of higher education and of our well-founded concerns about large-scale testing programs that do not engage the hearts and minds of either faculty or students.

What does our collective experience portend for the future of outcomes assessment? First, the call for introspection, analysis, and evaluation of our work in higher education is not a passing fad. As much as some faculty members and administrators might wish it would go away, for the foreseeable future the need to document what students are accomplishing as a result of their college experience will increase rather than subside. In all probability, assessment of outcomes will become an expected component of every new program proposal in higher education, and existing programs will have to be evaluated periodically to ascertain that they are continuing to contribute to the fulfillment of the institutional mission. We can no longer afford to invest our increasingly scarce resources in programs that do not serve valued purposes.

As more and more faculty members acknowledge the need for assessing outcomes, much of the experience described by my coauthors will be replicated in new settings. The use of locally designed tests, questionnaires, interview strategies, and portfolios will increase. More faculties will experiment with newer methods like assessment centers, self-evaluation, and identification of the effects of coursework using cluster analysis. On many campuses, efforts to apply total quality management will be linked to current outcomes assessment initiatives, and both approaches will be strengthened by the resulting synergy.

In addition to the anticipated increases in campus applications of existing instruments and methods, the measurement community must advance understanding of the issues involved and find new ways to measure cognitive and affective growth. Current dissatisfaction with the narrow focus of multiple-choice tests will deepen; thus, work on the development of cost-effective "authentic" measures must proceed. The full spectrum of possibilities for use of computer-adaptive testing must be explored.

Perhaps the most daunting challenge of all is to develop assessment strategies that simultaneously provide evidence of accountability and detailed information that faculty and staff may use to make specific improvements in academic programs and student services.

Outcomes assessment has the potential to touch every student and every faculty and staff member in every college in the United States. It could well become a subject of scholarship in every academic discipline and a topic for study and development by every professional association that counts college and university staff among its members. In the first decade of its history in the service of accountability and improvement in higher education, assessment has scarcely begun to attain its full potential. If it should realize that potential, one might argue at some point in the twenty-first century that assessment has made a greater difference for students than any other single influence in the history of higher education.

References

America 2000: An Education Strategy. Washington, D.C.: U.S. Department of Education, 1991.

Banta, T. W. "Toward a Plan for Using National Assessment to Ensure Continuous Improvement of Higher Education." *Journal of General Education,* 1993, *42*(1), 33–58.

Banta, T. W. "Using Outcomes Assessment to Improve Educational Programs." In M. Weimer and R. Menges (eds.), *Better Teaching and Learning in College: Toward More Scholarly Practice.* San Francisco: Jossey-Bass, forthcoming.

Banta, T. W., and Pike, G. R. "Methods for Comparing Outcomes Assessment Instruments." *Research in Higher Education,* 1989, *30*(5), 455–469.

Chickering, A. W. *Education and Identity.* San Francisco: Jossey-Bass, 1969.

Chickering, A., and Gamson, Z. "Seven Principles for Good Practice in Undergraduate Education." *Wingspread Journal,* 1987, *9*(2), 1–4.

Deming, W. E. *Out of the Crisis.* Cambridge, Mass.: Center for

Advanced Engineering Study, Massachusetts Institute of Technology, 1982.

Ewell, P. T. *The Self-Regarding Institution: Information for Excellence.* Boulder, Colo.: National Center for Higher Education Management Systems, 1984.

Ewell, P. T., and Jones, D. P. "Actions Matter: The Case for Indirect Measures in Assessing Higher Education's Progress on the National Education Goals." *Journal of General Education,* 1993, *42*(2), 123–148.

Hanson, G. R. "Critical Issues in the Assessment of Value Added in Education." In T. W. Banta (ed.), *Implementing Outcomes Assessment: Promise and Perils.* New Directions for Institutional Research, no. 59. San Francisco: Jossey-Bass, 1988.

Kuh, G. D., Schuh, J. S., Whitt, E. J., and Associates. *Involving Colleges: Successful Approaches to Fostering Student Learning and Personal Development Outside the Classroom.* San Francisco: Jossey-Bass, 1991.

Light, R. J. *The Harvard Assessment Seminars: Explorations with Students and Faculty About Teaching, Learning, and Student Life.* Second report. Cambridge, Mass.: Harvard University Graduate School of Education and Kennedy School of Government, 1992.

Pascarella, E. T., and Terenzini, P. T. *How College Affects Students: Findings and Insights from Twenty Years of Research.* San Francisco: Jossey-Bass, 1991.

Pike, G. R. "A Comparison of the College Outcome Measures Program (COMP) and the Collegiate Assessment of Academic Proficiency (CAAP) Exams." Unpublished research report, Center for Assessment Research and Development, University of Tennessee, Knoxville, 1989.

Index